Modernity

transitions
General Editor: Julian Wolfreys

Published titles
TERRY EAGLETON David Alderson
JULIA KRISTEVA AND LITERARY THEORY Megan Becker-Leckrone
BATAILLE Fred Botting and Scott Wilson
NEW HISTORICISM AND CULTURAL MATERIALISM John Brannigan
HÉLÈNE CIXOUS Abigail Bray
GENDER Claire Colebrook
POSTMODERN NARRATIVE THEORY Mark Currie
FORMALIST CRITICISM AND READER-RESPONSE THEORY
    Kenneth Womack and Todd F. Davis
IDEOLOGY James M. Decker
QUEER THEORY Donald E. Hall
MARXIST LITERARY AND CULTURAL THEORIES Moyra Haslett
LOUIS ALTHUSSER Warren Montag
RACE Brian Niro
MODERNITY David Punter
JACQUES LACAN Jean-Michel Rabaté
LITERARY FEMINISMS Ruth Robbins
SUBJECTIVITY Ruth Robbins
DECONSTRUCTION-DERRIDA Julian Wolfreys

ORWELL TO THE PRESENT, 1945–1999 John Brannigan
CHAUCER TO SHAKESPEARE, 1337–1580 SunHee Kim Gertz
MODERNISM, 1910–1945 Jane Goldman
POPE TO BURNEY, 1714–1786 Moyra Haslett
PATER TO FORSTER, 1873–1924 Ruth Robbins
BURKE TO BYRON, BARBAULD TO BAILLIE, 1790–1830 Jane Stabler
MILTON TO POPE, 1650–1720 Kay Gilliland Stevenson
SIDNEY TO MILTON, 1580–1660 Marion Wynne Davies

Forthcoming titles
NATIONAL IDENTITY John Brannigan
HOMI BHABHA Eleanor Byrne
POSTMODERNISM•POSTMODERNITY Martin McQuillan
ROLAND BARTHES Martin McQuillan
TRANSGRESSION Julian Wolfreys
DICKENS TO HARDY 1837–1884 Julian Wolfreys

Transitions
Series Standing Order
ISBN 0–333–73634–6
(*outside North America only*)

You can receive future titles in this series as they are published. To place a standing order please contact your bookseller or, in the case of difficulty, write to us at the address below with your name and address, the title of the series and the ISBN quoted above.

Customer Services Department, Macmillan Distribution Ltd Houndmills, Basingstoke, Hampshire RG21 6XS, England

transitions

Modernity

David Punter

First published 2007 by
PALGRAVE MACMILLAN
Houndmills, Basingstoke, Hampshire RG21 6XS and
175 Fifth Avenue, New York, N.Y. 10010
Companies and representatives throughout the world

PALGRAVE MACMILLAN is the global academic imprint of the Palgrave Macmillan division of St. Martin's Press, LLC and of Palgrave Macmillan Ltd. Macmillan® is a registered trademark in the United States, United Kingdom and other countries. Palgrave is a registered trademark in the European Union and other countries.

ISBN-13: 978–0–333–91455–7   hardback
ISBN-10: 0–333–91455–4   hardback
ISBN-13: 978–0–333–91456–4   paperback
ISBN-10: 0–333–91456–2   paperback

This book is printed on paper suitable for recycling and made from fully managed and sustained forest sources. Logging, pulping and manufacturing processes are expected to conform to the environmental regulations of the country of origin.

A catalogue record for this book is available from the British Library.

A catalogue record for this book is available from the Library of Congress.

10   9   8   7   6   5   4   3   2   1
16   15   14   13   12   11   10   09   08   07

Printed and bound in China

Contents

General Editor's Preface

Transitions: *transition* n. of action. 1. A passing or passage from one condition, action or (rarely) place, to another. 2. Passage in thought, speech,
or writing, from one subject to another. 3. **a.** The passing from one note to
another **b.** The Passing from one key to another, modulation. 4. The
passage from an earlier to a later stage of development or formation ...
change from an earlier style to a later; a style of intermediate or mixed
character ... the historical passage of language from one well-defined
stage to another.

The aim of *Transitions* is to explore passages and movements in critical
thought, and in the development of literary and cultural interpretations.
This series also seeks to examine the possibilities for reading, analysis
and other critical engagements which the very idea of transition makes
possible. The writers in this series unfold the movements and modulations of critical thinking over the last generation, from the first emer-
gences of what is now recognized as literary theory. They examine as well
how the transitional nature of theoretical and critical thinking is still
very much in operation, guaranteed by the hybridity and heterogeneity
of the field of literary studies. The authors in the series share the
common understanding that, now more than ever, critical thought is
both in a state of transition and can best be defined by developing for the
student reader an understanding of this protean quality.

This series desires, then, to enable the reader to transform her/his own
reading and writing transactions by comprehending past developments.
Each book in the series offers a guide to the poetics and politics of interpretative paradigms, schools and bodies of thought, while transforming
these, if not into tools or methodologies, then into conduits for directing
and channeling thought. As well as transforming the critical past by
interpreting it from the perspective of the present day, each study enacts
transitional reading of a number of well-known literary texts, all of
which are themselves conceivable as having been transitional texts at the

moments of their first appearance. The readings offered in these books seek, through close critical reading and theoretical engagement, to demonstrate certain possibilities in critical thinking to the student reader.

It is hoped that the student will find this series liberating because rigid methodologies are not being put into place. As all the dictionary definitions of the idea of transition above suggest, what is important is the action, the passage: of thought, of analysis, of critical response. Rather than seeking to help you locate yourself in relation to any particular school or discipline, this series aims to put you into action, as readers and writers, travellers between positions, where the movement between poles comes to be seen as of more importance than the locations themselves.

Julian Wolfreys

Acknowledgements

The author and publishers are grateful to the following for permission to use copyright material:

Farrar, Straus and Giroux, LLC for excerpts from Another Life by Derek Walcott, copyright © 1973 by Derek Walcott; and 'Essential Beauty' and 'Going, Going' from *Collected Poems* by Philip Larkin, copyright © 1988, 2003 by the Estate of Philip Larkin. All excerpts reprinted by permission of Farrar, Straus and Giroux, LLC.

New Directions Publishing Corp for excerpts from 'Pierre Vidal Old', 'The Game of Chess' and 'The Garden', from *Personae: Collected Shorter Poems* by Ezra Pound, copyright © 1926 by Ezra Pound. Reprinted by permission of New Directions Publishing Corp.

Faber and Faber Limited, for excerpts from 'The Wasteland' from *Collected Poems, 1909–1962* by T.S. Eliot; 'Essential Beauty' and 'Going, Going' from *Collected Poems* by Philip Larkin; and 'Pierre Vidal Old', 'The Game of Chess' and 'The Garden', from *Personae: Collected Shorter Poems* by Ezra Pound.

Margaret and Michael Snow, for excerpts from 'What Is The Language Using Us For?' by W.S. Graham.

Every effort has been made to trace the copyright holders but, if any have been inadvertently overlooked, the authors and publishers will be pleased to make the necessary arrangements at the first opportunity.

Introduction

The term 'modernity' has a long history. Indeed, one could argue that, not only in western culture but in many others, it is ubiquitous and unavoidable, in the simple sense that history itself may be seen as structured as a succession of moments at which the 'old' comes into conflict or tension with the 'new'. Without such moments, and the cultural recognition and realisation of such moments, it could be argued that it would be difficult to see history as in movement at all. There are, of course, many views to be taken of historical and cultural process and thus of the location of modernity. Among the most prominent, and the first to which I shall refer here, would be that which eventually derives from Hegel, which is the teleological idea that all of human history can be conceived as a type of progress, albeit dialectical, towards a future goal, which Hegel himself terms as, *inter alia*, the 'realisation of spirit' (Hegel 1966, 457). But Hegel himself was dependent on older views of history, some of which maintained that history is not a question of progress, but rather one of a continuing scenario of 'returns', a view which can be found most clearly expressed in the work of Giambattista Vico, of which Hegel was well aware.

A particularly sophisticated attitude towards this complex of ideas emerges in the poetry and prose writings of W.B. Yeats, who maintained, in his recurring image of the 'winding stair' or spiral staircase (Yeats 1965, 265), that there are indeed recurrences in human history, times when, as it were, the 'same things' seem to come round again, but they occur at a 'higher level' – more, therefore, spiral than circle – and can thus be accommodated to a general idea of progress. We thus constantly revisit the past, but in an increasingly 'enlightened' and advanced condition, from which we can look back and appreciate the changes of event and perception which have taken place as well as the uncanny similarities between past and present ages.

In the writings of Marx, one can find a different view of the resurgences and recycling of history, typically in his remarks on how a first occurrence which may present itself as tragedy will recur under the guise of farce. His cardinal example was the second 'French revolution', the bourgeois revolution which resulted in the installation of Louis Philippe on the French throne, and which served both as culmination and as parody of the 'original' revolution of 1789. One of the questions posed here is of how far a culture or civilisation can learn from the past – as in the familiar trope about having to learn from history in case previous 'mistakes' are repeated.

Further back behind all of these ideas there lie concepts which have their roots in religion. In Christianity since its beginnings, there has been an underlying programme of understanding history as an incarnation of divine purpose; as in the Hegelian and Marxist views, here there is a 'master-story' to be told, which in this case is of the working out of God's purposes – if unwittingly – through human agency, and a necessary concomitant injunction to patience if those purposes are not always transparent or beneficial. In these sorts of narrative, the 'new' or the modern cannot appear as *totally* new, whatever that might mean; that which appears to be new appears thus because it as yet awaits the interpretation which will fit it into the divine scheme of things, a mode of understanding which could return us again to Hegel and to his famous pronouncement that 'the owl of Minerva spreads its wings only with the falling of the dusk' (Hegel 1967, 13) which, through its reference to Minerva as the classical goddess of wisdom, affirms that the patterns of history are not seen at the time but become evident and available only through later interpretation – whether, in the case of religion, by the privileged agents of a priesthood, or through the intellectual activities of the philosopher.

The question of whether a phenomenon can be 'absolutely new' is crucial to notions of modernity through the ages; but it is put into question again in contemporary times by postmodernism, by the question of whether the 'shock of the new' (Hughes 1988) can be adequately accommodated by an overarching story of human or divine purpose. Perhaps after all the new, the modern, happens not through supernal planning but through a series of coincidences, through sets of conjunctions which cannot be predicted and which occasion changes in life and thought which would have been literally unthinkable in earlier times. For the postmodern, the new is always surprising and often catastrophic; the question of interpretation is suspended in favour of a radical admission of incomprehension, to which texts can only respond through recognising the supersession and fragmentation of past master-narratives.

And this again would lead to a series of speculations about what these 'earlier times' might be. It is frequently said, for example, that the European medieval world was one of comparatively slow change, or indeed that the very concept of 'change' held a different meaning, perhaps more menacing, less comprehensible than it has done since; another side of this argument would be one which claims that the rate of change has been growing – during, for example, the twentieth century – exponentially, that due largely to developments in the processes and outcomes of technology we now inhabit a world in which the rate of change is increasingly rapid, with specific implications for the ability of different generations to comprehend the state of the world in which they live. Here we begin to see that, although modernity is a question of cultural understanding, it is also crucially a question of technological evolution; the ways in which we interpret the world are critically interlinked with the ways in which we handle it, the ways in which it is amenable – or not – to our shaping.

In this book, I do not propose to investigate these changing conceptions of what might be modern right from the age of, for example, the ancient Greeks, because this would be unwieldy; instead, I propose to set as a beginning point the European eighteenth century, the so-called 'age of Enlightenment'. This is because, for the purposes of understanding the concept of the modern in the contemporary West, the Enlightenment marked a specific turning-point, one at which the modern consolidated its position as a highly valorised term. The Enlightenment myth – even if it *is* only a myth – was that humanity was on the point of decisively superseding its 'darker' origins; that the general process of civilisation (even if, at the time, this was seen as distinctively and exclusively the property of Europe and, within Europe, only of a more or less privileged caste) was in the process of annihilating an older world characterised by prejudice and misunderstanding.

We can find many ironic commentaries on this faith – which some would see as a quasi-religious faith – in an idea of modernity and progress founded on technological and intellectual enlightenment. One of the best-known twentieth-century examples would be Aldous Huxley's *Brave New World* (1932), where this process of enlightenment is seen as, naturally, providing immeasurable improvements in living standards and in the provision of mass entertainment, but at the same time as eliminating individuality and personality from the human condition. Huxley's parable is in part a satire on mass production, but it is also (emblematically through the elision in the novel of the names 'Ford' and 'Freud') a

satire on Freud, although Freud in fact held a radically different view
of progress, which we shall explore later but which will also provide a
continuing under-current to my argument.

Freud held crucially that, although civilisation, whatever we mean by
that vexed term, is necessary in order to banish the evil demons of the
past, they can never wholly disappear; instead they will recur in
repressed form. Civilisation for Freud, as he expresses it in his major text
Civilisation and its Discontents (1930), takes the form of a series of sub-
stitutive gratifications; in other words, the old problems of how to
survive and make our peace within a world which may in some ways be
radically inimical to human progress – or indeed survival – force us to
produce a kind of simulacrum of progress, but below this there lies
another level, in the world at large and also in the individual and collective psyche, which remains preoccupied with these 'original' problems.
We might suitably relate this way of thinking to some of the difficulties
encountered in the twentieth century with the idea of progress, emblematically in relation to instances of mass destruction such as the
Holocaust, and the accompanying suggestion that, far from contributing
to progress, the 'modernity' so beloved by European dictators and autocrats resulted directly in the most abhuman of violences. Can one write
poetry after the Holocaust, Paul Celan asks; or, how is it possible that a
nation, Germany in this instance, which has contributed some of the
most profound products of civilisation, in the form of, for example, the
music of Beethoven, can also provide us with the most vile of object
lessons in man's inhumanity to man?

To move, perhaps, from the sublime to the ridiculous, the most pervasive discourse of the modern in 1950s and 1960s Britain was of the
'labour-saving device', the machine, like the vacuum cleaner, the
washing-machine, even the car, which reduced the amount of time
human beings need to spend on the accomplishment of mundane tasks.
This, it was widely held, had two advantages. The more usually expressed
one was to do with the gender division of labour: such devices were
expected to liberate women from the irksome nature of household
chores and thus to give them more opportunity, more freedom to participate in the modern world, thus widening the pool of modernity's appeal.
We have only to see a film such as *The Stepford Wives* (1975), however, to
see that there is a very different possibility hidden within this notion of
'labour-saving', such that people without work can also lose their sense
of purpose, their individuality, and become manipulable by unseen
forces greater than themselves.

The subtext of the 'labour-saving device', however, was wider and implied that freedom in general from manual labour would improve the opportunities for 'self-betterment'. Without saying for a moment that this may not in certain cases have been true, it is worth again remarking how literature has anticipated the negative conclusions which may flow from this. One prominent example would be H.G. Wells' *The Time Machine* (1895), which envisages a future in which the human race is split even more irrevocably than it is in the 'present' between the 'have-nots' who continue to perform the manual labour (the Morlocks), and the 'haves' who live an 'aesthetic' and attenuated life on the back of this underclass (the Eloi). The fact that Wells provides us in the end with a sudden and startling reversal of the reality behind these apparent roles serves simply to further the argument about the delusions of technological advance.

Common to many of these examples and *topoi*, from the Enlightenment on but also occurring in earlier periods, is a discourse which talks of modernity in terms of 'the light' overcoming 'the dark', a discourse which is of course still very much with us in the mythpoeic structures of popular writers such as, for example, J.R.R. Tolkien, currently enjoying an extraordinary filmic revival. This *topos* occurs indeed in Freud as well, even with the reservation I have mentioned above; but it forms a broader and more compelling notion of modernity which, in the end, may be referred back to anthropology. Every invention is, in some sense, 'modern'; just so, we may reasonably assume that the most primeval inventions, including fire with all its promethean ramifications, could be seen as attempts to drive back the darkness, the 'dark materials' common to Freud's notion of the unconscious but also to literary texts from Milton to Philip Pullman, which might otherwise expose mankind to the power of the night, to the destruction threatened by the wild beast whose eyes are, after all, so much more nocturnally 'enlightened' than our own.

These, then, would be some of the figures within which the notion of 'modernity' might emerge. To examine them further, I will say something about each of the five quotations which the *Oxford English Dictionary* uses to illustrate its definition of 'modernity' which is, perhaps unsurprisingly though rather unhelpfully, 'the quality or condition of being modern; modernness of character' (it should be added that the definitions of 'modern' are considerably more interesting and I will return to them, if only implicitly, on later pages). The first of these illustrative quotations is from George Hakewill's *An Apologie or Declaration*

of the Power and Providence of God in the Government of the World
(1630), and reads: 'Yea but I vilifie the present times, you say, whiles I
expect a more flourishing State to succeed; bee it so, yet this is not to
vilifie modernity, as you pretend'. Even here, then, in the earlier part of
the seventeenth century, a distinction is being drawn between 'vilify-
ing' the condition of the present and a rejection of modernity as such;
modernity according to Hakewill and many of his contemporaries, we
might say, cannot be merely summarised as a single state, but rather it
presupposes a process, a *trajectory*. The moment of modernity, then, is
not merely the present, the here-and-now; rather, it is deeply embroiled
in the 'succession' of states, it is an always temporary term which
asserts both the *onset* of a condition of things and simultaneously the
passing-away of other things. From this beginning, we might go on to
assert the paradox that part of the complex structure of modernity will
always be a certain kind of nostalgia, a moment of regret for that which
is superseded – in Hegelian terms, *aufheben* – within the onset of the
new.

The second of the *OED*'s illustrations brings us on to 1782, and to a
comment by Horace Walpole on the poetry of Thomas Chatterton.
Chatterton's poetry, we may need to remember, was intimately bound up
with forgery; not, perhaps, in the sense that he did not write the poems
he claimed as his own, but rather in that he attributed to them an
archaic, medieval provenance. Walpole, writing after the exposure,
claims not to have been fooled: 'Now', he says, 'that [Chatterton's] poems
have been so much examined, nobody (that has an ear) can get over the
modernity of the modulations'. Of course, it may well be that Walpole is
here mocking those who were taken in by the forgery at the time yet
afterwards professed to have sensed danger all along; nevertheless, the
point is that there appears to him to be an ineradicable distinction
between the ancient and the modern. The modern can never properly
imitate or reproduce that which has gone before; the onward march of
knowledge, the development of what we may now refer to as the whole
technosphere, prevents us from being able to rehearse the past even as it
separates us from it. Thus, perhaps, another paradox: as modernity gives
us access to new forms of knowledge, new types of activity, just so it
marches us away from history, draws a veil over past ways of life and
thus, in a sense which the early twentieth-century modernists knew very
well, places us in a condition where, despite or even because of the
'improved' state of our knowledge, there is always an uncertainty behind
our backs.

The third illustration is from Samuel Pegge the Elder's *Anonymiana* (1798): Macrobius, he claims, 'is no good author to follow in point of Latinity, partly on account of his modernity, and partly of his foreign extraction'. We may for present purposes leave aside the questions of Macrobius' 'foreign extraction'; what is important is that, as a writer in Latin whose work was written around 430 A.D., his writing is perceived as inferior to the products of 'classical Latin'. Thus we may suggest another opposition: the modern is not merely opposed to that which is 'older than it', it is also opposed to the 'classical', a distinction which, as we shall see, was of crucial importance in and after the eighteenth century. What is classic about the classical is not merely its antiquity; rather, it is its canonisation, its adoption as a standard of taste. Thus, while the modern may be initially understood merely as the 'contemporary', it at the same time maintains – for a period of time – a certain distance from canonisation. At least, that has been historically true; arguably, with the exponential speeding up of technology, coupled with the commercialisation of the 'culture markets', this process has in a sense caught up with itself. While Picasso, Joyce, John Cage may indeed have enjoyed – or suffered – the pleasure for a while of being in the *avant-garde*, of being 'athwart' cultural standards, it no longer takes very long before the insights of modernity have, where possible, been absorbed into the mainstream, and the 'shock of the new' has been neutralised, cauterised.

The fourth illustration makes a similar point to the second: here an article in *The Athenaeum* in 1888 speaks of 'those unlucky stumblings into modernity which some archaising translators do not avoid'. Here, however, there is something more of an even-handed attribution of blame: the attempt falsely to 'archaise' is regarded as foolish, but this foolishness is brought out specifically by the impossibility of burying all trace of the modern. The modern thus becomes not merely a set of surface inflections within the 'tradition'; rather it figures as the very veins in the rock, a set of tell-tale signs which will betray us if we attempt to occupy another time than our own. The modern then, according to this view, would not be a conscious set of choices; rather it would be the inevitable outcome, the summation of all the forces which propel history along, of which we are unwitting witnesses; even though we may from time to time feel overwhelmed by a modernity which we cannot fully understand, nevertheless we are all part of that onward drive, passengers on a train from which we leap at our peril.

The final passage in the *OED*, written by May Sinclair in 1904, draws a further comparison: 'My dear fellow, modernity simply means democracy. And when once democracy has been forced on us there's no good protesting any longer'. Clearly this passage makes a strange and perhaps in this case politically unpalatable point about the link between modernity and democracy, but the more important issue is the more general one, namely that modernity is always, at all points and at all times, bound up with the political. What was seen as politically 'modern' in Britain at the beginning of the twentieth century would not, of course, seem so to us now, bearing in mind, as just one example, the limitations on the franchise then in force; neither could one possibly say that the version of modernity embraced with fervour by Mussolini and by the Italian futurists has any obvious bearing on democracy. Nevertheless modernity – or perhaps better, the cultural *recognition* of modernity – will always carry a political weight because it speaks of change; of the possibility of change, of forward movement, or perhaps, more radically, of the impossibility, the unsustainability, of non-change. Reverence for tradition may continually attempt to suppose that there is the chance of remaining forever within the present state; modernity comes to remind us that this is not possible, that change is happening always, everywhere, whatever different attitudes and stances we may choose to take towards it.

Partly on the basis, then, of these quotations I would like to offer five initial hypotheses about modernity which I shall test in a number of contexts in the following pages.

1. Modernity is different from the past but also, more crucially, it is not merely the same as 'the present'. It is therefore always different from 'what is', it comes to challenge stasis and to point up the ways in which even the present is passing away under the tides of the new. In most cases, indeed, it would be fair to say that modernity is also 'different from itself'; we cannot point to a particular age and identify exactly what is, or was, 'modern' in that age because since the modern is the essence of what is resistant to canonisation and codification it will always produce itself in the form of a plethora of projects and programmes, none of which are guaranteed to exert any specific dominance over the historical process.

2. Modernity has a particular relation to culture and, for the purposes of the present book, to the literary. This is because culture is always striated by the past and the future; where the world of labour may feasibly thrive on stasis and the need for stability in order to assess and fulfil economic need, the world of culture exists

in part as a testing-ground of possibilities. Some of those possibilities, as it were, 'take'; it is difficult to imagine the contemporary novel without the earlier modernities of, for example, Woolf or Lawrence; some do not, as in the exemplary case of the novelist B.S. Johnson, whose books, published without pagination, without order, collections of loose leaves in a cardboard box, seemed wildly experimental at the time they were published but have left little trace within further reticulations of the modern.

3. As is hinted in the quotation about Macrobius, modernity will very often have a complex relation with the 'foreign'. At the most obvious level, this is because cultures evolve at different rates in different places; thus 'imports' of foreign artefacts, whether these are from other 'civilised' cultures or from cultures perceived as primitive, will often be crucial as ways of voicing that within the host culture which might otherwise appear unable to be voiced. In this respect there will always be something uncanny about modernity, some sense that it is in opposition to the *heimlich*, that with which we feel 'at home'; modernity challenges us, as it were, in our own homes, it reminds us of other, frequently more disturbing possibilities of perception and it decentres and destabilises our everyday domestic assumptions.

4. The modern takes its place variously as an opposition to the 'ancient', the 'archaic', the 'classical', but it cannot live without a certain encounter with those forms. This encounter can take many paths: it may involve an absorption of the past, as in the case, for example, of Henry Moore's sculpture; it may involve a recasting of past symbols, as in the emblematic case of Francis Bacon's Screaming Popes; it may at least appear to reject the 'representationalism' of the tradition altogether, as in much abstract painting – although here it is worth remarking again on the cultural prejudices which tend to portray history in this way, forgetting the anti-representational stance of Islamic art down the centuries. But an encounter with the past there will always be, even if only, as in T.S. Eliot, with the fragments and remnants of that past, shards which have been stripped of their original meanings but which will nonetheless not 'go away', will never leave a cleared cultural site on which the modern can make a truly new beginning.

5. Modernity is always and everywhere political; it is consequently also inseparable from economic and technological conditions. Walter Benjamin in his crucial essay 'The Work of Art in the Age of

Mechanical Reproduction' (1935) suggests that the moment of modernity is the moment at which the work of art loses its 'aura', its uniqueness, becomes reproducible, but we may say that the history of western culture is striated by many such moments, from the invention of the printing-press through to the current possibilities for representation offered by the graphics of cyberspace. Modernity will, however, according to Benjamin also participate in a more general condition of culture, namely the obliteration or effacement of the grounds of its own production; there will be something phantomatic to it, something which is both haunted and haunting, progressive and nostalgic, in denial of its own material circumstances even at those moments when it seeks the most culturally materialistic of effects.

With those considerations in mind, I shall go on in the next chapter to examine in more detail four critical 'moments' of modernity in order to fill in something of the map we need to guide us around a world which all too readily conceives of itself as modern even while, in a manner similar to the famous image of overlooking the elephant in the living-room, it strives with the difficulties of dealing with a terrain which is always already occupied by the visible, physical and intellectual traces of the past.

Part I

Histories

1 Modernity and Enlightenment

In a lecture in 2000, the political philosopher John Gray offered the following comments on the relations between the Enlightenment and modernity:

> Modernity does not mean embracing the Enlightenment project. If you read early nineteenth century, mid nineteenth century and late nineteenth century European thinkers, if you read the great philosophers in the French Enlightenment, even if you read thinkers in the Scottish Enlightenment, it's often taken that in becoming modern a society thereby adopts or embraces an Enlightenment worldview or Enlightenment values. I think that's a mistake. It's a mistake to think that modernisation and the acceptance of Enlightenment values go inescapably together, that a society that's not adopted some version of the Enlightenment project has, for that reason, failed to become modern.   (Gray 2000, 3)

What is of interest here, as we begin to look at the notion of modernity over the last three hundred years, is the assumption, to which Gray still has to address himself, that there is an intrinsic link between the Enlightenment and modernity; and we need to ask what the basis of this link might be. We can see it in four specific areas.

1. Perhaps the most outstanding work of the Enlightenment, certainly the most emblematic, was the great *Encyclopédie* (1751–72). This massive project claimed to be able to represent the entire sum of human knowledge; it claimed to shed light into the dark spaces of incomprehension which, it was suggested, had held back human development until this time. Implicit in this effort was also a notion of *categorisation*: knowledge should not be regarded as a mere jumble of facts, rather it should be seen as an ordered and

orderly approach to the world, within which facts and details did not merely stand alone but were related one to another in terms of what we might call, following Linnaeus' concomitant efforts to categorise the plant and animal kingdoms, a *general taxonomy* of human affairs. This encyclopaedia was in no sense to be a mere 'catalogue'; rather, it was to offer a map onto which these facts and details could be inscribed. As such, it was not merely a summary of the current state of knowledge; rather, it set itself up as a template onto which future knowledge *could also be mapped*, as a set of paths towards the future.

2. The Enlightenment set itself firmly in opposition to religion. Religion was reconceived not as a path upwards towards spiritual understanding but rather as a path downwards towards mystery. An opposition was set up between a public, transparent system of knowledge, to which all could (supposedly, and according to one of a long series of 'universalist' myths) have access, and a secret, arcane system which was the purely the property of priests and other initiates. Science, on this model, was not a recondite study, the privilege of the educated few; rather, it should be judged by its intellectual and, more to the point, practical benefit to mankind. Intellectual activity became, on this reading, a public service and a public duty; it was not something to be performed away from the scrutiny of the people but rather a matter of expanding the potential for general knowledge and understanding.

3. The guiding principle behind all this was reason, which was conceived during the Enlightenment as a sure guide to understanding both the human situation and the greater cosmos. Faith was merely subjective; reason has access to greater rules by which human lives can be suitably governed. All this, of course, was at least incipiently political; for if mystery were removed from human affairs, then this did not merely affect religious faith, it also affected the people's belief in the divine right of their rulers, and thus the French Revolution emerges from history as the consequence of this stripping away of ancient mystique in favour of a more 'modern' apprehension of the human position. The old is perceived as oppressive, the new as at least potentially liberating.

4. This entire discourse of enlightenment was predicated on scientific and technological advance. The philosophers of the Enlightenment saw themselves as living in a time of unprecedented progress – in the medical sciences, in the world of manufacture, and concomi-

tantly in that realm in which rational political and social systems could be devised which would proclaim themselves – so the hope went – as self-evidently superior to the inequities and mystifications of the past. It would become possible to produce a system of government based on the 'first principles' of reason, one which would address the tyrannical past; this 'new system' would not, so the theory went, necessarily require the force of revolution to promulgate itself; rather, its mere existence would make the inadequacies of the past so obvious that it would naturally succeed in persuading people that it was the next necessary step towards the future.

The European Enlightenment was, according to some standards, a short-lived phenomenon; in literary terms, it was rapidly overtaken by romanticism, a structure of intellect and feeling which had a considerably more ambivalent attitude towards the past and towards, in particular, the feudal and the medieval, all those sources of mystery and inequity which the Enlightenment came to try to sweep away. And thus one might point here to a specific 'dialectic of enlightenment', to quote the title of the great book on the subject by Max Horkheimer and Theodor Adorno: namely, the question of what happens to all the material which is swept away by modernity. For the Enlightenment thinkers, myths and symbols were mere fairy stories told to keep the people happy; what romanticism came to demonstrate was that, even if this may be true, there might nonetheless be a real social and psychological need for stories of this kind, that the realm of the cultural could not survive on reason alone. Alexander Pope, interestingly, is very clear about this, about the co-necessity for reason and what he calls 'self-love' as the twin engines of human betterment. In his *Essay on Man* (1733), he attempts to situate the 'myth of reason' among other myths of human coherence:

> Know then thyself, presume not God to scan;
> The proper study of Mankind is Man.
> Plac'd on this isthmus of a middle state,
> A being darkly wise, and rudely great:
> With too much knowledge for the Sceptic side,
> With too much weakness for the Stoic's pride,
> He hangs between; in doubt to act, or rest,
> In doubt to deem himself a God, or Beast;
> In doubt his Mind or Body to prefer,

> Born but to die, and reas'ning but to err;
> Alike in ignorance, his reason such,
> Whether he thinks too little, or too much:
> Chaos of Thought and Passion, all confus'd;
> Still be himself abus'd, or disabus'd;
> Created half to rise, and half to fall;
> Great lord of all things, yet a prey to all;
> Sole judge of Truth, in endless Error hurl'd:
> The glory, jest, and riddle of the world!   (Pope 1966, 250–1)

Pope, therefore, appears to seek to steer a psychological and cultural 'middle way', a course which will enable the realm of the human to be considered as a compound of reason and passion. It is interesting that he uses the terms 'abus'd' and 'disabus'd', for these are surely very complex words. Does he mean, for example, that whatever mankind does there is a comparable risk of being 'abus'd' by false beliefs and by the oppressive governmental and religious systems which might follow from false premises, or of being 'disabus'd' by a kind of enlightenment which Pope himself might still regard negatively, as a tool by which people are stripped of their sense of wonder, that essential moment of awe which prevents us from acceding to the pretensions of omniscience?

Certainly Pope is arguing against those pretensions, the notion that reason and science can, or one day will, render all of nature open to our understanding, and in doing so he is precisely operating against the position of 'enlightenment', which founds itself on holding that there is an onward, progressive march of reason. One can find many examples of this belief, and therefore of the process of enlightened 'disabuse', in the emblematic *Conversation between D'Alembert and Diderot* of 1769. We might consider, for example, Diderot's remarks on the processes of birth and maturation. He is here taking as his own example the quasi-anthropological processes by which an eminent thinker may emerge from his forebears:

> What I mean is that before his mother, the beautiful and scandalous Madame de Tencin, had reached the age of puberty, and before the soldier La Touche had reached adolescence, the molecules which were to form the first rudiments of our mathematician were scattered about in the young and undeveloped organs of each, were being filtered with the lymph and circulated in the blood until they finally settled in the vessels ordained for their union, namely the sex glands of his mother and father. Lo and

behold, the rare seed takes form; it is carried, as is generally believed, along the Fallopian tubes and into the womb. It is attached thereto by a long pedicle, it grows in stages and advances to the state of foetus. The moment for its emergence from its dark prison has come: the new-born boy is abandoned on the steps of Saint-Jean-le-Rond, which gave him his name, taken away from the Foundling Institution and put to the breast of the good glazier's wife, Madame Rousseau; suckled by her he develops in body and mind and becomes a writer, a physicist and a mathematician. How did all this come about? Through eating and other purely mechanical operations. Here is the general formula in a few words: eat, digest, distil *in vasi licito et fiat homo secundum artem*. And anyone lecturing to the Academy on the stages in the formation of a man or animal need refer only to material factors, the successive stages of which would be an inert body, a sentient being and then a being who can resolve the problem of the precession of the equinoxes, a sublime being, a miraculous being, one who ages, grows infirm, dies, decomposes and returns to humus.   (Diderot 1966, 152–3)

I have chosen to quote this marvellous passage at length because in it, I believe, it is possible to capture the entire strength and excitement of the Enlightenment project. The intellectual world captured here is one which has no need of recourse to divine causation or to primal myth. Instead, it is possible to account for the advent of a great thinker through the employment of purely 'material agents', the normal – but only recently scientifically described – processes of conception, birth and growth. It is, of course, interesting that here there is an interruption in these processes, namely the abandonment and subsequent adoption of the infant; but what is even more interesting is that to Diderot and to his Enlightenment colleagues such events in no way affected the sequence through which human life must pass. On the contrary, the fact that life does indeed pass through such disruptions provides further evidence of the underlying rule of progress; far from being thrown backwards or, as it were, athwart by such events, there is the ground here for the further proof that scientific evidence is inviolable, that 'anyone lecturing to the Academy on the stages in the formation of a man or animal need refer only to material factors'.

It is important to emphasise that, if this is a version of materialism – which it is – then it is of a very different kind from some other materialisms. In other words, Diderot does not conceive of this materialistic explanation as constituting some kind of bondage to the past, to the 'material conditions of being', to the ineluctable pressures of the flesh; rather he sees reliance on material evidence as a way of counteracting those intellectual and political forces which would have us forever bound by a sense of mystery.

Another way of approaching this constellation of Enlightenment thought would be through the notion of the secret. For Diderot and many of his philosophical contemporaries, the significance of advances in scientific and technological understanding was that they 'laid bare' the innermost workings of the human and natural worlds. And this was, by definition, a political argument: the power of tyrants, autocrats, and – at the end of the day, or more certainly at the end of the eighteenth century – monarchs, is based on hiding secrets from the people. The alternative is a power which derives from knowledge; to paraphrase Adorno, that kind of knowledge which is itself power and knows no obstacles, neither in the enslavement of people nor in compliance with the world's rulers. Technology is the essence, of course, of this knowledge.

And thus we can make a smooth transition from the Enlightenment to the key concepts of modernity; for modernity, from one point of view, stands as that which resists the holding of the secret. Perhaps one archetypal, though much later, example would be the modernist construction of buildings where all that has previously been hidden becomes obvious: buildings where pipes, heating ducts, service phenomena of all kinds, are no longer subjected to concealment but are instead displayed on the outside, manifested as fully constituent parts. In this kind of architecture – and the same could be said of some kinds of modernist poetry – an entirely different arrangement between the aesthetic and the technical is proposed. Where, the theorist of modernity would say, in earlier and more traditional epochs the principal function of the aesthetic has been to conceal, to erase, the trace of the technical, modernity comes to celebrate the technical, to make it crystal clear that architecture, sculpture, poetry are 'works of man' and that there is a kind of bad faith involved in concealing these facts from the outside world, or from the viewer's gaze.

Yet it is also important to bear in mind that in asserting the value of the 'new', the dismissal and replacement of the old, the Enlightenment thinkers were not suggesting that this directly conferred power on man. Rather the contrary: the 'enlightened' attitude consisted in removing the traditional blinkers from the human gaze and opening oneself to what is already there, but as yet unperceived, in nature, even if that proves, in fact, to be intensely problematic. In a brief interchange in the

Conversation, D'Alembert suggests that Diderot's system does not make it clear how we form syllogisms or draw inferences; to this rather abstruse query, Diderot responds with robust common sense:

> As a matter of fact we don't: they are all drawn by nature. All we do is describe connected phenomena, the connection between which is either necessary or contingent, and these phenomena are known through experience. They are necessary in the case of mathematics, physics and other exact sciences, contingent in ethics, politics and other speculative sciences. (Diderot 1966, 161–2)

Thus Enlightenment is not a matter of claiming an overweening inventive power for mankind; it is rather the reverse, suggesting that what is required for advancement is minute, detailed, patient attention to nature – and to human behaviour. The important thing is to approach the phenomena with an unclouded mind, and this necessarily entails eschewing unnecessary reverence for the past; if we pay too much attention to accepted practices, traditional models of explanation, then we will find ourselves merely repeating past error.

Here, then, we see a major root of the idea of modernity. The past, of course, will not and cannot go away, and we would be greatly the worse if it did. But we need to consider the conclusions drawn by past philosophers with a sceptical eye; it is indeed their very errors which, if we consider them aright and in their proper historical context, can help us with our own further enlightenment. And behind all this there lies the question of power, and at whose service knowledge lies. It is here – and indeed throughout their book – that Horkheimer and Adorno raise a further critique of Enlightenment thinking, where they 'unpack' it, as it were, from a future historical perspective.

For, they claim, the problem with Enlightenment thinking is that, even as it opens new possibilities to us, it is at the same time necessarily blinkered by its own historical circumstances. For Diderot, it seemed as though the investigations being undertaken in his contemporary world were genuinely at the service of the whole population of mankind, and that the fruition of these intellectual and technological labours would be a universal emancipation. Not so, say Horkheimer and Adorno. Technology is, indeed, the essence of knowledge; it 'does not work by concepts and images ... but refers to method'; but therefore it also refers to 'the exploitation of others' work, and capital', and discoveries are apt to transform themselves in ways which may appear unexpected but which are in fact in the service of wider economic and ideological forces:

> ... the radio as a sublimated printing press, the dive bomber as a more effective form of artillery, radio control as a more reliable compass. What men want to learn from nature is how to use it in order wholly to dominate it and other men. That is the only aim. Ruthlessly, in despite of itself, the Enlightenment has extinguished any trace of its own self-consciousness. The only kind of thinking that is sufficiently hard to shatter myths is ultimately self-destructive.   (Horkheimer and Adorno 1972, 4)

This is a heavy indictment indeed, even though it must be noticed that Horkheimer and Adorno use the phrase 'in despite of itself'. What, then, does this rejection of Enlightenment imply, and what might it signify for the ongoing – or at least intermittent – processes of modernity?

One answer might be that modernity has always, and at all times, to do with the development of technological process; but it also, inevitably, thus confronts the processes of nature, but in 'other' forms. We might consider, for example, the contemporary form of 'enlightenment' signified by the 'cult of fitness' and related matters, on which Jean Baudrillard, in an essay called 'Mass-Media Culture' (1970), comments in these terms:

> Medical recycling: the check-up. Bodily, muscular, physiological recycling: Le Président for men; diets and beauty care for women; holidays for everyone. But we can (and *must*) extend this notion to much broader phenomena; the very 'rediscovery' of the body is a corporeal recycling; the 'rediscovery' of Nature, in the form of a countryside trimmed down to the dimensions of a mere sample, surrounded on all sides by the vast fabric of the city, carefully policed, and served up 'at room temperature' as parkland, nature reserve or background scenery for second homes, is, in fact, a recycling of Nature.   (Baudrillard 1998, 100–1)

From this we might derive the thought that Enlightenment is not necessarily a matter of a 'step change' in thinking; rather it is what the major theorists of modernity Gilles Deleuze and Félix Guattari might refer to as a 'reassemblage' of items, elements, phenomena, which are in some sense pre-existent. The move of Enlightenment is to suggest the new, while at the same time that which precedes Enlightenment continues to 'press back', continues to perform that activity in which, to use a rhetoric to which I shall refer again later, the old 'beast-flesh' goes on returning, albeit in transmuted form.

What is also revealed here is the way in which Enlightenment is, precisely, a set of rhetorical devices. For the transmutation of nature, of human flesh, into a 'new' arrangement can be seen from a different perspective as a reassertion of the law, but under a new guise. 'Enlightenment' claims to 'do away with the dark'; but the dark remains very much present. Another way of looking at this would be through a certain notion of artistic perspective. Enlightenment claims that the older darkness, the darkness of prejudice and terror, can be somehow relativised, or even framed, by 'new thinking'; but what if, at the end of the day (or of the night) it comes to appear that the 'light' itself is further framed by the endless return of the dark, the impossibility of escape or removal from a world of primitive imperatives? As Baudrillard goes on to say:

> [Nature] is no longer an original, specific presence at all, standing in symbolic opposition to culture, but a *simulation*, a 'consommé' of the signs of nature set back in circulation – in short, nature *recycled*. (Baudrillard 1998, 101)

By this point, we may seem a long way from eighteenth-century Enlightenment thinking, but the dialectic between modernity and nature nonetheless keeps recurring. For example, it is very reasonably asserted that the major political achievement, or perhaps the major 'descent', of the Enlightenment is to be found in the establishment of a notion of 'America' as the home of enlightenment, as a nation founded on enlightened principles where political freedom is enshrined and religious and other bigotries and persecutions are eschewed. From a contemporary perspective, of course, we may now find this a surprising proposition, and this is again a matter to which I shall return; for the moment, however, it is perhaps interesting to quote a short passage from Harold Rosenberg's seminal book *The Tradition of the New*, published in 1959. In the course of an essay about American poetry, he suggests that

> Whoever speaks the American language is forced into romanticism. His strictest discipline is itself a spiritual oddity and gives birth to an oddity – witness *The Scarlet Letter*, Emily Dickinson, the early gas engine. The American landscape is not easily mistaken for an endless wallpaper of nymphs and fountains – in the American language it takes hard application to achieve academic deadness. (Rosenberg 1962, 91)

Of course, Rosenberg is here writing about a highly specific phenomenon, namely what he sees as the incapacity of the American poet to respond in a 'new' or modern way to the fresh circumstances of his or her environment. Nevertheless, he touches upon an enormously important point about the Enlightenment, which we may see replicated through the various forms of modernity down to the present day.

We may put it in terms of a paradox, or perhaps better in a rather shaky syllogism, which goes like this. The onward march of reason demands the eschewal of old 'structures of feeling' (to use Raymond Williams's phrase). It therefore propels us to set off towards the new – 'to boldly go', to indulge in a rather different act of quotation. But as we set off towards the new we are, surely, gripped by a certain excitement, an excitement which involves loss, uncertainty, hope, ambition – precisely all those 'old' romantic feelings which we are supposed to be leaving behind.

What then needs to be said is that the Enlightenment is itself, seen in a certain light, in the light of a certain 'difference', a 'romantic' phenomenon. What, after all – as has been proved in fiction down the ages, from Homer through Defoe to *Pirates of the Caribbean* – can be more exciting than adventure, discovery, the hope of occupying the place of 'stout Cortez' when he first beholds a new world from 'a peak in Darien' (Keats 1990, 32)? Modernity, therefore, cannot be considered as a subjugation of event to an abstract principle of reason; it is rather, from almost the inception of the term, a complex compound of innovation and fear, escape and convention, transgression and return. Above all, perhaps, it is an act of *beckoning*; it suggests the possibility of a move from *this* place to *that* place.

A definition of the verb 'to beckon' reads thus: 'To make a mute signal or significant gesture of head or hand to (a person), as commanding his attention or action, and esp. his approach; hence, to summon or bid approach by such a gesture'. In its insistence on new worlds of understanding which we may enter or occupy if we have the will, the Enlightenment commits itself to such a set of gestures; but in doing so, it also again reveals its links to the secret. After all, if we are beckoned 'mutely', then we are not immediately vouchsafed the evidence of what scene we are being encouraged to enter or survey; we are being encouraged to take a 'romantic', possibly fatal risk, a situation which is underlined by the frequent fictive association of beckoning with ghosts, phantoms and similarly uncertain narrators. To beckon, the dictionary reminds us, is also to 'summon', with all the ambiguities, in terms of the 'summoning of spirits', which have historically surrounded that term. The 'sleep of reason' may, indeed, produce monsters; but, at least arguably, reason itself, in its Enlightenment manifestation – and as seen clearly by romantic artists and writers such as Blake and Fuseli – produces its own brand of monster, into whose exciting, forbidden company we cannot help but fall if we accept the lure and the temptation of the modern.

2 Modernity and Decadence

It would be fair to say that the complex trajectory of 'enlightenment' in the British context in the eighteenth century, its mutual involvement with modernity and with the 'trace' of the ancient, reached its apotheosis in Mary Shelley's *Frankenstein* (1818). *Frankenstein* is usually, of course, taken to be a novel emblematic of the fate of an overreaching technology, a use of science so quasi-divine in its attitude that it inevitably produces its own disastrous consequences. The actual scenario of the novel, however, is more complex than that. For one thing, it is framed within the narrative of one Walton, who is an adventurer, a romantic explorer of previously unknown regions. For another, the sort of overweening, Promethean search for knowledge which Mary Shelley apparently criticises is probably represented as much by her husband, the arch-romantic poet Percy Shelley, as by any particular scientist. And for a third, although it appears that in the person of Victor Frankenstein the author may be wishing to criticise science and technology, such – inevitably for a young woman in the early nineteenth century – was her lack of knowledge of scientific discourse and practice that the actual processes in which Victor engages in the construction of his creature owe – as he himself says – as much to the archaic, mysterious world of alchemy as they do to those more modern regimes, such as galvanism, with which the novel is ostensibly concerned.

Frankenstein's take on modernity, then, is curiously oblique, and reflects some of the paradoxes and contradictions which we have already encountered in Enlightenment thinking. These tensions continue throughout the nineteenth century – in, for example, Tennyson's resonant premonitions of a technologised future – but here I would like to turn to a specific moment towards the end of the century when, in a variety of forms, modernity again comes to the forefront of the public imagination. Here, for example, we encounter a plethora of fictional scientists engaged in dubious modernising processes. One of them is the central figure in Wells's novel of 1896, *The Island of Doctor Moreau*. In this text Prendick, the narrator, finds himself washed up on a mysterious island; he encounters, to his surprise, a white man called Montgomery, who informs him of the presence on the island of one Moreau, and Prendick is initially puzzled as he thinks he recognises the name from some scandal:

> 'The Moreau – Hollows' was it? 'The Moreau –'? Ah! it sent my memory back ten years. 'The Moreau Horrors'. The phrase drifted loose in my mind for a moment, and then I saw it in red lettering on a little buff-coloured pamphlet, that to read made one shiver and creep. Then I remembered distinctly all about it. ... I had been a mere lad then, and Moreau was, I suppose, about fifty; a prominent and masterful physiologist, well-known in scientific circles for his extraordinary imagination and his brutal directness in discussion. (Wells 1993a, 32)

What Prendick goes on to remember is that Moreau was regarded as a vivisectionist of a particularly cruel kind and that, as a result of what seemed to be revelations of his working practices, he was 'howled' out of the country, even though he 'had published some very astonishing facts in connection with the transfusion of blood, and, in addition, was known to be doing valuable work on morbid growths'. In this respect (as in almost all others in the novel) Prendick turns out to be both right and, more significantly, wrong. He is right in that Moreau conducted, and is still conducting, experiments on animals, but wrong in his conjectures as to the purpose of these experiments. Far from attempting simply to investigate animals' responses to pain, what Moreau is in fact trying to enact is an archetypal modernising project, nothing less than turning the beast into the human. In this respect, Moreau claims when he explains his work to Prendick, he has some eminent forebears,

> And yet this extraordinary branch of knowledge has never been sought as an end, and systematically, by modern investigators, until I took it up! Some such things have been hit upon in the last resort of surgery; most of the kindred evidence that will recur to your mind has been demonstrated, as it were, by accident – by tyrants, by criminals, by the breeders of horses and dogs, by all kinds of untrained clumsy-handed men working for their own immediate ends. I was the first man to take up this question armed

with antiseptic surgery, and with a really scientific knowledge of the laws
of growth.   (Wells 1993a, 70)

And so Moreau figures in the text as an arch-moderniser, as a new kind
of scientist who can bring modern discoveries to bear on age-old problems. Prendick, perhaps quite naturally although in a somewhat
unreflective fashion, finds these processes, and more particularly the
particular examples of 'beast-men' that he encounters, all of them
deeply faulty in one way or another, disgusting and inhuman; perhaps
Wells does too, but as we might expect from an author whose lifetime
mission was to explore the implications of scientific and technological
advance, his condemnation of Moreau seems at times curiously half-
hearted, and there is a sense that although Moreau's methods might
indeed be pain-inducing to the point of suggesting a characterological
pathology nonetheless the goal he seeks, which would be nothing less
than a rejuvenation of the human race, may be worthy of more complex
consideration.

What the text overall appears to suggest is that the modernising
advances of science must know their limits. Obviously there are enormously close connections here with more recent scientific developments.
The same people, presumably, as those who 'howled' (an interestingly
bestial phrase!) Moreau out of the country now dig up graves in order to
persuade the relatives of the dead that they should cease to breed guinea-
pigs for scientific experimentation. The same argument about whether it
may be necessary to experiment on animals in order to better the human
condition still proceeds, sometimes democratically, sometimes violently.

One might say that a crucial modern distinction here is between
animal experimentation which is devoted to the eradication, or at least
the management, of human disease, and that which conduces merely to
the perfection of a range of cosmetics, but the point is that in the march
of modernity these two aims are not always easy to distinguish. Behind
them both there lies a thoroughly Enlightenment view that the human is
the pinnacle of achievement, and that whatever is done to progress the
species – and, crucially, to extend its life-span – can be potentially
justifiable. Yet, of course, there is a certain circularity to this argument,
for at the root of it can be discerned the most archaic, irrational motiva-
tion of all, namely the survival of the species. It could be argued, for
example, that animal experimentation – the name that now appears to
have almost completely supplanted vivisection, even though the activities performed may be identical – is simply a new, 'improved' form of

hunting, designed to ensure and vindicate human supremacy at the expense of the beast – by which means we may punish the threatening beast within ourselves as well as other members of the animal kingdom.

In these ways, then, the arguments in *The Island of Doctor Moreau* about modernity have strong and continuing connections with the present day, with the critical exception, perhaps, of the fact that Moreau is – more or less – a lone scientist, whereas contemporary arguments would focus more on the role of, for example, the giant corporation and its ability to defy both law and 'natural' morality. But the end of the nineteenth century saw also another modernising challenge. It took most obviously the form of the 'New Woman', by which we may signify the emergence of a debate about gender equality which, again, has ramifications down to (and no doubt beyond) the present day.

Frankenstein, as is well-known, is subtitled 'The Modern Prometheus'; at the other end of the nineteenth century, we might see its natural counterpart Bram Stoker's *Dracula* (1897) as also, and perhaps more startlingly, addressing issues about modernity. We might consider, for example, the issue of degeneration in *Dracula*, the fear often expressed in the text that the danger awaiting modern man is of returning down the evolutionary spiral. It would be difficult to overestimate how pressing a fear, in the wake of Darwinian revelations about human kinship with the apes, this was towards the close of the nineteenth century. One of the major figures in this debate was Max Nordau, whose *Degeneration* was translated into English in 1895 and contains passages such as the following:

> One epoch of history is unmistakably in its decline, and another is announcing its approach. There is a sound of rending in every tradition, and it as though the morrow would not link itself with to-day. Things as they are totter and plunge, and they are suffered to reel and fall, because man is weary, and there is no faith that it is worth an effort to uphold them. Views that have hitherto governed minds are dead or driven hence like disenthroned kings, and for their inheritance they that hold the titles and they that would usurp are locked in struggle. Meanwhile interregnum in all its terrors prevails; there is confusion among the powers that be; the million, robbed of its leaders, knows not where to turn; the strong work their will; false prophets arise, and dominion is divided among those whose rod is the heavier because their time is short. (Stoker 1998, 470)

It is of course easy to see in this startling rhetoric echoes of biblical apocalypticism, but there are other traces here which relate to a fear of modernity. For the 'morrow' not to link itself with today it would, pre-sumably, have to be *totally* different; the anxiety here is of a future emerging for which we are not prepared, which will catch us by surprise: a realm of the future, perhaps, even what we might now call, in the strictest sense, a realm of science fiction, for which we have no maps, in which we shall not know where to turn for guidance. The apparent battle, again, between the divinely sanctioned – 'enthroned' – forces of the past and the 'usurpers' who may come to challenge this 'divine right' can be represented as a battle between those forces which resist the challenge of modernity and those, unexplained and inexplicable as they may be, who represent this dangerous path into an uncertain future.

What we may deduce from this, then, is another significant paradox about modernity. On the one hand, modernity asserts the dominance of – scientific or rational – knowledge; it promises to banish the dark places of the mind, to lay the ghosts to rest and to exterminate the monsters. But on the other, it beckons us towards an unknown future, where old certainties will no longer hold and the old writs will no longer run. Modernity is thus deeply imbricated in what we might fairly call an uncanny struggle between knowing and unknowing, between a notion of restrictive certainty and one of libertarian doubt. It is certainly this 'lib-ertarian doubt' which afflicts Nordau:

> Men look with longing for whatever new things are at hand, without presage whence they will come or what they will be. They have hope that in the chaos of thought, art may yield revelations of the order that is to follow on this tangled web. The poet, the musician, is to announce, or divine, or at least suggest in what forms civilisation will further be evolved. What shall be considered good to-morrow – what shall be beauti-ful? What shall we know to-morrow – what believe in? What shall inspire us? How shall we enjoy? ... (Stoker 1998, 470)

What Nordau is in part calling attention to here is the value assigned to sheer – or mere – novelty; he is predicting, with perhaps uncanny accu-racy, a condition of society in which the 'new' has credibility in and of itself, and in which the business of looking into its credentials, its prove-nance, is short-circuited by a kind of overarching glamour. What is at least as interesting here, however, is the role he ascribes – with, of course, the utmost suspicion – to the artist as the avatar of modernity. It is for the artist to 'announce, or divine, or at least suggest' the future – even though those three verbs carry very different freights of meaning on a spectrum of presumed creative authority. This is a kind of thinking which we shall come across increasingly as we trace the trajectory of modernity in its later formations, and it will fall in with some extremely uncomfortable political bed-fellows (in the shape, for example, of Vorticism and futurism); but for the moment, I will return to the connections between this kind of thinking and the text – and quasi-myth – of *Dracula*, considered as emblematic of a certain perspective on modernity.

The first point to make is that *Dracula*, perhaps as a matter of surprise to the first-time reader, is replete with technology. In her edition of the text, Glennis Byron quotes Jonathan Harker, referring to his shorthand diary: 'It is nineteenth century up-to-date with a vengeance', he says. Byron goes on to say:

> The claim could equally be made of *Dracula* itself. From telegraphs, typewriters, and telephones, to shorthand, phonographs, and kodaks, Bram Stoker's *Dracula* flaunts its modernity: it is concretely embedded in the ever-growing late Victorian world of information technology. ... Newspaper cuttings, telegraphs, ships' logs, journal entries, letters, interviews – all come together in the typescript Mina produces in triplicate. Even Dracula is aware of the need to collect data and avidly seeks the power it confers. (Stoker 1998, 12)

One of the interesting features of this list is that many of its elements are technologies which are specifically used for communication *at a distance*, as the Greek root *tele* indicates. The modernity of *Dracula* thus consists, at one level, of the representation of a stage of evolution or progress which allows for an escape from the domestic or national confines of traditional life and thus of the traditional novel; and this element of progress stands in stark contrast to the figure of Dracula himself, who signifies a clinging to older roots of power. Seen in this light, the novel demonstrates the superiority of modern technology over older ways of life, the replacement of an order of power based on the 'ancient house', in all senses of that word, by a different order, the replacement of a surviving aristocracy by a technocracy, the 'Team of Light', focussed on the scientist figure of Van Helsing but also, and importantly, including a representative of America, symbol of a new age, in the calm, reasonable form of Quincey Morris. Behind this there also lies the notion of a power based on extreme individualism – the Count is, in one sense, the last of his race – being supplanted by a power based on teamwork and cooperation: no one individual is strong enough to withstand Dracula, but the kind of working together permitted by new technologies permits a modern flow of information which eventually proves successful in the quasi-epic struggle.

It is, however, worth noticing that the flow of modernity runs in two directions in the text. As has often been said, the role of women in *Dracula* is deeply ambiguous. To an extent, they are portrayed as passive victims, even as the weak spot in the team's armour; on the other, there is a sense in the novel that one reason why they need to be rigidly controlled is precisely because of a fear that they might become, indeed, 'out of control', and this reflects contemporary anxieties about the 'New Woman', the emergence in the late nineteenth century of a significant set of demands for gender equality, which also signifies a version of modernity, but one which Stoker himself, and the novel, are evidently reluctant to accept.

And behind this again there lies a coded fear of degeneration, an anxiety about the continuing pull, signified in the vampires, back to a more archaic form of life. If the modernising elements of *Dracula* beckon the reader forward into the future, then vampirism signifies a countervailing beckoning back into the past. Similarly, the conquest of Dracula clearly requires an effort, a harnessing, of will; to succumb to the vampire involves a relinquishing of this strenuousness, a return to a somnambulistic world which might appear menacing before it is entered but is afterwards restful, trancelike, standing for a dream of history from which we might never need to be awakened.

And this, we might further say, is both the fear and the lure of decadence. Climbing upwards towards the modern is difficult, engaging all the faculties of the intellect; it might be easier, the novel reflects – while ending by sternly repudiating this thought – to relapse into the past, to let the vampire – which, in this sense, represents the past itself – do its work and allow for a certain forgetfulness in the face of the difficulty of handling the ever-increasing flow of information which is characteristic of the modern world.

We can notice aspects of a similar constellation in that other best-selling phenomenon of the 1890s, Conan Doyle's Sherlock Holmes stories, which are ostensibly devoted to the expulsion of mystery – not here necessarily by technological means but by the exercise of a deductive reason so elevated that it can seem, to the uninitiated, divinely inspired. We might consider, for example, some remarks Holmes himself makes to his colleague Watson – another doctor – in 'The Crooked Man':

It is one of those instances where the reasoner can produce an effect which seems remarkable to his neighbour, because the latter has missed the one little point which is the basis of the deduction. The same may be said, my dear fellow, for the effect of some of these little sketches of yours, which is entirely meretricious, depending as it does upon your retaining in your own hands some factors in the problem which are never imparted to the reader. Now, at present I am in the position of these same readers, for I hold in this hand several threads of one of the strangest cases which ever perplexed a man's brain, and yet I lack the one or two which are needful to complete my theory.   (Conan Doyle 1974, 147–8)

There are many points of interest in this passage. Perhaps the most obvious one is the way in which Holmes's version of reasoning serves to split apart the surfaces, the appearances, of things and to replace them with a clear, differentiated set of points, arguments, pieces of evidence. What seems mysterious at first sight appears so only because it has not been reduced to its constituent elements; we might again think of this as an 'architectonic' process, one which prohibits the concealments which are an effect of more traditional methods of thinking. What is distinctively 'modern' in this is the refusal to accept pre-given data; everything must be subjected to rigorous, 'dissective' scrutiny.

Once this has occurred, Holmes claims, then even the wildest dreams of the encyclopaedists may be fulfilled: one of the 'strangest cases which ever perplexed a man's brain' may be solved. What is also interesting here in terms of modernity is the way in which Holmes's remarks effectively break apart the surface of the story itself, the story which Watson tells, for what is happening here is that Watson, as the narrator of 'The Crooked Man', is recounting comments Holmes is making on his, Watson's, own story-telling and its accompanying withholding of information. It would be fair to say that there is here a harbinger of a distinctively modern *mise en abŷme*: if Watson's story-telling methods are indeed as Holmes claims, then what, the reader may reasonably ask, is being withheld in this particular instance? And all this is further compounded by the way in which Holmes is placing himself, or claiming to place himself, precisely in the position of one of these uninitiated, even perhaps manipulated, readers; although in this case it is not a story-teller who is withholding facts but rather the texture of life itself which proves resistant to having its secrets teased out.

We see here, then, a version of modernity as a form of *exposure*, and we could relate this to a kind of psychoanalytic explanation. Broadly speaking, we might say that the process of modernity is one of placing behind us the ghosts, the phantoms which we would prefer to regard as merely things of childhood; instead of these we have the bracing breath of reason, the possibility of total explanation. In this guise, one could then say that modernity sets itself firmly against a notion of the unconscious; the dark forces which ruin individual lives and human history can be surmounted if only we can see them in a proper 'light', a dream of technological benefit which has certainly lasted to the present day. Yet even here, it is interesting that in the Holmes stories there are frequent hiatuses, gaps – cases, for example, which Watson mentions but which he fails to recount in full – 'I still retain', he says in 'The Naval Treaty', 'an almost verbatim report of the interview in which [Holmes] demonstrated the true facts of the case to Monsieur Dubuque, of the Paris police, and Fritz von Waldbaum, the well-known specialist of Dantzig, both of whom had wasted their energies upon what proved to be side-issues. The new century will have come, however, before the story can be safely told' (Conan Doyle 1974, 209).

Quite what Fritz von Waldbaum was a specialist *in* is not recounted; neither is 'The Adventure of the Second Stain', which is the episode to which Watson claims to be alluding, and which, in another sense, does not exist at all since it does not fall prey to his story-telling. What is, however, significant is that passages such as this deepen and complicate our sense of both exposure *and* concealment in the Holmes stories: modern though his techniques may be, there still remains an apparent vast hinterland of untold, or insufficiently told, stories, together with the hint that grave matters of state may prevent the telling of these and other stories until 'the new century', until, that is, the condition of the modern has 'caught up' with events. It would be possible then in the Holmes stories to see a new 'dialectic of enlightenment', one in which apparent solutions to human problems only lead us into new depths, new areas where the supposed spread of a successful regime of explanatory discourse falters before the sheer weight of experience, while at the same time demonstrating the inevitable partiality which, as Holmes says, characterises Watson's attempts at objective recounting.

Watson, however, is of course not objective, and presumably neither is he striving for objectivity. On the contrary, his stories are geared towards demonstrating Holmes's extraordinary powers of reasoning; whether the impact of this partiality is towards a more general demonstration of the potential reasoning power of modern man is perhaps a moot point, but certainly there is a suggestion that the 'dark places' so graphically named in the titles of the stories – Boscombe Valley, The Priory School, The Abbey Grange, Thor Bridge, perhaps most emblematically of all Shoscombe Old Place – can be penetrated. These places may contain ancient secrets, they may indeed be the generators of secrets; but it is not beyond human power to explain these secrets, and this perhaps is one of the main sources of the power of the stories. As Holmes says, it is in fact the case that many of the 'cases' recounted do not involve anything at all which could be called, in conventional social terms, a 'crime'; Holmes's abilities and activities as a detective lie athwart such categorisations, and his work is a work of the pure intellect, regardless of legal and other implications, dedicated to 'enlightenment' wherever mystery may be found.

To return to Wells, we can find a further reticulation of modernity as conceived in the 1890s in *The Time Machine*, which has long been accepted as one of the earliest works of what has since come to be called science fiction. Here the Time Traveller goes forward to the future, and he there encounters what at first sight appears to be a paradise, a paradise achieved through the modernisation of the human species. He muses on it thus:

> The science of our time has attacked but a little department of the field of human disease, but, even so, it spreads its operations very steadily and persistently. Our agriculture and horticulture destroy a weed just here and there and cultivate perhaps a score or so of wholesome plants, leaving the greater number to fight out a balance as they can. We improve our favourite plants and animals – and how few they are – gradually by selective breeding ... Some day all this will be better organised, and still better. That is the drift of the current in spite of the eddies. The whole world will be intelligent, educated, and cooperating; things will move faster and faster towards the subjugation of Nature.   (Wells 1993b, 31)

And so the continuing progress of modernity will eventually iron out all human problems, eradicate the friction between the human and the natural, and will produce a golden future society, of which the Time Traveller, as he thinks, has evidence:

> I saw mankind housed in splendid shelters, gloriously clothed, and as yet I had found them engaged in no toil. There were no signs of struggle, neither social nor economical struggle. The shop, the advertisement, traffic, all that commerce which constitutes the body of our world, was gone.   (Wells 1993b, 32)

But of course this evidence is in no way what it seems. While it is true that the Eloi, the post-human race which enjoys these privileges, do indeed lead a toil-free life, a life dedicated to beauty, they are at the same time, as the Time Traveller notices, curiously enervated and childlike. The reason for this emerges when he realises that there is, in addition, another race in the future, the Morlocks. It is the Morlocks who in fact do the necessary work to keep the species going; it is significant that whereas the Eloi live in the open, the Morlocks live underground, in the underworld, which signifies the degradation of human labour and the way in which a myth of human superiority is again associated with a problem of what then happens to the 'dark places', those aspects of human nature which resist modernisation. The fact that the Morlocks signify all that is 'unregenerate' in mankind is further underlined by their cannibalism; this is significant at a social level, but it also reminds us of one of the most primordial and anti-social desires identified by psychoanalysis.

Before he fully realises the terrible relationship between the Morlocks and the Eloi, the Time Traveller hits upon a different potential explanation for the state of the future world which he has discovered. He speaks of the widening gap between rich and poor which appears to be attendant on modernisation, and adds:

> So, in the end, above ground you must have the Haves, pursuing pleasure and comfort and beauty, and below ground the Have-nots, the Workers getting continually adapted to the conditions of their labour. Once they were there, they would no doubt have to pay rent, and not a little of it, for the ventilation of their caverns; and if they refused, they would starve or be suffocated for arrears. Such of them as were so constituted as to be miserable and rebellious would die; and, in the end, the balance being permanent, the survivors would become as well adapted to the conditions of underground life, and as happy in their way, as the Upper-world people were to theirs.   (Wells 1993b, 50)

We need to see here a relation to the social thought of Marx; the separation of the classes, the dehumanisation of labour, an extreme form of human alienation. But the Time Traveller, at this point in the book, is not aware of the way in which, over the course of history, the Morlocks have re-established their dominance over the etiolated Eloi, although even his current perception of the situation is alarming enough:

> The great triumph of Humanity I had dreamed of took a different shape in
> my mind. It had been no such triumph of moral education and general co-
> operation as I had imagined. Instead, I saw a real aristocracy, armed with a
> perfected science and working to a logical conclusion the industrial system
> of today. Its triumph had not been simply a triumph over Nature, but a
> triumph over Nature and the fellow-man.   (Wells 1993b, 50)

Quite how complete this triumph has been is something the Time
Traveller only comes to realise later on, as he becomes aware that the
actual pattern of society he is observing is the reverse of its appearance,
that this dystopia is more radical, more profound, more destructive of
any fiction of modernity than he had ever dreamed, and that the Eloi
indeed resemble and enact the extreme conclusion of decadence.

Modernity then in the 1890s, we may say, is in a state of tension. On
the one hand, technological advance appears to pave the way for the possibility of the general improvement of the human lot; on the other, the
discoveries of Darwin and Freud, whether known directly by individual
writers or not, both in their different ways suggest that mankind is tied
to the past, the past of the species or the past which continues to exist in
the form of ineradicable social (and antisocial) desires in the depths of
the unconscious.

As we have mentioned, it was later, in 1930, that Freud wrote one of his
last works, *Civilisation and its Discontents*, but nevertheless some comments he makes there are relevant to this particular constellation of
modernity. He concludes the text with the following observation:

> The fateful question for the human species seems to me to be whether and
> to what extent their cultural development will succeed in mastering the
> disturbance of their communal life by the human instinct of aggression
> and self-destruction. It may be that in this respect precisely the present
> time deserves a special interest. Men have gained control over the forces of
> nature to such an extent that with their help they would have no difficulty
> in exterminating one another to the last man.   (Freud 1964, 145)

And this comment on the possible terminus of the human species can, of
course, suitably move us on to a further major epoch in the progress of
modernity, the one now known precisely by the name of 'modernism'.

3 Modernity and Modernism

The Enlightenment, it might be said, asserted its modernity through an attempt to bring (rational) order into what was perceived as intellectual chaos. The modernity of the end of the nineteenth century, it might equally be said, sought to assert the possibility of a progressive future against the background of the regressive human tendencies adumbrated by Darwin and Freud. The movement called 'modernism' has often been considered to be a reaction against, or a response to, a more concrete eruption of the chaotic, the disorderly and the inhumane, in the form of the First World War, which was widely believed, at least during the 1920s, to represent a nadir of human brutality which threw the very possibility of human progress into radical question.

In an influential essay published in 1965 as the Preface to a book called, significantly, *The Modern Tradition*, Richard Ellmann and Charles Feidelson spoke of modernism in these terms:

> If we can postulate a modern tradition, we must add that it is a paradoxi-
> cally untraditional tradition. Modernism strongly implies some sort of his-
> torical discontinuity, either a liberation from inherited patterns or, at
> another extreme, deprivation and disinheritance. ... Committed to every-
> thing in human experience that militates against custom, abstract order,
> and even reason itself, modern literature has elevated individual existence
> over social man, unconscious feeling over self-conscious perception,
> passion and will over intellection and systematic morals, dynamic vision
> over the static image, dense actuality over practical reality ... Interwoven
> with the access of knowledge, the experimental verve, and the personal
> urgency of the modern masters is ... a sense of loss, alienation, and
> despair.   (Ellmann and Feidelson 1965, vi)

This is obviously a very complex, and in some ways puzzling, definition. The point about historical discontinuity is well taken; there is no doubt that in the work of many of the modernist masters – Eliot, Ezra Pound and Franz Kafka among them – one can find a deep dislocation from the past. In an emblematic play like Samuel Beckett's *Waiting for Godot* (1986), it would seem fair to doubt whether the past, in any recognisable sense, exists at all. In *Waiting for Godot* everything is frozen into a single interminable moment; there is no causal link between events but only a sense of isolation and repetition as the two protagonists, Vladimir and Estragon, try without much hope to make sense of their situation and to establish who or what it is that the continually deferred arrival of Godot might represent.

There is certainly nothing in *Waiting for Godot*, or in any other of Beckett's plays or novels, which suggests 'liberation' from the oppressiveness of the past; but one can indeed find in his work evidence of 'deprivation and disinheritance'. It is as though a world which, at some previous stage of human history or the individual life, has been perceived as succouring and nurturing has been radically withdrawn – or redrawn; there are no longer any certainties on which to rely. To a certain extent, one might see this (and the point is underlined by Godot's name) as a modernist reflection of the collapse of moral certainties as underlined and sanctioned by religious belief, and as a diagnosis of a 'modern' condition it is interesting to refer this back to the Enlightenment, for the Enlightenment too serves as a reminder of the fate of the human in the presumed absence of divine certainties; the eighteenth-century term in which this sense was apprehended and encapsulated was *deus absonditus*, the notion of a hidden God, who might indeed, for all we know, have created the universe but who has now, as far as we can tell, 'hidden' himself and left the human race to make sense of things as best it can.

Where matters become more puzzling, however, is when Ellmann and Feidelson refer to that which stands against 'custom, abstract order, and even reason itself', for of course this suggests a kind of modernity very different from that which held sway in the eighteenth century. We can certainly see the truth of this in some writers who are now labelled 'modernist'. Perhaps the most obvious example would be D.H. Lawrence. Lawrence's novels are certainly radically opposed to 'custom'; indeed, the entire series of well-known events surrounding the publication and trial of *Lady Chatterley's Lover* (1928) can be seen as clear evidence of, firstly, how deeply athwart custom and tradition Lawrence's fiction was but also, secondly, how powerful those same forces of custom and tradition proved to be in their opposition to this particular form of modernity, couched as it was in terms of a certain form of sexual liberation but also in terms which violently supported, in more general terms, the demands of passion in opposition to those of a 'bloodless' reason.

And we can see some sense too in Ellmann and Feidelson's opposition between 'individual existence' and 'social man' – in Beckett obviously, but also in the various ramifications of philosophical existentialism emanating from such writers as Jean-Paul Sartre and Albert Camus. In these forms of writing – and long before Margaret Thatcher surprisingly proclaimed a superficially similar (but also superficial) credo – society has ceased to exist; or, perhaps better, it has become fatally corrupted, so that the only way of retaining any level of self-coherence is by proceeding in a willed ignorance of societal demands. We can see some of this kind of thinking too in the notion, pioneered above all by Woolf, of the novel as a 'stream of consciousness'.

But it is worth pausing for a moment on the case of Woolf; because, in emblematic novels like *Mrs Dalloway* (1925) and *To the Lighthouse* (1927), despite their elevated position in the modernist canon, it is not at all that society has ceased to exist, nor is it necessarily regarded as corrupt. Woolf's achievement is certainly to allow the reader extraordinary insight into the workings of particular psyches, a level of insight probably only paralleled by Henry James; but the psyches she depicts are not at all divorced from society. On the contrary, they are precisely the constructs of that society, and the most fascinating moments in Woolf's writing are arguably those where we sense individuals quailing and reeling before the social pressures exerted upon them. Certainly Woolf's discourse is 'internal' in a way which would be very foreign to the narratorial assumptions of Jane Austen or George Eliot; but the world which her characters inhabit is vividly depicted and bears none of the outward marks of alienation which would be typical of Beckett, Kafka, perhaps Joyce, or certainly that relatively unknown arch-modernist I have previously mentioned, B.S. Johnson.

Perhaps some of these issues can be best further addressed by looking at some of Pound's poetry. Here, for example, is his well-known short poem, 'The Garden' (1916):

> Like a skein of loose silk blown against a wall
> She walks by the railing of a path
>   in Kensington Gardens,
> And she is dying piece-meal
>   of a sort of emotional anaemia.

And round about there is a rabble
Of the filthy, sturdy, unkillable infants of the very poor.
They shall inherit the earth.

In her is the end of breeding.
Her boredom is exquisite and excessive.
She would like some one to speak to her,
And is almost afraid that I
                    will commit that indiscretion.   (Pound 1948, 92–3)

What is firstly noticeable about this poem is its title, 'The Garden', which might appear at first glance to refer us back to a long tradition of English-language garden poems and tropes, of which the most famous would be Marvell's 'green thought in a green shade' (Marvell 1972, 101). But clearly Pound's poem, while acknowledging this tradition, diverges widely from it. For one thing, it differs in formal terms: there is no rhyme here, no formal metrical pattern, instead a version of the patterning of speech or, at any rate, of thought. For another, there is none of the peacefulness which has been conventionally attached to the garden in the history of literature since, at least, the Renaissance. The 'difference' of this take on the garden is already signified from the very beginning, with the 'wall' and the 'railing': these are images not of freedom or contentment but rather of confinement and frustration.

The poem also enacts, not a consummation of self-communing as in the Marvell example, but rather the reverse, a pervasive non-communication: the poet may or may not be correctly interpreting the wishes of the protagonist, but whether he is or not the fact remains that real communication is here under a sign of prohibition, a type of erasure. What is portrayed instead as an image of the modern world is a state in which speech and communication have become precarious, problematised; there is an irony bordering on sarcasm in the poet's summary of the condition of his 'object' ('her boredom is exquisite and excessive'). And this, of course, is because of a specific social and political perspective. The 'she' of the poem may indeed be an aristocrat, or a member of the upper middle classes; but we are left in no doubt that her time is finished, she is merely a bewildered and unwelcome survivor into a different, more modern age. Yet for Pound, here as elsewhere, it is not as though this 'new world' is itself to be welcomed; instead it is summarised in the notorious phrase 'the filthy, sturdy, unkillable infants of the very poor', which summarises a whole new social order which is in no way preferable to the past, a fact further summarised in the satirical use of the biblical phrase 'They shall inherit the earth'.

This is a bitter poem, which represents no hope for the future; instead it depicts a sterile lock between past and present. When it is claimed that the lady represents the 'end of breeding', the reader needs to appreciate that the meaning of the word 'end' as purpose and the alternative meaning of 'end' as conclusion are fatally interlocked in this outmoded figure. The modernity of this world, then, represents a kind of supersession; but it does not represent a clear trajectory into an improved future. Rather, the shards of civilisation are being overwhelmed, possibly inevitably; but what they are being overwhelmed *by* is itself, as any Augustan writer would have suggested, merely a new access of barbarism.

What if anything, then, does Pound set up against this pessimistic trajectory in modern culture? One of the other approaches he takes is that signified in the idea of 'vorticism'. Vorticism was a literary and artistic movement which attempted precisely what Ellmann and Feidelson suggest above when they speak of the elevation of 'dynamic vision over the static image', and one of the emblematic poems is Pound's 'The Game of Chess' (1916), which is subtitled 'Dogmatic Statement Concerning the Game of Chess: Theme for a Series of Pictures':

> Red knights, brown bishops, bright queens,
> Striking the board, falling in strong 'L's' of colour.
> Reaching and striking in angles,
>   holding lines in one colour.
> This board is alive with light;
>   these pieces are living in form,
> Their moves break and reform the pattern:
>   luminous green from the rooks,
> Clashing with 'X's' of queens,
>   looped with the knight-leaps.
>
> 'Y' pawns, cleaving, embanking!
> Whirl! Centripetal! Mate! King down in the vortex,
> Clash, leaping of bands, straight strips of hard colour,
> Blocked lights working in. Escapes. Renewal of contest.
>   (Pound 1948, 122)

This is, in the first place, a poem which is vividly, even violently, coloured; not for nothing is it imagined in terms of a 'series of pictures'.

This vividness is not reflective; it is designed to produce, to enact or incarnate, an immediate scene, as though poetry, if it is sufficiently 'strong', can actually *produce* the world it seeks to describe – hence the concatenation of exclamations and imperatives in the second stanza. At the same time the subject of the poem, although it is ostensibly a game of chess, also constantly reminds us of a set of military manoeuvres; the reality of the world presented here is one of warfare and conflict, from which all softness and indeed all emotion has been removed. Poetry here becomes one of a number of versions of attack, even if, as is suggested in the final line, that attack can never be completely successful; it is not the role of poetry to explore the human psyche, but rather to discern the underlying dynamic material shapes of the world, stripped of human sympathy. That world is a matter not of emotion or even reason but rather of shape, perspective, proportion, form; the poet – and implicitly also the visual artist – does not have as his or her duty the revelation of hidden depths but rather the accurate portrayal of the hard shapes of the observable world, just as advances in technology continually serve to replace the softness and vulnerability of the human body by an invulnerable, violent carapace – and as tanks and aircraft replace infantry and cavalry in newer, more 'distanced' but also more violent, forms of physical warfare.

But what is equally interesting about Pound's poetry – and, one might say, most other manifestations of modernism – is that the insistence on a modern clarity of vision is never fully separable from the traces of the past. A great deal of his work is lyrically moving, as it were, despite itself, and alludes to a vast range of historical backdrops, ranging from ancient China to medieval Provence. Here, for example, are the opening stanzas of 'Piere Vidal Old' (1909), in which Pound takes us back to the world of the Provençal troubadours:

> When I but think upon the great dead days
> And turn my mind upon that splendid madness,
> Lo! I do curse my strength
> And blame the sun his gladness;
> For that the one is dead
> And the red sun mocks my sadness.
>
> Behold me, Vidal, that was fool of fools!
> Swift as the king wolf was I and as strong
> When tall stags fled me through the alder brakes.

> And every jongleur knew me in his song,
> And the hounds fled and the deer fled
> And none fled ever long.   (Pound 1948, 55)

Essentially this poem looks back to a past order of things, one in which the poet and his curious equivalent the hunter had a 'natural' place in the world and were respected for their varying kinds of 'strength'. But here, as perhaps also in 'The Game of Chess', one can sense the difficulties into which Pound's views were to lead him in his well-known flirtation with extreme right-wing politics. For the kind of romanticisation of a heroic past in which Pound is here engaging can lead naturally to a call for the restoration of that past, of a world in which the strong flourish and the weak go to the wall. 'O Age gone lax!' writes Pound towards the end of the poem,

> O stunted followers,
> That mask at passions and desire desires,
> Behold me shrivelled, and your mock of mocks;
> And yet I mock you by the mighty fires
> That burnt me to this ash.   (Pound 1948, 57)

In the rhetoric of an 'age gone lax', one can certainly discern the lineaments of modernism's constant outrage against the 'discolouration' of the world; but one can – and must – also discern a fascistic rhetoric, a discourse which by criticising the present for its 'laxity' permits and encourages the emergence of 'strong leadership', whether that leadership attains and keeps its power by democratic means or not.

This version of modernity, then, is very far from a vision of democracy and profoundly likely to stray into authoritarianisms of one kind or another; while appearing to represent and privilege the freedom of the intellect, it also paradoxically promotes an idea of power which will in the end – as was so visible in the years leading up to the Second World War, and has been equally visible in many parts of the world since – precisely close down those possibilities of freedom. And these kinds of lamentation are by no means the preserve of the 'modernists' themselves; if we are thinking here of a *concern* with modernity as much as of *advocacy* of it, then we can find this concern even – or perhaps especially – in so unlikely a poet as Philip Larkin. His poem 'Going, Going' (1972), for example, is precisely a lament for the changes endemic to modernisation:

I thought it would last my time –
The sense that, beyond the town,
There would always be fields and farms,
Where the village louts could climb
Such trees as were not cut down;
I knew there'd be false alarms

In the papers about old streets
And split-level shopping, but some
Have always been left so far;
And when the old part retreats
As the bleak high-risers come
We can always escape in the car.   (Larkin 1988, 189)

Of course, Larkin's rhetoric may seem to us now curiously more old-fashioned than Pound's, couched as it is in terms of a specific age ('split-level shopping', 'high-risers') which has already been long superseded by a more 'modernistic' cultural rhetoric of malls, atria, waterfront developments and studio flats. But the combination here of fear of the modern and a hankering for a past – even when, as with the 'village louts', that past is presented in less than flattering terms – is a recognisable offshoot of modernity, and the reference to these 'louts' seems no more democratic than Pound's to the infants of the 'very poor'.

We might say, then, that there is a tendency within modernism towards certain forms of elitism: towards, certainly, the figuring of the poet, novelist, artist as possessing a specific and unique perspective on the present age (although this, of course, is in itself hardly the specific preserve of modernism), but also towards a post-neoclassical awareness of the imminence of the barbaric. In this respect again, modernism demonstrates its doubleness: in beckoning us towards the future it simultaneously gestures towards a safer, saner past, a past which, to be sure, stands in continuing need of (re)interpretation but which also, as Eliot powerfully reminds us his essay 'Tradition and the Individual Talent' (1919), provides us with the only background for contemporary culture and the only yardstick by which it may be safely measured.

There are, however, other strands in modernism. We might, for example, return to Virginia Woolf and consider the puzzling case of her novel *Orlando* (1928). The most obvious sense in which *Orlando* is puzzling – and has been considered scandalous – is that it recounts the adventures of a protagonist who is variously male and female; but what it also does is take the reader on a journey through a peculiar version of history, from the sixteenth century to the 'present day', thus exploring a succession of waves of modernisation – and sometimes its reverse – as though they are being experienced by a single character. One typical moment of transition occurs at the end of the fourth chapter. A clock begins to strike over London; as it does so,

> a light breeze rose and by the time the sixth stroke of midnight had struck the whole of the eastern sky was covered with an irregular moving darkness, though the sky to the west and north stayed clear as ever. Then the cloud spread north. Height upon height above the city was engulfed by it. Only Mayfair, with all its lights shining, burnt more brilliantly than ever by contrast. With the eighth stroke, some hurrying tatters of cloud sprawled over Piccadilly. They seemed to mass themselves and to advance with extraordinary rapidity towards the west end. As the ninth, tenth, and eleventh strokes struck, a huge blackness sprawled over the whole of London. With the twelfth stroke of midnight, the darkness was complete. A turbulent welter of cloud covered the city. All was darkness; all was doubt; all was confusion. The Eighteenth century was over; the Nineteenth century had begun. (Woolf 1993, 156)

What does this passage imply? Principally, we might say that it represents a certain dialectic of modernisation. Although, of course, the reign of Queen Victoria did not begin in 1800, the fact remains that the 'image' of the nineteenth century in Britain has been indelibly coloured – or stained, as some would say – by Victoria's later lengthy mourning over the death of her husband, a mourning in which the majority of the population were forced, in some sense, to share. Thus here the 'enlightenment' of the eighteenth century, the sense of a future towards which we might move, is replaced by a stultifying cloud which threatens the death of modernity; it is indeed no coincidence that it was precisely the grip of Victorian culture and morality which the modernists exerted themselves to lift.

Yet Woolf's attitude towards modernity in *Orlando* is curiously striated. Arriving at a time very near to the 'present day' (or in other words to 1928, when the book was first published) Orlando finds herself waiting to cross a road in central London:

> ... the traffic was heavy that spring afternoon, and kept her standing there, repeating 'ecstasy, ecstasy' ... while the wealth and power of England sat,

as if sculptured, in hat and cloak, in four-in-hand, victoria and barouche landau. It was as if a golden river had coagulated and massed itself in golden blocks across Park Lane. The ladies held card-cases between their fingers; the gentlemen balanced gold-mounted canes between their knees. She stood there gazing, admiring, awestruck. ... What she now beheld was the triumph of an age.   (Woolf 1993, 200)

What is, however, crucially interesting about *Orlando* is that the long historical and wide geographical perspectives of the text allow for a deeper response to this 'triumph of an age'; for this is a book which is critically aware of how the triumphalism of the Victorians and the new triumphs of the twentieth century have been constructed. Woolf is aware that such prosperity as her character sees is far from evenly divided even within Britain; but she is also aware of the foundations on which this prosperity is itself based, with the whole issue of empire and its vexed relation to modernity in a crucial position.

Over many years, it was customary among historians to regard the empire as crucial to the evolution of Britain in nationalistic terms, in terms of international strategy and power; but it has only been more recently that economic historians have shown that the importance of empire ran deeper than that. A more common view now is that, without the empire to provide cheap imports and, perhaps even more importantly, a captive export market, Britain's financial power, certainly in the nineteenth century and perhaps for many centuries before that, could not possibly have developed as it did. Furthermore, the suggestion is now made that even the famed 'inventiveness' of Britain was fuelled by possibilities offered by the empire; the case most usually quoted is that of the railways, where the development of the British network was obviously of critical importance but a small matter when compared with the growth of the Indian railway system.

It will, I hope, have already been seen that capturing 'modernism' within a single period of time is difficult to the point of impossibility. Beckett, for example, is writing considerably later than Woolf, and the heyday of modernism is often said to be the 1920s, but the fact is that it has ramifications both later and earlier. A relevant earlier text, Conrad's *Heart of Darkness*, was published in 1902, but here we have a test case in which the dialectic of modernity and the absolute imbrication of Britain with its empire is very much in the foreground. It is present, for example, at the very beginning of the book, when Marlow is beginning to recount his tale. He and his audience of amateur sailors are moored in a yawl at the mouth of the Thames, awaiting the turn of the tide, and the narrator is musing on the past and present of London:

> What greatness had not floated on the ebb of that river into the mystery of an unknown earth! ... The dreams of men, the seed of commonwealths, the germs of empires.
>
> The sun set; the dusk fell on the stream, and lights began to appear along the shore. The Chapman lighthouse, a three-legged thing erect on a mud-flat, shone strongly. Lights of ships moved in the fairway – a great stir of lights going up and going down. And farther west on the upper reaches the place of the monstrous town was still marked ominously on the sky, a brooding gloom in sunshine, a lurid glare under the stars.
>
> 'And this also', said Marlow suddenly, 'has been one of the dark places of the earth'.   (Conrad 1983, 29)

As is so common in Conrad, there is a multitude of contradictions at work here. The lighthouse, for example, stands 'erect', apparently firm and secure, a work of symbolic and practical 'enlightenment'; yet it is based upon a mud-flat. London is a 'brooding gloom', yet it is simultaneously a 'lurid glare'. Marlow's main point, however, is that it is the labours of empire that have 'produced' London, they have lifted it from its darkness and obscurity onto a new plane; and this will, of course, contrast sharply with the 'darkness' which still prevails, in so many senses, in the Africa to which we are introduced in the text. The modernisation of London is as unstable as the three-legged lighthouse; its 'lurid glare' has been purchased at the expense of the lives and fortunes of both the slaves of empire and the Britons who have given their service to it. It is worth pausing for a moment to reflect on the fact that, in some ways, little has changed since Conrad's day; recent satellite images of the earth, for example, show that, while large parts of the world show up vividly at night, almost the whole of Africa, with the exceptions of Cairo, Lagos and the South African conurbations, remains in entire darkness, a result of the absence of electricity – and, of course, other ramifications flow from that: there is less mileage of telephone cable on the continent of Africa than there is on the island of Manhattan. It is perhaps worth adding that a climate-induced sea-level rise of one metre would require the evacuation of London as a human settlement.

However: to talk of Conrad is almost automatically to bring up the name of the African writer Chinua Achebe, who in an influential essay accused Conrad of racist attitudes in his work. And Achebe's work too is filled with references to modernity, and naturally more specifically to its impact on West Africa. In *Anthills of the Savannah* (1987), for example, one of the characters speaks of modernity in this way:

> The sweeping, majestic visions of people rising victorious like a tidal wave against their oppressors and transforming their world with theories and slogans into a new heaven and a new earth of brotherhood, justice and freedom are at best grand illusions. The rising, conquering tide, yes; but the millennium afterwards, no! New oppressors will have been readying themselves secretly in the undertow long before the tidal wave got really going.
>
> Experience and intelligence warn us that man's progress in freedom will be piecemeal, slow and undramatic. Revolution may be necessary for taking a society out of an intractable stretch of quagmire but it does not confer freedom, and may indeed hinder it.   (Achebe 1988, 99)

We are now, of course, a very long way away from modernism considered as a formal or stylistic revolution, but at the same time there are aspects of what Achebe is talking about which are relevant not only on a political, social and cultural level, but also when thinking about the underlying principles of modernism. The major example here is his allusion to 'grand illusions'. It has become conventional, in the wake of Lyotard and others, to speak of postmodernism in terms of an abandonment of, or at least a certain scepticism about, these 'illusions' or grand narratives; there is a sense that whether or not, as in the particularly emblematic case of Marxism, they appear to offer the possibility of liberation, they rarely impact on people's lives in the ways one might expect or hope.

But this resistance to 'grand narratives', an insistence that no single intellectual or ideological framework would suffice to interpret the world, emerged long before the constructions to which we now refer as 'postmodern'. One aspect of modernism itself was a radical scepticism in the face of received beliefs, coupled with a profound questioning of the powers of language. Although it could be said that in the cases of Pound and Eliot this radical thinking in the end led them in surprising directions, nonetheless one can find in them the partial origin of a more continued questioning throughout the middle and later years of the twentieth century. One suggestive case is the poet W.S. Graham, whose small corpus of poetry is almost entirely devoted to examining the workings of language and to the question of whether any kind of truth is obtainable through it or whether it is in fact language itself which shapes us to its will, as would now be held by most theorists of language from the structuralists onwards. Here is the opening of the first poem in a set of three under the provocative heading 'What is the Language Using us For?' (1977):

> What is the language using us for?
> Said Malcolm Mooney moving away
> Slowly over the white language.
> Where am I going said Malcolm Mooney.
>
> Certain experiences seem to not
> Want to go in to language maybe
> Because of shame or the reader's shame.
> Let us observe Malcolm Mooney.
>
> Let us get through the suburbs and drive
> Out further just for fun to see
> What he will do. Reader, it does
> Not matter. He is only going to be
>
> Myself and for you slightly you
> Wanting to be another. He fell
> He falls (Tenses are everywhere.)
> Deep down into a glass jail.
>
> I am in a telephoneless, blue
> Green crevasse and I can't get out.   (Graham 2004, 199)

The figures here of the fictional explorer Malcolm Mooney, of the poet/narrator, and of the reader are inextricably entwined; this is a kind of poetry which seeks to lay bare the workings of poetry and thus of language itself. There is an extraordinary irony in the way in which Graham proclaims the impossibility of ever writing anything satisfactory; instead, he presents us with a visualisation of a *mise en abŷme* in the shape of the fall into the 'telephoneless, blue/Green crevasse', which is an image of the perilousness of language which Graham represents here as in many of his other poems in terms of an adventure, often into the Arctic or Antarctic wastes or onto the high seas.

Here, then, would be evidence that modernism remains, as it has always been, strung between two poles: on the one hand, the 'high view' of the author in his or her cultural role, on the other a profound scepticism as to whether language can ever really be bent to new uses. It may be that it is possible to call new worlds into being; but if so, it is not easy to tell what they might be like; it may be possible to escape from the bondage of tradition, but it is also always possible that we may find ourselves suffering from new kinds of restriction, confinement, even imprisonment. But what can certainly be said of modernism is that it was concerned with these issues, with pushing at the boundaries of what might be considered sayable or unsayable, even if that often required a certain consorting with stylistic or ideological disaster.

4 Modernity Now

It will, I hope, have become obvious by now that modernity if not a simple term, but rather one which has been constantly remade. At times it has gone out of fashion, and there is a major school of thought that suggests that in recent decades it has been superseded by 'postmodernity'; however, despite the best and most scrupulous efforts of critics of various hues to keep the two terms apart there remains a constant 'bleeding' of one into the other, which suggests that it is not possible to place modernity in the past, to relegate it wholly to the strata of the ghostly or the archaic.

One of the most compelling formulations of the 'problem of modernity' comes from Fredric Jameson who, to put his complex arguments in their simplest form, claims that there is an intrinsic historical link between modernity and capitalism; as early forms of capitalism emerge in association with techno-development from the eighteenth century on, so the discourse of the modern also emerges as a set of representations of capitalism's present and future. Jameson does, however, make the point that

> if I recommend the experimental procedure of substituting capitalism for modernity in all the contexts in which the latter appears, this is a therapeutic rather than a dogmatic recommendation, designed to exclude old problems (and to produce new and more interesting ones). (Jameson 2002, 143)

What might some of these new and more interesting ones be? One would certainly be whether the 'new world order' of the last fifty years, increasingly based on previously unimaginable data-flows and the instantaneous exchange of information, on virtuality and tele-technology, rather than on older systems of manufacturing and transport, is still most aptly described under the label 'capitalism' at all; certainly a form of capitalism is still with us in the classical Marxist sense of the extraction of surplus profit, now largely by multinational corporations rather than via economies at the service of the nation state, but it is increasingly difficult to see these processes leading to anything that could resemble their Marxist conclusion, namely the reappropriation by the workers of the means of production. Various critics have called into use the term 'late capitalism'; but by supposing that this is a belated or terminal situation they have in fact begged the question.

This is, of course, in part because the geography of the world is in a state of radical change – or perhaps series of changes. A major aspect of this has, in the most immediate past decades, been the export of labour power to developing economies where life is still cheap and health and safety issues do not put a brake on untrammelled productivity. Another has been the breakdown of the Soviet Union and the emergence within its successor states of a variety of 'gangster capitalism' steered by a corrupt collusion between governmental and corporate forces. A third has been the continued impoverishment of Africa, a situation which the dominant powers have now, belatedly, come to recognise as dangerous – not, most would say, because of the evil of poverty and disease in itself but because an impoverished continent provides no outlet for manufactured goods from the 'developed' world. A fourth has been, and remains, the 'modernisation' of China (and, to a lesser extent, India); although this may have happened on the back of China's advantages in terms of productivity, whether such 'modernisation with Chinese characteristics' will tend in the medium term towards economic triumph or social and national breakdown – or, feasibly, both – remains imponderable. The age of the 'Asian tigers', although it was but a short while ago, now seems to belong to a long-gone era, although some of those economies – Taiwan, Singapore, Hong Kong insofar as it can still be regarded as a single entity – remain contenders on the world stage and are firmly embedded within the processes of modernity – which, as may now seem obvious, has in some circles come to seem an equivalent term to 'development' rather than to 'capitalism'.

A further, and pressing, example of the contemporary vicissitudes of modernity would be the so-called 'rise of Islam'. Baudrillard, contemplating the historical phenomenon of Istanbul, has this to say:

> The Bosphorus. The line of unification of two seas and continents, and at the same time, a fault line where civilisations, religions, peoples and empires step on one another like tectonic layers ... Once, the Roman Empire was established by stepping over Asia. Later it overran Europe and

withdrew again. Today the modernity emanating from Europe carries the
empire toward the Asian continent ...   (Baudrillard 1999, 2)

What does this mean for Istanbul? For Baudrillard, it entails the need to
read a city, even one which, like most cities, is modern in some of its
appearances, as a palimpsest, as a place where different cultures, different
changes, have 'overwritten' each other, such that the façade of modernity
will always be a painted face (although Baudrillard does also make the
point that 'the primitive stage of New York is modernity and the city itself
is the stage of modernity' [Baudrillard 1999, 2], an argument which he
links with the symbolic 'necessity' of the destruction of the twin towers).
And from this source among others flows Baudrillard's key idea of the
'simulacrum'; the way in which modernity is characterised by an increasing replacement of the 'real' by the 'virtual', as exemplified in the transmission and reception of television news or in the prevalence, sometimes
subliminal, of commercially driven advertising.

Interestingly, we may turn this notion of the 'simulacrum' to an
account of modernity itself. For it would clearly be ludicrous to say that
the arrival of the first radio in an Indian village is modernity of the same
type as corporate reliance on mobile technology; the question would
more aptly be about what the 'appearance' of these changes signifies. In
other words, modernity is relative; but that may not mean that we cannot
identify certain key elements. The sociologist Peter Berger lists these key
elements, which he calls 'carriers', as, among others, urbanisation, privatisation and globalisation, but even as we contemplate that list we may
suspect that, in fact, there are countervailing tendencies going on.
Certainly 80% of people in Britain live in an urban environment; but the
need for this to be the case is being gradually eroded by the onset of tele-
working, the removal of jobs to offshore sweatshops and call centres, and
the high costs of urban housing, to name but three issues. Privatisation,
by which Berger means the rolling back of state control, has certainly
been a feature of many 'advanced economies'; but when we look at the
multinationals, it is difficult to see in what other sense – other, that is,
than being 'offshore', and to an extent off-limits, to the power of the
nation state – they are 'private' at all (except, perhaps, insofar as 'private'
means 'secretive').

Globalisation is an even more complex term, which can be used – and
has been used – by politicians for years to refer to directly contrary phenomena. To take one example, it is certainly true that the mass production of flowers for developed markets has transformed parts of the

economy of Kenya; but on the other hand, are we equally willing to credit the appalling working conditions, the poor health of the workers in the vast hothouses and the way in which their masters filch water from an already desperate situation of shortage as part of the effects of globalisation? Messages from all around the world can now be transmitted and received in the blink of an eye, it is said; but not, obviously, if you live in one of the thousands of areas of the world where there is inadequate electricity, or none at all.

One of the major writers on globalisation and its consequences is Zygmunt Bauman. In his book *Liquid Modernity*, published in 2000, he draws a useful distinction between a kind of modernity which is 'heavy' or 'solid' and one which is 'light' or 'liquid'. The first kind of modernity he identifies on the intellectual plane in the work of such thinkers as Marx and Max Weber: its motifs would be the factory, the concentration of labour, the manufacture and transportation of heavy goods. The second, more recent kind has more to do with flexibility of work, dispersal of information and the transmission of data. Perhaps more interestingly, he associates 'heavy modernity' with a kind of belief structure; not, perhaps, in a conventional religious sense, but more in terms of a belief in progress, however tortuous its advance may seem and however remote its advantages may be to the worker. 'Liquid modernity', on the other hand, is uncertain, provisional, subject to constant change. Another conventional way of looking at this would be by alluding again to the exponential growth of technological change. Under a 'heavy' regime, one might say, testing of product tended on the whole to happen before its delivery; in a liquid regime, where products are in a constant state of development, products are launched and it is for the market to respond by buying or not buying them. In the previous regime, it may have been possible for the consumer to tell whether he or she was in possession of a piece of domestic equipment which was 'state of the art'; now this is impossible, the 'art' may be changing as we speak, as the mountains of discarded computers and VCRs littering the rubbish tips and landfills of the western world testify, not to mention the rotting hulks of big ships which clutter beaches from southern India to Taiwan.

Lying behind this is a deeper and more troubling question, which is nothing less than the question of the 'human', and its accompanying terms the 'inhuman', the 'abhuman' and the 'post-human'. In its most radical forms – for example, in the works of Donna Haraway – concern with these defining issues takes the form of a radical questioning of the sense of whether, or at least in what form, we are still 'human' at all.

Freud made many interesting remarks years ago on man's need for prostheses, artificial aids, in order to stave off the ubiquitous perils of life,
whether under barbaric or 'civilised' conditions; it is possible that life,
again at least in the developed world, is now lived in a continuous 'prosthetic state' – we move, as we go through the day, from states of being
'person plus coffee-maker' to being 'person plus car' to 'person plus computer' to 'person plus television'. Strong recent evidence for this theory of
modernity as an advance into an increasingly prosthetic state would come
from the mobile phone phenomenon, which has had, at the very least, a
radically reductive effect on the possibility of communicative street
encounters, which may be seen as an emblem of communitarian collapse.

Again, however, there are countervailing forces; it is conventional to
speak of the understandable envy felt in parts of the developing world for
the modern material goods which are unavailable to them, and arguably
it is precisely this envy which constitutes the principal driver for multinational corporations, but the effects on national identity and destiny are
more complex than this. As Homi Bhabha observes in *Nation and
Narration* (1990), a nation's political unity is

> a continual displacement of its irredeemably plural modern space,
> bounded by different, even hostile nations, into a signifying space that is
> archaic and mythical, paradoxically representing the nation's modern
> territoriality, in the patriotic, atavistic temporality of Traditionalism.
> (Bhabha 1990, 300)

To put it at its simplest, this line of thinking would suggest that the
attempt to live in the modern world drives you mad. It does so because it
confronts you constantly with such a panoply of difference (and apparent
choice) that it is paradoxically impossible to handle except by the most
reductive of means; hence, if we take Bhabha's argument at an intra-
rather than an inter-national level, we have the recourse of people who
consider themselves threatened by the intrusion of a world which they
would prefer to think of as external to the violent histrionics of the
British National Party. An even more pertinent example might be the
Little Cuba of Miami, where people attempt to inhabit lifestyles which
have long vanished from the very nation most of them continue to call
their own, and which the majority of them have never seen.

From this very different angle, then, we might suspect that modernity
is troubled by a tendency within it towards dehumanisation. Michel
Foucault sees the issues from a related perspective which is, however,

again different. Essentially, his vast range of work is a development of ideas drawn from structuralist theories of language and translated into other institutional realms. Regimes of power, such as prisons or clinics, are not there, Foucault claims, to be at the service of the citizen; rather, they operate objectively to transmit power down to the subject. The subject, for Foucault, is in every case and everywhere 'subjected'; his best-known image is the 'panopticon', which was an innovative idea for a prison, developed by Jeremy Bentham, according to which every inmate would be under constant surveillance from a central control tower ('the object of information, never the subject in communication', as Foucault puts it in *Discipline and Punish* [1975] [Foucault 1977, 200]).

If this is a version of modernity, then it is one we can also see represented in fictional texts such as George Orwell's *1984* (1948) and Huxley's *Brave New World*, where the power of the modern – or in these cases, the future – state is devoted to removing privacy from every individual. The illusion of a private life is transformed into the ultimate heresy, it is that which the state cannot withstand – as indeed various social revolutions, in for example Eastern Europe, have recently shown – and therefore in the end, according to Foucault, surveillance and punishment become the most significant forms of modern power. All this, of course, can be implemented in the name of the apparently socially 'good', such as crime reduction; just as the presence of surveillance cameras on every urban street corner is similarly justified even while it nonetheless provides a minute record of our movements, whether innocent or not.

And here there is, then, a modern paradox. People do not want to live in fear of crime; but also, people do not want to be watched. If we were to turn to current controversies such as the one about speed cameras, for example, however trivial it may initially seem the argument gets even more complex. There appears to be no doubt that speed cameras save lives; but the permission to judge one's own driving speed seems to have become enshrined in the self-definition of every motoring member of the public. And this in turn is sanctioned by the car manufacturers; there is, to my knowledge, no car currently in production which does not advertise on its own speedometer that it is capable (along with, of course, the cyborg/human driving it) of exceeding any speed limit yet imposed. My own modest car claims to be capable of 120 m.p.h.; where, how, and with what penalties attached I would ever be able to discover the truth of that claim remains, to me at least, imponderable.

To return to camera technology; this is obviously particularly interesting as a phenomenon of modernity, partly because of its potential

scopophiliac implications; partly because of its ability to function precisely in the ambiguous and vacillating space which encompasses both
the 'long view' and the 'close-up'; partly because it lays claim to a 'reality'
which surpasses that of the human eye. The human eye is of special
interest in a brilliant, disturbing and, indeed, revolting film by Michael
Powell and Emeric Pressburger, made many years ago, which draws
attention to all three of these aspects in a narrative of a film-maker who
delights in killing his victims while he photographs them; the current
wave of 'happy slappers', who knock their victims about, and sometimes
worse, while filming their reactions on cameras inset into mobile phones,
are clearly successors to Powell and Pressburger's protagonist, and
although so far as I am aware they have not yet, in Britain, killed
anybody there can be little doubt that they soon will. In saying that, I am
not evincing a general pessimism about human nature; I am drawing
attention to an argument about modernity, which is that if something is
technologically possible it will occur. For a product to sell, one or both of
two things have to happen: it has to appeal to the desires of the consumer, or it has to manage to form that desire itself, often by association,
which is one definition of the function of advertising.

And this is a point which was underlined many years ago, in 1928, by
Walter Benjamin, in the course of a challenging essay called 'This Space
for Rent':

> Fools lament the decay of criticism. ... Criticism is a matter of correct dis-
> tancing. ... Today the most real, the mercantile gaze into the heart of
> things is the advertisement. It abolishes the space where contemplation
> moved and all but hits us between the eyes with things as a car, growing to
> gigantic proportions, careens at us out of a film screen. ... People whom
> nothing moves or touches any longer are taught to cry again by films. ...
> What, in the end, makes advertisements so superior to criticism? Not what
> the moving red neon sign says – but the fiery pool reflecting it in the
> asphalt.   (Benjamin 1996, 476)

This is an extraordinary passage and, as frequently with Benjamin, it is
difficult to gauge the depth of its scepticism. Certainly it dramatically
demonstrates a key feature of modernity, which is that it is not possible,
in a developed society, to avoid it; one cannot say 'No' to advertisements,
even if one can choose whether or not to see a particular film. Benjamin
is also drawing attention to a certain kind of immediacy, an absence of
subtlety which may nonetheless be being very subtle about precisely its

own absence, a process at which advertisers have got considerably better over the years to the point where an advertisement, given sufficient time to sink into the popular imagination, can cut itself completely free from the name of its product and yet remain financially effective. Perhaps a further, and more frightening, hint of Benjamin's is that the space which advertisements and similar material now fill is that which has been vacated, forcibly or not, by criticism – is criticism, in any of its former senses, still even possible under conditions of modernity?

Herbert Marcuse, in *One Dimensional Man* (1964), argued fiercely that is was not, that advanced capitalism had reduced the social and cultural space to such an extent that it was no longer possible to find a vantage point from which to offer effective critique (although there is a paradox inherent in his argument, in that if he were right it would have been silly of him to write his book). But perhaps we may take some of these arguments further, if on a slightly different track, by referring to an interesting essay called 'Hybrid Cultures and Communicative Strategies' (1997), about the 'crisis of modernity' in South America, in which Néstor García Canclini writes thus about a photomural and video called 'Montezuma's Foreboding' by the Italo-Venezuelan artist Paolo Gasparini:

> Based on a manuscript in which Montezuma announces the catastrophe of the Mexican capital, on Walter Benjamin's text about Paul Klee's Angelus Novus, and on an exasperated montage of Pre-Columbian, colonial, and modern images of Mexico City, Gasparini indicates that the brazen multiculturalness of this metropolis is the result of a national project based on inequality. By combining the street sign that indicates Montezuma Street, folded and twisted by an anonymous inhabitant; a mask of the great fighter himself alongside other masks being sold on the street; and a photo of a Zapatista wearing a balaclava, next to indigenous and mestizo faces and bodies ... he offers, as he says, 'a selection of post-battle images: all the civilising corpses are scattered about and the various cultural strata interweave and coexist in the crossroads of the urban scene: from the Pre-Columbian debris and the ruins of modernity to the already-decomposing pastiche of globalisation'. (García Canclini 1997, 6)

If this passage seems complex, that is because it is, and the phenomena to which it refers are at least equally so. Here we have an interweaving of the archaic and the modern which refuses to separate them or to allow the fiction that supersession, whether by conquest or by any other means, necessarily erases that which preceded the moment of modernity.

What we also have is a suggestion that it is impossible for the modern to attain its goal, which is seen as a pure, clear world where the messy, 'heavy' details, the 'debris' of previous epochs has been surpassed and left behind. Here, indeed, the modern project is itself already in ruins even though one could argue that, from another angle – and one to which we shall return – it is precisely the persistence of ruin which modernity tries to deny. And so, at the end, back also to globalisation, seen as an 'already-decomposing pastiche', an attempt to patch together a world which is visibly falling apart at the seams and in which the pretence of equality, at any level, is under continuing pressure.

If we were to connect these images together in a slightly different way, we would arrive at a theory of modernity as mask, but this mask could be seen to have a surprisingly Gothic inflection. It would not be clear whether it was a mask which could be taken off and set aside, or whether, behind the mask, there is no longer a face; or whether, indeed, what lies behind the mask would reveal itself as 'decomposition', all that side of, for example, a city which has to be disguised or forcibly ejected when it finds itself 'on show' as, for instance, host to the Olympic Games or named as European City of Culture.

There is, then, an uneven participation in modernity; the various critics I have cited do not on the whole point this out because they are not prey to any kind of nostalgia for a time when life was 'nasty, brutish and short', they are concerned rather to point up the task of the critic of modernity to continue to lay bare the deficiencies of the system, especially where those deficiencies may themselves be considered to be 'systemic' – that is, essential elements of the system rather than accidental adjuncts to it. Seen in this light, it is significant that so many 'critics' of modernity are in fact just that – critics rather than advocates. There are however, of course, exceptions. Jonathan Glancey, in a recent *Guardian* article, offers the following comment on the current relation between politics and aesthetics in Britain:

> Throughout Britain, and up until the eighties, local councils, education authorities, universities and other public or publicly minded bodies fused Modern architecture to Modern ideologies ... not simply to create the shiny and new, but to modernise class-divided, low-wage Britain ... New Labour has inherited [the] Thatcherite penchant for fancy dress and has yet to separate in its mind the New from the Modern. The former is all about fashion; the latter about the health of the body wearing the latest clothes.   (Glancey 1997)

According to this argument, in Britain at least mid-twentieth-century modernisation was one branch of a genuine attempt to root out ancient practices and prejudices. The planners and architects who moved people from run-down terraces with no inside toilets into high-rise flats with what were then the latest modern amenities did so in good faith; and indeed it is on record that the majority of people thus moved were genuinely pleased with their change of circumstances. We can also agree with Glancey that the merely 'new' may indeed be only about fashion; modernity, as practically enacted by local councils and the like, aims for both a deeper and a longer transformation of working and living conditions, even if, as Glancey suggests, this distinction is not always easy to perceive.

And thus to a further paradox within modernity. For on the one hand, modernity recognises transience; we are far more sure now than our forefathers could possibly have been that the world when we leave it will be radically different from the world into which we were born. But at the same time, there has to be a certain resistance within modernity to a notion of continual change, of 'permanent revolution'; after all, resources are limited, and it is now – and perhaps has been for a long time – a fact of life that most Britons, when asked to choose, would prefer to live in a manner – largely based on detached houses and bungalows – which would be quite unfeasible without a radical modification of existing urban spaces and/or the 'development' of substantial areas of the countryside, the latter being a phenomenon which these same interviewees claim is the last thing they want.

And this too is an intrinsic part of 'modern' culture, namely the process of cultural *consultation*, whatever the significance one attaches to its results. This is something which was, in a sense, foreseen by one of the earliest thinkers of modernity, Max Weber, who devoted much of his thought to the origins and consequences of modern bureaucratisation and its relation to the processes of dehumanisation. One way in which he puts his arguments is this:

> [The calculability of decision-making] and with it its appropriateness for capitalism is the more fully actualised the more bureaucracy 'depersonalises' itself, i.e., the more completely it succeeds in achieving ... the exclusion of love, hatred, and every purely personal, especially irrational and incalculable, feeling from the execution of official tasks. In the place of the old-type ruler who is moved by sympathy, favour, grace, and gratitude, modern culture requires for its sustaining external apparatus the

emotionally detached, and hence rigorously 'professional', expert. (Weber 1954, 351)

There is a social and legal dilemma here which is typical of modernity, which centres on the question of how it is possible to exert and maintain justice. The modern method, according to Weber, is to work essentially according to 'calculation', and this can work in all sorts of ways: by calculating what is a reasonable amount of interest to pay on a debt, by calculating what an injury is worth, by comparing punishments handed out for different crimes, by determining levels of social benefit afforded to people on low wages. Some such kind of justice, we might reasonably suspect – and anthropologists would agree – has as far as we know always been a feature of the organisation of human communities. But in pre-modern times, according to this analysis, there were other factors also to be taken into account: emotional ties within the community, oral records of past transactions, the value of service previously performed, the health of the person concerned.

Modern justice does not, of course, entirely ignore such factors; but nevertheless, Weber argues, the premium is on 'calculability' and thus on that distinctively modern phenomenon, the 'professional expert'. Recent cases involving cot death, to take but one example, have brutally exposed how misplaced this reliance can be, but it is nonetheless a cornerstone of the system of modernity, and in some ways this is contiguous with Foucault's ideas: the individual is again a 'subject', a subject of information, or perhaps more exactly a point of intersection, a node of different flows of information, knowledge and power. This, of course, is why in so many court cases there is a delay between conviction and sentencing while the subject is 'referred for reports'; it is also why, for a child protection service to work effectively and well, so many professionals, so many experts have to come together in order to discuss and offer final, or even provisional, judgements.

But we need again to return to the vexed question of whether, in our age, 'modernity' is somehow 'over' – 'abandoned – destroyed, liquidated' (Lyotard 1984, 111), as Jean-François Lyotard claims in *The Postmodern Condition* (1979). Various thinkers from Jürgen Habermas to Anthony Giddens would claim that this is a misprision, and that we still live in some sense within the project of modernity. But the real issue here is again of what 'modernity' means, and of what its relation is to 'grand narratives'. If modernity stood for grand narratives, if Marx, Weber, Freud are the key figures of recent modernity, then we might well argue that the postmodern, with its insistence on the temporary, the unanswerable, the ephemeral, stands in stark contrast with this version of the modern. The problem, however, with this argument is that early twentieth-century modernity never was totally in thrall to the 'grand narratives'; when we think of a quite different canon of writers, ranging from Baudelaire to Eliot and Kafka, what we see is a version of modernity itself built on and shot through and through with contradictions.

Writers like these are painfully, even agonisingly, aware of the ruinous nature of the past; not only that the past may be in ruins, which is not an improbable supposition to entertain in mid-twentieth-century Europe, but also that that past continues to exert its ruinous effect on the present. Thus the need for a 'clean break'; but at the same time the awareness that no such clean break is truly possible, that there is no escape from the past's baleful legacy. And here, it would seem, it would be difficult to uphold the view that the 'postmodern' has somehow moved a stage beyond the earlier modernist projects; one might equally argue that the postmodernists are 'in retreat' from – or even in denial of – the attempts of their predecessors to carve out a distinctively modern space from the 'ruins of empire'.

Giddens, in *Modernity and Self-Identity* (1991), uses his habitual identification of the contemporary period as one of 'late modernity' to put what may seem at first glance to be a disarmingly simple series of questions:

> What to do? How to act? Who to be? These are focal questions for everyone living in circumstances of late modernity – and ones which, on some level or another, all of us answer, either discursively or through day-to-day social behaviour.   (Giddens 1991, 70)

But what lies behind these questions is not at all simple; for Giddens's point, and it is surely correct, is that it is only under certain specifically modern circumstances that such questions can – or need to – be posed at all. However one labels particular sub-epochs of the 'modern period', it remains the case that we are dealing here in societies and cultures which are 'non-traditional'. This is not a reference to their particular age; there are still 'traditional' societies on the planet, though their already very small space is being almost terminally eroded by the demands of mineral extraction, the oil industry, and tourism. It is rather a reference to that 'moment' in the life of a culture, as in the life of an individual, when it becomes clear that, in fact, there are choices to be made; that it is not *necessary* to live as one's forefathers have done.

Of course, it is perfectly possible nonetheless to make a 'choice' to continue in the 'old ways'; but this changes nothing. Once the *question* of
choice has been raised, the *answer* to the question is hardly relevant;
what is crucial is that the authority of tradition has been addressed, it no
longer executes a divine or quasi-divine power over our lives. This may
be the very essence of a 'progressive' view of human development, but it
is concomitantly true that it also represents a loss, a perhaps terrible if
unthought loss which, Freud would say, will continue to reverberate at
the unconscious level even if – or indeed to the extent that – it is unac-
knowledged in conscious cultural interchange.

It will have become apparent in much of what I have said so far that
any attempt to assert a consistent, globalised spread of modernity across
the world is fruitless; it would not be a reflection of the fractured and
imbalanced world in which we live. Everywhere one looks, one cannot
help but see what we might call 'modernity's others' – what Bauman
refers to as the 'stranger'. It would be intellectually and emotionally futile
to return to earlier, romantic notions of the 'outcast'; nevertheless,
modernity now undoubtedly encompasses – and partly realises – the
danger of 'leaving behind' large parts of the world which, in its more
messianic moments, it claims to be trying to save. On the macro-level, as
we have suggested, this involves whole continents; but it also presses, in
more immediate ways, all around.

The 'mall rats' who are continuously excoriated by the tabloid press, for
example, are not some kind of accidental by-product of modern consumer society; on the contrary, they are its direct result, the outcome of a
modernity that bases itself in a certain type of material desire and defer-
ment of satisfaction. The current debate about 'hoodies' is also directly
appropriate: a large shopping mall has recently banned people – young
people, of course – from wearing them 'on the premises' on the two
grounds that, first, they intimidate 'respectable' shoppers and, second,
they make the wearer invisible to the CCTV cameras which are ubiquitous
in this mall, as in every other. Yet there are shops in the same mall which
sell these clothing items; it is therefore legal to buy one but not to put it on
until one is, rather as in the case of a firework, at a 'safe' distance.

The point, however, is that these phenomena are a direct and
inescapable concomitant of modernity, which can never be a fully inclu-
sive movement. One might be tempted to feel that as modernity continues with its attempt to clean up the world, to render it a place of
technologically engineered light and grace, so its 'strangers' – and they
are not necessarily rebels, subversives, terrorists, or even criminals, just

'strangers' – will become even more extreme in their actions, in their attempt to find a position from which – in practice rather than in discourse – to critique the world which they see in front of them but of which they can never be fully part.

Another cardinal example here is graffiti. Regarded, of course, by many as sheer hooliganism and the defacement of property, some people have come forward to defend the best examples as 'works of art'. But this rhetorical exchange is entirely beside the point, as indeed is the largely unintelligible content of most graffiti themselves (unintelligible, that is, to all but a small esoteric community, the epitome of the discursively 'local'). What is to the point is that graffiti are 're-signatures', they are acts of defiance; they say, You may have the planes and trains, the modern high-tech stuff, but we can come and take our bit too, you can't endlessly protect it from us. As in the case of Conrad's view of the 'natives' in *Heart of Darkness*, who do not kill and eat European traders even though they may (according to Conrad) wish to, it is possible to admire the *restraint* of graffiti artists: there is, they hint, so much more we could do as we slip through the night, unrecorded on CCTV, but no: we will content ourselves – for the moment – with *this*, this surreptitious and yet so public reminder of an alternative source of modern power, another ramification of the endless proliferation of power in the absence of the authoritative master-narrative.

Nevertheless, it is obvious that none of this will prevent the flow in the direction of modernity. In a recent interview, Bauman put it like this:

> … modern states did not emerge from inter-communal conferences, or as federations of parishes and townships. They were born and grew up in dogfights with 'local particularisms', and at the expense of expropriating the locally based powers of a greater part of their pre-modern authority. One wonders whether the same operation won't have to be repeated, two centuries later – but this time on a global scale. I suspect that non-governmental movements and organisations, deliberately ignoring state boundaries and paying little attention to state institutions, could be seen as manifestations of that premonition, and as experimental, trial-and-error attempts to act on it.   (Leighton 2001, 11)

It is possible to imagine that foremost among the examples of which Bauman was thinking was 'Médécins sans Frontières', a loose organisation of doctors who operate in disaster areas and, where necessary, across state boundaries, and thus effect an entirely beneficial consequence of the mobility attendant upon 'light' or 'liquid' modernity. But in some ways, what is most interesting about Bauman's views at this point is that, if extended in a certain direction, we could find a curious but perhaps all-important link between the 'stranger' of modernity and an apparently quite different figure, the 'nomad' who figures so largely in the work of Deleuze and Guattari.

Deleuze and Guattari's major work, the two parts of *Capitalism and Schizophrenia* subtitled *Anti-Oedipus* (1983) and *A Thousand Plateaus* (1987), describe a 'collision' between the forces of the State, which are always, and must always be, dedicated towards delineating and securing boundaries, and the forces of nomadry, by which they mean those prac-tices of life which do not respect – and perhaps cannot understand – these boundaries. Behind this there lies, of course, a certain archaism: the kinds of conflict of which one might initially think would involve the Bedouin, or the aborigines of Australia, attempting to maintain their 'nomadic' way of life in spite of the incursions and 're-draftings' of the State.

What has this to do with Bauman's point about NGOs? Perhaps, superficially, not a great deal, because most NGOs are highly 'respectable' organisations; but the question would more be about how to describe the 'hinterland' of the NGOs – for example the loose groups of anarchists, anti-capitalists and single-issue activists who increasingly gather around sites of military and ecological contention. These, perhaps, are the 'strangers' – or, perhaps better, the symbols of the stranger – which cannot be accommodated within modernity; modernity's 'other', which is inexorably constructed as any other hegemony builds its own opposi-tion in a logic of the phantom, of the 'stranger', of the uncanny repetition and reversal of power.

Other critics would argue, however, that the central issue is not one of what is 'within' and what is 'outside' modernity, but rather that moder-nity itself is not a 'movement' but rather in itself precisely a site of con-tradictions. Iain Boyd Whyte, for example, in an essay called 'Modernity and Architecture' (2004), makes the following proposal:

> ... four themes might be identified as characteristic of modernity, which align themselves into two diametrically opposed groupings. Individualism and relativism on one hand – understood as the absence of any absolute values – are challenged by the authoritarian demands of instrumental reason and capitalism on the other – the demands of technological progress, cost-efficiency, and a docile labour market. Each of these four

conditions is essentially modernist, yet in a state of total opposition to its inimical pair. (Hvattum and Hermansen 2004, 44)

Whyte goes on to quote Marx's observation of 1856, that

On the one hand there have started into life industrial and scientific forces which no epoch of human history has ever suspected. On the other hand, there exist symptoms of decay, far surpassing the horrors of the latter times of the Roman Empire. In our days everything is pregnant with its contrary. (Marx 1978, 577–8)

This proposes a complex field for modernity indeed. One might of course suspect, with Foucault among others, that the appearance of 'individualism' and 'relativism', with the kinds of freedom from control which they imply, is partly a mask for the underlying forms of power manifested through instrumental reason and capitalism. A pertinent example might be the rise of 'youth culture', which promises all kids that they too can vent their individualistic, anarchistic, rebellious streak provided they all wear *the same* type of jeans. Or one might mount a more psychoanalytic reading, and suggest that what we see here is one aspect of a continuing battle within the psyche, between the urge towards differentiation on the one hand and, on the other, the pleasure of losing one's will, of abandoning oneself to external control, as when the psyche subjugates itself to the demands of the superego.

Certainly as one looks around the modern city, it is possible constantly to discern this ongoing dialectic of decay and replacement, ruin and reconstruction, a contrast between the sleek office block and towering hotel and the run-down areas of the inner city. One might even, if one had suitable technical equipment, trace modernity physically as a continual flowing, such that as one part of a city is renewed, so another takes its place at the bottom of the social heap. And this would indeed be an obvious effect of capitalism, one of the major imperatives of which is to assert and retain a steep gradation between employer and worker, profit-taker and profit-maker. Capitalism cannot sustain itself on a level playing field; surplus profit can only be squeezed out when there is a 'gap' – a gap between the 'haves' and the 'have-nots', a gap which renders labour, even of the least likeable kind, desirable as a route towards material well-being, a gap of desire whereby the goods of society can be proffered as consistently within reach, consistently unattainable. A bitter poem of Larkin's perhaps expresses this point as well as any treatise on the economics of advertising. It is called, with an irony that obviously reminds us of the modern implausibility of Platonic ideals, 'Essential Beauty' (1962):

In frames as large as rooms that face all ways
And block the ends of streets with giant loaves,
Screen graves with custard, cover slums with praise
Of motor-oil and cuts of salmon, shine
Perpetually these sharply-pictured groves
Of how life should be. High above the gutter
A silver knife sinks into golden butter,
A glass of milk stands in a meadow, and
Well-balanced families, in fine
Midsummer weather, owe their smiles, their cars,
Even their youth, to that small cube each hand
Stretches towards. These, and the deep armchairs
Aligned to cups at bedtime, radiant bars
(Gas or electric), quarter-profile cats
By slippers on warm mats,
Reflect none of the rained-on streets and squares

They dominate outdoors. Rather, they rise
Serenely to proclaim pure crust, pure foam,
Pure coldness to our live imperfect eyes
That stare beyond this world, where nothing's made
As new or washed quite clean, seeking the home
All such inhabit. There, dark raftered pubs
Are filled with white-clothed ones from tennis-clubs,
And the boy puking his heart out in the Gents
Just missed them, as the pensioner paid
A halfpenny more for Granny Graveclothes' Tea
To taste old age, and dying smokers sense
Walking towards them through some dappled park
As if on water that unfocused she
No match lit up, or drag ever brought near,
Who now stands newly clear,
Smiling, and recognising, and going dark.   (Larkin 1988, 144–5)

What this poem does is to mark out the area of difference between the kinds of desire of which modernity so frequently tries to persuade us, the visions of a purer, whiter, cleaner, clearer life, and the actuality of ruin and death which stands in stark contrast to the advertisers' claims. We live, the poem suggests in a way uncannily redolent of Baudrillard, a life ruled by images, by a virtual reality to which we can, in fact, never really attain. And worse than this: what the poem suggests is that what lies behind this manipulation of fantasy is a hidden cultural death-drive, not only in the sense that some of the products themselves – the cigarettes, Granny Graveclothes' Tea – might actively promote our death, but also in that we are encouraged by them to avert our gaze from the rain-soaked reality around us. Within the poem there is the identification of a massive contempt; a contempt on the part of the advertisers, certainly, but also an inner contempt which allows us to subscribe to these mockeries of desire even as we think we are seeing through them.

If this is part of modernity – and it is, of course, only a part – we might ask what, under conditions of modernity, is 'real life'? One route to an answer would lie through an investigation of 'reality television', by means of which we are apparently meant to be persuaded that attention-seeking individuals placed in a goldfish bowl are likely to provide us with models of human behaviour. Another would be that there is no longer any possibility of 'real life' at all: we are so thoroughly 'interpellated', to use Louis Althusser's term, by the mechanisms of consumption that there is no escape – the projected consummation signified in, for example, the 'glass of milk' standing in a 'meadow' is in reality a patch to cover our despair.

The apotheosis of these ways of thinking could be found in a film like *The Truman Show* (1998). Here the protagonist, who imagines himself to be living a 'real life', is shown to be merely an object of spectacle, watched by millions every week as he goes about his daily business. His realisation leads him too to an attempt at escape, but there is no way of passing from the inside of the show to the outside; all ways of escape are barred. This again might relate to Foucault's panopticon: the purpose of this virtual incarceration is not in any obvious sense punitive, but it is a version of total surveillance, as is the fiction of life that goes on in the 'Big Brother House' and in other cognate TV shows (and the word 'show' itself, of course, is not without its interest here).

And the rhetoric of 'Big Brother' takes us straight back again, as it is knowingly designed to do, to Orwell. A similar image for our times might come from Ray Bradbury's *Fahrenheit 451* (1954). What is best known about this book is probably the role of the 'firemen', whose role in this future scenario is no longer to put out fires but to set fire to books wherever they are found, because books remind us of the possibility of other lives, lives that might be lived beyond the boundaries of state control. But there is another powerful image in *Fahrenheit 451*, which is of the wife of the protagonist, Montag, who spends almost her entire time watching a television show, about the lives of an 'ordinary family', which is projected onto (almost) every wall of the living-room.

There is here an extraordinary doubling. In one sense, one might follow Baudrillard in identifying the modern age as an 'age of spectacle'; but on the other, it seems as though what we want is not merely to be constantly entertained by 'celebrities' but also to be able to see ourselves, as it were, 'from the outside'. Thus magazines like *Hello!* deal entirely in the lives and loves of celebrities; but they do so in such a fashion as to make it appear as though these too are also, in some sense, 'ordinary people' and that we can, if we look closely enough, see our own lives reflected in them.

In 'Essential Beauty', with one exception, Larkin does not name real or even virtual products; clearly matters have gone much farther since 1962, when this poem first appeared. There are now whole sub-genres of fiction where the naming of products – Gucci, Dior, Rolls-Royce – is essential; it provides the fabulated background of the plot as the same time as it exerts a powerful fascination over the desires of the reader. And of course it goes farther than this as well: corporations have long paid film-makers for visible 'product placement', and an eminent airport bookshop novelist recently admitted that she too had been paid for the same service. There is an amusing, if rather crude, short story by Irvine Welsh which consists of two interlaced scenarios, in one of which his typical low-life Edinburgh characters are conversing in respectable accents while the celebrities whom they are admiring, or rather lusting after, speak the half-intelligible urban Scots for which Welsh is justly famous.

Another way of summarising some of these features would be in the words of Marshall Berman, who defines modernity as

> ... a mode of vital experience – experience of space and time, of the self and others, of life's possibilities and perils – that is shared by men and women all over the world today ... To be modern is to find ourselves in an environment that promises us adventure, power, joy, growth, transformation of ourselves and the world – and, at the same time, that threatens to destroy everything we have, everything we know, everything we are. Modern environments and experiences cut across all boundaries of geog-

raphy and ethnicity, of class and nationality, of religion and ideology. (Berman 1982, 15)

But one would need to place a strict qualification on this apparently joyful and celebratory definition. While we have seen that it is true that modernity has a global dimension, what is crucial is that *different* social and cultural groups are located *differently* in regard to it. In this respect, of course, modernity may appear inseparable from any kind of traditionalism, for older and more embedded forms of social organisation also relied on steep social gradations; but the crucial difference is that now it is possible to see the possibilities of other ways in which one's life might be lived, even if one lacks the material means to fulfil one's fantasies. Thus we might again further think about modernity in terms of *envy*; it is not possible for modernity to spread throughout the world, but it can still serve an ideological function by persuading us that what is, in fact, *not possible* is within a fantasised realm of possibility.

As Benjamin's work repeatedly suggests, modernity is the world dominated by its phantasmagorias. Or we could look back to Marinetti's crucial *Futurist Manifesto* of 1909:

> We say that the world's magnificence has been enriched by a new beauty; the beauty of speed. A racing car whose hood is adorned with great pipes, like serpents of explosive breath – a roaring car that seems to ride on grapeshot – is more beautiful than the *Victory of Samothrace*. (Marinetti 1991, 49)

What is perhaps most interesting about this passage – and it is true of many others in the *Futurist Manifesto* – is the immersion of modernity within an imagery of technologised warfare ('grapeshot'). One might say, at the least, that Marinetti was predicting the appeal, composed of a mixture of weaponry, speed and sexual allure, of the long and popular sequence of James Bond films; but this combination of modernity and war also has further ramifications.

To this I shall return: in the meantime, however, it is perhaps worth paying attention to a formulation on modernity by one of its most trenchant recent commentators, Gianni Vattimo:

> .... living in history and feeling oneself as a moment that has been conditioned and sustained by a unitary process of events is an experience that is possible only for modern man: reading the newspapers is, in this sense,

the morning prayer of the truly *modern* man. Only with the advent of modernity – or the Gutenberg era, as McLuhan has called it – are the necessary conditions created for the construction and transmission of a global image of human affairs. (Vattimo 1988, 10)

Modernity, then, would according to this reading be not only a sense of the present and the future, but also a specific kind of awareness of the past – as, one can only assume, a continuing process of *differences*. And here one might embark upon a description of modernity as a function of specific changes in the concept of *recognition*. Clearly 'recognition' is a complex term, alluding as it does to repetition; the possibility of 'knowing again' that which, perhaps, one has known before; and a certain kind or scope of intimacy. The immediate question, though, is of how one might – or might not – recognise oneself in the context of modernity. Consider the rather specific twentieth-century question of the family photograph. Here it may be true that one could recognise the bare lineaments of oneself in the faces of one's progenitors; but it is equally true that one would have to go through a process of 'recognition' which is not only a matter of 'finding a likeness', but involves also a necessary accommodation of difference which is responsible to the technological means available: the older black-and-white – or sepia – photograph may indeed be recognisable, but only after a certain translation process has been applied – translation, one might say, 'out of the past'.

Vattimo muses further upon what we might call this reflexive point of modernity when he makes the claim that 'modernity is the epoch in which simply being modern became a decisive value in itself' (Vattimo 1992, 1). He places the origin of this mind-set a long way back, at the end of the fifteenth century, but rapidly moves on to exemplify it from the age of the Enlightenment. But Vattimo's work is also deeply and intricately bound up with a set of speculations about what he calls the 'end of modernity':

> … modernity ends when – for a number of reasons – it no longer seems possible to regard history as unilinear. Such a view requires the existence of a centre around which events are gathered and ordered. We think of history as ordered around the year zero of the birth of Christ, and more specifically as a serial train of events in the life of peoples from the 'centre', the West, the place of civilisation, outside of which are the 'primitives' and the 'developing countries'. In the nineteenth and twentieth centuries

philosophy has launched a radical critique of the idea of unilinear history, exposing the *ideological* character of these views. (Vattimo 1992, 2)

This is obviously an interesting claim, but in several ways it appears to be faulty. For one thing most people – everywhere, one suspects, but certainly in the west – still continue to regard history as unilinear: an apotheosis of multiplicity may be on the way, but it is taking a long time coming, and the number of children in Britain being taught the history of the great black African empires can still be counted on the fingers of very few hands. For another, one could argue that the question of 'exposing' ideology is a loose conception: ideology, of whatever hue, has a habit of digging its heels in when threatened with exposure, and it would be difficult to see the viewpoint of the 'modern' west as one which assigns equal positions to all ideological viewpoints; the position of Islam in current political discourse is a case in point.

One can perhaps get a little further, while also returning to the question of the problematic but inevitable links between modernity and war – as well as speed, to return to an earlier topic – by considering the work of Paul Virilio. Virilio bases part of his complex and brilliant analysis of modernity, perhaps surprisingly, on the words of a British Second World War commander, one Major-General J.F.C. Fuller:

> Every animal breathing today under the sun owes the survival of his species to adroitness, to courage, or to speed. Now, in the age of atomic energy opening up, of these three prerequisites, it is speed that is the most important. (Fuller 1948)

At first glance, it is difficult to see what the good soldier might mean; after all, speed is of remarkably little avail in the case of a nuclear attack. But Virilio glosses it thus:

> … in the modern arsenal, everything moves faster and faster; differences between one means and another fade away. A homogenising process is under way in the contemporary military structure, even inside the three arms specifications: ground, sea, and air is diminishing in the wake of an *aeronautical coalescence*, which clearly reduces the specificity of the land forces. But this homogenising movement of combat techniques and instruments of warfare is coupled to one last movement. This is, with the 'weapon-vehicle' *contraction* and the cybernetisation of the system, the volumetric reduction of military objects: *miniaturisation*. (Virilio 1994, 18)

One might initially think that this 'reduction' of modernity to a series of
events within techno-military history is quite incompatible with wider
movements, but Virilio is quite clear in asserting that military necessity
is the driving force, as it were, of the modern movement (and we have
already seen some support for this idea, albeit from a widely different
quarter, in the thought of Marinetti). We would need to think back, at
least, to the thought of Marcuse and other writers of the 1960s on the
'military/industrial complex'; we might also need to take into account the
fact that what we now know as the 'world-wide web' was originally developed in the USA as a means of developing, sharing and protecting military intelligence.

Many people, of course, would see military development as a spin-off
from, or accompaniment to, technological advance; Virilio, on the contrary, sees military concerns – by which he means, in the broadest sense,
control over territory and populations – as the driving force behind technical advance. But he goes further than this, and into more complex
intellectual territory:

> As can be seen, military space is today undergoing a radical transforma-
> tion. The 'conquest of space' by military and scientific personnel is no
> longer, as it once was, the conquest of the human habitat but the discovery
> of an original continuum that has only a distant link to geographical
> reality. From now on, the warrior moves at once in the infinitely small
> space of nuclear physics and in the infinitely huge outer space. The reduc-
> tion of warring objects and the exponential increase in their performances
> bring to the military establishment that *omniscience* and that *omnipresence*
> it has from the beginning wished to acquire.   (Virilio 1994, 18)

The 'conquest of space' here appears to be a curious term. On the one
hand, as is clear, it refers to what used to be known, in the days of the
Cold War, as the 'space race'; but at the same time, and perhaps more
importantly, it refers to the general realignment of territorial boundaries which is the aim of most, if not all, of modern warfare, invasion
and insurrection. The sophisticated means which are at the disposal of
modern man are still, Virilio claims, being aimed towards the oldest of
human aims: the control of resources which are deemed necessary to
the survival of the tribe, or, as time has gone on, the nation or the state.
One would hardly have to think twice to see in Virilio's analysis a clear
explanation – and one which many thinkers have made – for the recent
invasion of Iraq in order to take control of its oil supplies, a scenario

now being constantly repeated in many locations in, for example, Africa.

What is equally important here, however, is the way in which superior force of arms not only enables this kind of conquest but also allows the most powerful entities to 'distance' through modern means their geographical links. Here we return to the whole question of the relation between modernity and the 'tele-': the most powerful expression of modernity, we might say, is the supersession of the need to 'be there'. Modernity allows those in possession equally of its armaments and of its media to view 'the struggle', whatever it may be, from a distance, not to have to be visibly involved. This works at a military level; but it works too at the wider level of human experience, in which television news or the more 'personal' news one may be receiving via text-messaging on the mobile phone take precedence over more traditional notions of 'lived experience'.

Thus a further paradox within modernity: as Virilio would put it, 'omniscience' and 'omnipresence' are achieved not through a vast global spread but through 'miniaturisation'. One might consider some of the architectural consequences of this situation:

> The representation of the modern city can no longer depend on the ceremonial opening of gates, nor on the ritual processions and parades lining the streets and avenues with spectators. From here on, urban architecture has to work with the opening of a new 'technological space-time'. In terms of access, telematics replaces the doorway. The sound of gates gives way to the clatter of data banks and the rites of passages of a technical culture whose progress is disguised by the immateriality of its parts and networks. Instead of operating in the space of a constructed social fabric, the intersecting and connecting grid of highway and service systems now occurs in the sequences of an imperceptible organisation of time in which the man/machine interface replaces the facades of buildings as the surfaces of property allotments.   (Virilio 1984, 13–14)

Is it, one may be permitted to wonder, a coincidence that Bill Gates's name is what it is? It is, certainly, interesting that this sound of doors and gates opening and closing – 'clunky' is the usual techno-term to describe old-fashioned, outmoded systems – gets contrasted with the relatively silent, weightless whirring of the technosphere as the 'modern' replacement for the older, 'heavier' forms. It is perhaps also of interest, however, how the newer forms of communication and data storage continue to use older elements of discourse: one of the most common ways of referring to a means of access to a website is the ancient term 'portal', which probably carries as much signification of fantasy and the supernatural as it does of the insides of a computer – although it is, perhaps, exactly collocated with the notion of the 'gate'.

Virilio *defines* modernity as speed; he recounts an incident when a 'young media figure' was asked what really filled him with dread and replied, 'The idea that everything might become static, that the machine might grind to a halt. That's why I never take more than ten days' holiday. I'm terrified of immobility'. Yet within modernity also there are other expressions of what we might fairly call that 'terror of loss', and also of the potential grandeur of approaching it. Here is a brief passage from Giorgio Agamben on one of the very first 'prophets' of modernity, Baudelaire:

> It is in the context of this crisis of experience that modern poetry finds its place. For, on close scrutiny, modern poetry from Baudelaire onwards is seen to be founded not on new experience, but on an unprecedented lack of experience. Hence the boldness with which Baudelaire can place shock at the centre of his artistic work. It is experience that best affords us protection from surprises, and the production of shock always implies a gap in experience. To experience something means divesting it of novelty, neutralising its shock potential. Hence Baudelaire's fascination with commodities and *maquillage* – the supremely inexperiencible.   (Agamben 1993, 41)

Perhaps this passage best captures where we have got to so far in our analysis of modernity. There is the question of experience, 'real life', and of the value which we place on it. There is the possibility that modern conditions remove us from an 'inward' understanding of what is going on around us – and within us. There is the issue of the 'shock of the new', and of what we might do when beckoned towards the unpredictable. There is the question of the 'gap', the inevitable uncertainty as we leave the safety of 'traditional' frameworks. And there is the move towards commodities, the inevitable fetishistic outcome of the subject within capitalism. But beyond this there is also the attraction, the fascination of a radically altered world, a world 'made anew', in which we might be free spirits, unattached adventurers, possessed of an ultimate mobility which defies earthly trammels.

Part II

Structures of Contemporary Modernity

5 Post

One of the crucial structures of contemporary modernity, as we have already glimpsed, is the notion of the 'post': the three critical 'postal' terms, we might say, are 'postmodern', 'poststructuralist' and 'postcolonial'.

The concept of the postmodern relies on a version of modernity which claims it to be still held in thrall to the 'grand narratives' – Marxist, Freudian, historicist – whereas the postmodern is regarded as liberated from that servitude and as operating instead through a 'rhetoric of localisation'. At the same time, the postmodern is held to take the technical innovations of modernist writers and artists – and architects, town planners and so forth – into new areas: insofar as the modernist remains attached to the 'traditional', and colludes in concealing the mechanics of writing or art, the postmodern exposes these workings and does not attempt to set up a 'smooth surface'.

Poststructuralism similarly engages in a complex dialectic with structuralism. Where structuralism in its classic formulations – in the anthropology of Lévi-Strauss, for example, or in the linguistics of Saussure – sought a kind of master-code behind human behaviour and language respectively, poststructuralism offers a more nuanced account which no longer holds to the possibility of a 'key' to all knowledges and mythologies. We may cite Roland Barthes, and more specifically the later Barthes of, for example, the fragmentary text *A Lover's Discourse* (1977), as a poststructuralist critic; but the principal influence on poststructuralism is the work of Derrida and the many types of 'deconstruction' which have flowed from it.

The postcolonial is a more vexed site. Some would claim that the postcolonial moment in writing begins from the historical point of 'independence' from colonial rulers. Others would claim that it instead measures a certain level of reflexivity in writers writing in colonial situations as well as later ones, and here the archetypal texts would be the bitter, trenchant writings of Frantz Fanon, especially *The Wretched of the Earth*

(1961). Still others would claim that the truly postcolonial, if such a thing can be, is not yet with us, that the situation of states, especially African states, after their apparent liberation remains haunted by the aftermathic distortions of the colonial condition.

What, however, all three of these approaches have in common is the notion that we now inhabit at a social and cultural level a kind of 'after-life', and it is interesting to see how this rhetoric continues to go through such further modulations as 'after 9/11', as though, to cite Francis Fukuyama, we have reached an 'end of history' and are now living beyond it, in a peculiar kind of stasis in which the prospects for real change are no longer on the agenda. This would suggest a view of modernity as a levelling or flattening of the old conflicts caused by class, nationalism and religious proselytisation. It does not, however, require much inspection to tell us that many of these 'traditional' conflicts are still very much with us, and that the concept of the 'end of history' is a kind of fantasised wish-fulfilment, an attempt to expunge an 'event horizon' which in fact remains ever more pressing.

A psychoanalytic interpretation of this drive for the 'post' would say that it embodies, on the one hand, a belief in the maturation of society, and on the other a desire for a kind of exemption from the continuing disasters of human history. The belief in maturation ignores the continuing – and indeed, in many cases, developing – inequities which characterise the global system sometimes referred to as the 'new world order'; just as the maturing person's wish to put behind him or her the things of childhood only results in a repression which is bound to flare up again as this repression proves partial and inadequate. The desire for exemption could be related similarly to infantile wishes: not to have to go through and deal with the difficulties of maturation but to wish instead for a world in which conflicts are effortlessly resolved and the workings of the reality principle can be ignored.

The question of the 'post' has been through a vast variety of forms, but the linguistic relation between 'post' as 'after' and 'post' in the sense of the mail – emblematised in Derrida's *The Post Card* (1987) – remains to the fore, and demonstrates again how much modernity has to do with distance, the 'tele'; a minor example would be the way in which the steady decline in the numbers voting in UK general elections has been at least marginally reversed by the broadening of the opportunities for 'postal voting'. But this perhaps also reminds us of the extent to which notions of the 'post' are predicated on the continuing erosion of face-to-face contact, of the ways in which cyborgisation proceeds apace, so that the 'machine' is required in order to ensure that, in this case, the most basic functions of representative democracy are performed.

Modernity, then, seen in this light constitutes an advance into an age when communicative interaction is dependent on *techne*, where the face and the voice are occluded, reduced to the status of mere ghosts in the machine. In this 'post-age', it is interesting to see the outmoded force of the individual signature being replaced by a set of (personal identification) numbers; the introduction of identity cards would be part of a similar constellation, in which guarantees of identity are no longer provided by the intimacies of 'local knowledge' but rather by a specific system of 'accounting' from which nobody can opt out.

The move towards localisation thus proposed by the theorists of the 'post' can thus be seen as a counter-movement, indeed perhaps a reactionary one, against the erosion of real 'local knowledges' in the name of the establishment of a set of data-bases – perhaps eventually, so the fantasy runs, a single universal data-base, although here *techne* can be seen to be running behind itself – within which all individuals will be fully 'subjected'. In one sense, it would be possible to see this as an apotheosis of modernity: human fleshly actuality, 'meat' as it is referred to by some writers, would be subjugated to a massive flow of information; one of the great symbols here would come from the imaginary glossary to Greg Egan's novel *Diaspora* (1997), in which a 'citizen' is defined thus:

> Conscious software which has been granted a set of inalienable rights in a particular polis. These rights vary from polis to polis, but always include inviolability, a pro rata share of processing power, and unimpeded access to public data.   (Egan 1997, 363)

It does not take a great deal of imagination to see in this a delineation of what we might call a future 'polis state'.

6 'Differend'

The 'differend' is a term which first emerges in Lyotard's book, *The Differend: Phrases in Dispute* (1988). Lyotard's central claim is predicated on his belief that the great master-narratives, from the late eighteenth century to the present day, have decisively lost their legitimacy: that Hegel's belief in the progress of the human spirit, Marx's in the supremacy and ultimate goals of the class struggle, Humboldt's in the civilising function of the university, along with may other teleological ideas, no longer exert their previous force.

What then happens in modernity, according to Lyotard, is that there is no absolute 'ground' on which to claim or assert the validity of 'facts'; instead, we are adrift in a world of competing discourses. His chief example is the Holocaust, where he says that the continuing arguments about the historical facts can never come to conclusion because there is no common rhetorical ground between them. It seems probable, although perhaps never quite clear, that Lyotard intends us to infer from this that, where there is no 'appeal' from different discourses to a truth outside themselves, the argument will be *de facto* 'won' by the side in the position of greater power; as he puts it, 'I would like to call a differend the case where the plaintiff is divested of the means to argue and becomes for that reason a victim' (Lyotard 1991, 9).

What we have here is a suggestion of a more or less total moral relativism. The 'differend' is not merely a 'difference', because 'difference' is locked into a dialectic of which the other side is 'similarity'. To put it very simply, common sense would say that it is, at least at some point, possible to say how different and how similar one phenomenon is to another. But this, Lyotard says, is no longer an operable philosophical hypothesis: words, terms do not have meanings in themselves, their meanings are only generated within the specific systems of power and knowledge in which they are located.

At least in part, this situation would stem from increasing technological complexity. One pertinent example might be the current debates about global warming, where there are clear differences of view between various states and between their leaders. But these are not simply differences of opinion: nobody, for example, claims that global warming is a 'good thing'. The question is rather about whether or not it is currently important; the timescales on which it might operate; and to what extent, if at all, national self-interests would need to be overridden in order to address it. Each side of the debate produces different scientific opinion to back up its case; in the end, all that can happen is that the state with the most power will have its way. Thus the entire process of debate becomes revealed as specious, as what a different rhetoric would refer to as a clash of incommensurable ideologies.

Or one might consider the recent debate in the UK about the utility of juries in complex fraud trials. The argument for retaining them is based within a discourse, of some considerable antiquity, which holds sacred the notion that a person has the right, whatever the circumstances, to be judged by his or her peers. The argument against is based on wholly different grounds, involving the sheer difficulty of understanding issues which may arise in the course of examining corporate fraud. This is not, Lyotard would no doubt say, a situation in which previous systems of 'rational argument' can be called upon to adjudicate; rather, it is a case of two entirely different regimes of discourse being used.

What has this to do with modernity? In each case, it is obviously to do with the rise of the 'expert'; with the enormous surplus of technical knowledge over the presumed mental capacities of the 'man in the street'. These huge bodies of knowledge (of which now, of course, the largest is the Worldwide Web) are not only beyond the reach of the average citizen; they also have their own dynamic and are constantly evolving in ways which are beyond individual comprehension. The 'differend' therefore has also to do with what we might call the 'problem of untranslateability': a familiar, if old-fashioned, rhetoric would speak of the various 'branches of knowledge', as though they were all linked to a single central tree, and that therefore links and connections could be made among them. Indeed, Hegel's attempt in his *Phenomenology of Spirit* (1807) was precisely this: to demonstrate that the history of the individual, the history of (western) society and the history of the cosmos are interlinked in a series of parallels and repetition which, in the end, guarantees man's place at the centre of the universe.

To more modern thinking, this appears as a 'supreme fiction', an attempt to anthropomorphise a world which is far more diverse, far more resistant to interpretation than appears to 'common sense'.

Concomitantly with a growth of knowledge has come a growth in the awareness that, first, that knowledge can never be in any sense 'complete' (and thus that the original 'encyclopaedic' venture of modernity is impossible), and second, that there is a prevailing danger that what we take for knowledge is merely an effect of our need to 'put a human face' on things which are fundamentally not human.

An example of the 'differend' to which Lyotard does not refer, although it is all around us, is the relation between the human and the 'domesticated animal', the pet. Here it should be above all obvious that we are dealing with different 'regimes of discourse'; yet it is clearly crucially important – and has been for millennia – to suppose, or believe, that the 'language' used by cats and dogs is somehow 'translateable' into human terms. The 'differend' is the world of absolute difference, where power relations are both the driving force but also, and simultaneously, the object of the most powerful forces of obfuscation. Here again one may discern the outline of the most central problem of modernity since, at least, the time of Darwin: how to assert man's power within and over the world while remaining at the same time increasingly aware of how limited this power actually is.

7 Hauntology

One of the most interesting features of recent theories of modernity is the extraordinary emphasis they have placed on the ways in which the modern is 'haunted' by its own past. This emerges in postcolonial writing and theory; it emerges in Derrida's notion of 'hauntology' (by which he intends a pun on 'ontology', two words which sound identical in French); it emerges also in the whole repertoire of hauntings, crypts and phantoms which characterise recent advances in psychoanalytic theory and technique.

Consider, for example, this paragraph from Nicolas Abraham and Maria Torok's psychoanalytic work, *The Shell and the Kernel* (1978):

> The phantom is a formation of the unconscious that has never been conscious – for good reason. It passes – in a way yet to be determined – from the parent's unconscious into the child's. …The phantom's periodic and compulsive return lies beyond the scope of symptom-formation in the sense of a return of the repressed; it works like a ventriloquist, like a stranger within the subject's own mental topography.   (Abraham and Torok 1978, 173)

There are of course many things which could be said about this passage in the psychoanalytic context. For example, the very process of analysis could be seen to be challenged by such a statement, and by the more powerful ones offered by Jean Laplanche in his work on the 'message', for if this 'sub'-unconscious has never *been*, then what role can analysis play in unearthing it for inspection, and thus in the putative 'cure' of the patient?

However, our concern here is with modernity, and here we may take Abraham and Torok's comments as themselves symptomatic of a certain view of the modern condition. According to this view, the very enterprise of the modern in shifting the weight of tradition, in breaking free from the trace of the past, is itself in some sense 'phantomatic'; just as the child remains at all times the 'product' of the parent, so new cultural movements serve to contain within themselves, albeit in 'unknown', or at least in unthought, forms the relics of a past which cannot be buried, or re-buried, because the corpse itself is unavailable on any specific topography.

This thought might lead us in two directions. One would be towards the notion of the 'secret history' (to use the title of a relevant novel by Donna Tartt). It might be claimed within modernity that a 'secret history' is all there is: that the history we all imbibe as a result of cultural and educational processes is merely a cover-story for something quite different. Indeed, we could see the seeds of this view being laid precisely within the moment of Enlightenment, with the 'secret history' of the Rosicrucians and the Illuminati serving as the 'real' text to which the world has been working even while claiming to be pushing in another direction entirely. Thus there is a 'sealed knot' upon enlightenment: while it appears to seek openness and transparency, it can also be seen to be in fact in thrall to a quite different expedient, which has more to do with the endless persistence of the past, albeit in covert form.

The other direction would engage us directly with topographies, and maps. Indeed, a primary image of modernity would be the map, the clear grid onto which everything can be (to use a suspect term) 'plotted'; but it could equally be said that each map is simultaneously the erasure of another map. Here we might think about the state's insistence on impos-ing a map onto previous aboriginal territorialisations, ones which have nothing to do with maps as conceived by the western, 'enlightened' mind: Bruce Chatwin's work on 'song-lines' might come to mind as an attempt to conceive and translate the vortices of a nomadic existence into the terms of a mind-set which respects and indeed enforces rigid, state-controlled boundaries.

In both of these cases, it would be the case that modernity is haunted by its other; but perhaps what is more important is the series of ways, including Derrida's analysis of 'hauntology', in which modernity has tried precisely to come to grips with its own other, with this constant seepage whereby the gesture towards precision seems to end up contam-inated by its own 'imprecise' past. This kind of self-reflexive modernity thus moves a decisive step beyond the motifs of severance and experi-mentation which characterised its earlier avatars; it recognises what we might usefully term the 'impossibility of banishment' and recognises also that the primordial philosophical gesture offered in the very term 'ontol-ogy' is immediately destabilised as one realises that there is no supernal point from which to gain fresh leverage upon a world – cultural, historical, national – which is already formed.

There is, we might say, always a ghost. That ghost might be *Hamlet*'s emblematic ghost, the ghost of the undead father; or it might be the ghostly lines signified on the map as the boundaries of postcolonial countries, which were traced there long ago by the imperial need for power-driven geographical clarity – perhaps it might be appropriate to call them 'deadlines', since this would conjure up a certain phantomaticity of time as well as of space. We can see the trace of the ghost also in the emergence of 'virtual reality', and in the persistence of apparently archaic terminology in the newest of virtual spaces – and this again is 'nothing new': from 'typewriting' to the 'writing' of an e-mail message, and thus to the concept of 'texting', the terms remain with us, dragging their echoes from the past even as we think we might be thankfully emerging into a new space.

Hauntology suggests that there is no 'new space'; there may be new perspectives particular to modernity, but as they become more sophisticated they will pick up, as the original exploits of photography so often claimed to do, ghosts from the past, ghosts, of course, 'in the machine'; and this might also be what such a prevalent theme in science fiction, the residual or reborn humanity of the robot, touches upon. Modernity, indeed, touches at all points upon the 'post-human'; but in order for us to be able to recognise this phenomenon, then the 'human' itself has to be there, as trace, as legend, as phantom. The notion of the 'haunt', of course, also figures as the very concept and underpinning of the concept of neighbourhood; it is thus a dialectical trope which suggests that in our most intimate and quotidian relationships there is always a ghost present at the feast.

8   Global Language

As I write, in late August 2005, the results of GCSEs in Britain are being announced. One of the most remarkable features is an enormous (13–14%) drop in the number of schoolchildren taking GCSEs in French and German; this is in no way compensated by take-up rates in other languages, such as Spanish and Mandarin Chinese, which might be seen as having contemporary commercial use. On the radio, a commentator is also remarking on the recent difficulties experienced – certainly in Britain, but probably also throughout the western world – in finding experts in Arabic languages who might be able to assist in the identification and pursuit of Islamic 'terrorists'. It is also noticeable that the name of the Brazilian electrician, shot at an underground station not long ago on being mistaken for such a terrorist, has at the time of writing been pronounced in six different ways on the BBC; it appears that a phonological consensus is yet to emerge.

What is significant in each of these cases is the emergence and consolidation of English as a global language and the connection between this phenomenon and the structures of modernity. One can point to three distinct phases in this development. The first occurs in the nineteenth century, when an education in 'English' – by which is meant the language and, in particular, the attendant literary culture – became inextricably linked with a notion of national mission. This national mission was in turn dependent upon a certain concept of civilisation, which was 'naturally' associated with an expansionist imperialism.

During this phase, of course, English was not the only possible contender for linguistic domination. French, Spanish and other European languages were also exported, modified and creolised through the empires of their host nations. Indeed, the very idea of a 'global language' would at this stage have seemed meaningless: imperial cultures had their own spheres of influence within which their language spread and grew. Within these spheres of influence, on the other hand, there were enormous instabilities; varieties of English occurred, for example, within the

Caribbean which were to become barely recognisable to the host culture, but these varieties remained 'unofficial', informal: the goal of British imperial education – and a particularly striking success was produced in the Indian subcontinent – was the perfection of the English language and the consequent export of the supposedly supreme culture and literature which had been expressed therein.

The relative equity of the major European languages came to an end, however, in the second phase: just as the British empire had been the driving force behind the first phase, so in the early and middle years of the twentieth century it was the United States which provided the political and military muscle to ensure a further step in the dominance of English. Some previously powerful languages, including French and German, were driven back towards their original metropoles, where institutions like the Académie Française sought, and still seek, to maintain their insularity and purity. Others, like Spanish and Portuguese, remained hugely dominant in terms of sheer populations, but since these populations were, and remain, largely impoverished these numbers failed to translate into global clout. The most popular language of all, of course, Chinese, figured little on the world stage: partly because of the insularity of mainland China, partly because of what was – and still is – perceived by the west as its impenetrable difficulty, partly again because during these years China was not an economic force to be reckoned with.

Just as the first phase was driven by empire and the second by political and economic national dominance, so, according to the inexorable logic of modernity, the third phase is now driven by technology and corporate culture. The international language of the computer – because market leaders like Microsoft and Google are US-based – is English, and the larger and more monopolistic these corporations become, the less likely it is that serious competitors to English will remain. Chinese faces particular difficulties here for two reasons: one is the vast gap between the spoken Chinese of the various regions and worldwide communities and the 'official' Mandarin which is the conduit for political and economic thought and development, the other is the fact that since global technologies have largely emerged geared to the alphabet, the western perception of Chinese as 'too difficult' is unlikely to be eroded in the foreseeable future. This apparent 'difficulty' is, of course, not a universal 'given'; rather, it is an *effect* of the balance of national and corporate power.

At the linguistic level, then, it would appear that modernity is tending towards an increasingly monopolistic condition, and it is clearly this that

GCSE students are responding to, even if they might not choose to artic-ulate it in these terms. The archaic phenomenon of the Englishman abroad who is convinced that, if only he shouts loudly enough, the 'for-eigner' will eventually understand him is rewritten in the languages of e-mail and text-messaging, with other languages progressively reduced to remote outcrops, to be saved for their quaint nostalgic value.

At the same time, it needs to be pointed out that the divergence between this 'official' convergence and the spread of dialects, argots, creoles, suggests again that there is a ghost in the machine. Part of official UK governmental policy, as I write, is to produce a situation wherein all British citizens are capable of speaking English, thus expos-ing the fact that in several minority communities, including Pakistani, Bangladeshi and above all Chinese, this is not currently the case. But these difficulties, modernity claims, will eventually die out; it is the older echelons, often of first-generation immigrants, who retain their 'other' linguistic roots. This, however, is of course not the reason for insistence on speaking English, which is rather the fear that, in the midst of the modern state, other languages are being spoken and are being made to carry a freight of resistance to modernity, typically now in the form of extremist Islamic preachers.

Here we sense the presence again of Foucault's panopticon, modern society conceived as a regime within which everything can be observed and understood, and there is clearly a delicate balance here between freedom of expression and the production of a police (or 'polis') state. Modernity, we might say, believes in an ultimate transparency, and that which resists such transparency, whether it be the anarchic individual who wishes to withdraw from state control or the 'foreigner in our midst' who wishes to teach and enact values which are remote from western democratic assumptions, has to be crushed so that such transparency can exist, to produce, in other words, a 'totalitarianism of transparency' from which 'resistant materials' are banned.

9   Development

In an interesting essay in *The Future of Knowledge and Culture: A Dictionary for the 21ˢᵗ Century* (2005), Majid Rahnema writes:

> In the last sixty years, few words have been as intensely discussed, glorified or attacked as 'development'. At the end of the Second World War, the word came to symbolise the hopes of almost every human being dreaming of a future liberated from colonialism, hunger, destitution, exploitation and all other forms of injustice and suffering. Today, for the billions who shared these hopes, the dream has become a nightmare. The increase in the world's productive capacity has made it possible, indeed, to provide enough food for nine billion people, that is one and a half times the population of the earth; yet more than one billion are today suffering from hunger and malnutrition.   (Rahnema 2005, 70)

There is, of course, no denying Rahnema's point: one has only to think, for example, of the terrible health problems which I have already mentioned suffered by Kenyans growing forced flowers for western consumers, or of the millions of Chinese peasants displaced by enormous hydroelectric projects, to see that 'development', whatever it might once have meant, has now come to play a large part in a dehumanisation of the world, in the removal of populations and the destruction of the environment.

What is most important, however, is to see this as part of the dialectic of modernity. Modernity seeks what is clean, pure, transparent; it wishes to remove old traditions, inequities and prejudices; it looks towards a future free from ill health, intolerance and 'darkness' of all sorts. But at the same time, and this is the critical element in the dialectic, in seeking to fulfil its mission of 'bringing the light to dark places' – of replacing, to use an obvious and more local example, slum terraces with high-rise towers – it has to mobilise forces which are themselves in hock to quite different missions. And in this process it becomes clear that modernity tells several very different stories: the emphasis in modern cultural theory on multiplicity of narrative is not merely an interpretative device for unpacking modern culture, it is also an *effect* of a multiplicity of narrative which is commonplace, even inevitable, under modern conditions, where there is always a secret story to be told as well as the overt tale.

We might consider, for example, the recent western invasion of Iraq. The official story here would be one with which we are all familiar: a mission to bring civilisation by ending a barbarous regime, a welcome into the light of democracy of a people suffering helplessly under the heel of a brutal dictator, a gesture even to help a largely impoverished Arab world (despite the colossal wealth of some of its elites) into a better economic order. What is critical as one approaches this story is not to denounce it as untrue: there are undoubtedly many people in the world – and a great number in the armed forces – who have believed this story, and many who still do. To call them wrong is, at the moral level, to denigrate a huge amount of human self-sacrifice, and at the intellectual level to settle for too simple an answer to a question which is complex in the extreme and which hinges again on the notion of the 'differend'.

Another story which can be told about the Iraq invasion would be about oil. According to this narrative, it is not the possibility of a renaissance of Iraqi civilisation which is being sought, but the securing of a version of society based on the US model and involving the continuing consumption of huge quantities of oil which can, at the moment, only be imported. Followers of this line would point to the involvement of the US Vice-President, Dick Cheney, with the giant oil conglomerate Halliburton; they might also, as a sideline, want to point to the death threat made by a major supporter of the US government, the televangelist Pat Robertson, to the President of Venezuela, Hugo Chavez, who controls vast alternative oil reserves but who is political anathema to the US establishment (and thus, by extension, to the new global order). Turning back to the specificities of Iraq, it is of course not lost on the tellers of either tale that Iraq has an enormous symbolic significance to the west and to Abrahamic theological and cultural tradition, as the west's choice as the 'cradle of civilisation' (despite the alternative and scientifically much sounder claims of Africa).

How, then, might we approach these two stories of the effects of development and modernity (and of course there are many others)? One approach would be through an aspect of the work of Deleuze and Guattari. In *A Thousand Plateaus* and elsewhere, they contrast a model of thought based on 'arborescence' with one based on the 'rhizomatic'.

By the 'arborescent' they mean to refer to the development of the tree, which proceeds from the roots through the trunk to the branches and leaves in an endless upward motion; here we have the concept of development in embryo, an underlying principle which suggests that growth is inevitable, beneficial, but necessarily 'uneven', in the sense that the branches are superior to the roots, that culture continues to move upwards. The 'rhizomatic', by contrast, refers to a horizontal process, one in which there is no classification of 'superiority' and 'inferiority', but instead a 'spread' which is, in a sense, not 'developmental' at all but rather obeys a principle of aboriginal equality. A model for the arborescent would be the western hierarchised managerial institution; a model for the rhizomatic would be the network in which no one unit is superior to another.

In these contexts it is perhaps worth remembering that the Christian tradition has been based throughout its history on authority; traditionally, in Catholic form, on the authority of the priesthood eventually sanctioned by the divine power of Rome, in Protestant form on the authority of the Bible, of the sacred text. Islam is a very different religion; there is of course authority in Islam – the authority of the prophet Mohammed himself, the authority of the Koran – but these are not mediated through an established priesthood but rather through a restless – and indeed restive – assemblage of teachers, who need to convince their audiences that their interpretations are correct rather than relying on an assumed authority.

We may seem to have moved here a little way away from the problematic of 'development', but certainly some such notion is crucial to current relations between 'Christendom' (to revive an old-fashioned but thoroughly relevant term) and Islam. What, it is constantly asked, will be sacrificed in the name of development? Or, to put the same question a different way, what is 'fundamental'? According to the logic of modernity, nothing is fundamental, everything is capable of beneficial revision; but we need to see 'fundamentalism' not as a hidden reservoir of feeling which the 'modern' west has stumbled upon as if by accident, but rather precisely as an *effect* of the logic of development. It is not as though in the Middle East one finds a world which has never itself produced or felt the benefits of scientific or technological discovery – indeed, in many ways, of which the west's habitual use of Arabic numerals is only the most obvious, many of the world's great discoveries have been the result of unexpected symmetries, synergies and convergences between European and Arab technology. What one does find, however, is that modernity is here again producing its own alternate, its own distorted mirror image. For development to matter or to mean anything at all, there obviously needs to be something to be developed: hence the rhetoric of the 'developed world', and the comparatively recent shift from describing what was formerly known as the 'third world', and then as the 'undeveloped world', into the 'developing world'. In one sense, of course, one could see in this phrase a statement of hope; but inevitably such a statement is haunted by its own other, which is that such development has to proceed to a point of arborescent supremacy in which the 'fundamentals' of economies, of cultures, of ways of life have to be surpassed in the name of a common global goal wherein all local knowledges and proclivities will be subsumed, sublated – or lost.

10 Hong Kong

Hong Kong has for a long time been a global symbol of modernity, and remains so even now, although it has in many respects been overtaken by a resurgent Shanghai liberated (as it has been on several foiled occasions in the past) from central Chinese control and the envy of Beijing. We can look at Hong Kong's modernity in several different ways.

Most obvious, perhaps, is the architecture: the gleaming facades of the finance houses of Central District, the towering hotels of Tsim Sha Tsui, the seemingly endless residential skyscrapers of the new towns inland. There is also the purity and cleanliness expected of a thoroughly modern city, the effortless travel on the MTR, the neatly ordered parks; and of course there are the systems behind all this which keep it going, the rapid flow of money, the virtually tax-free status of the big corporations. Also, perhaps, the seemingly effortless mixing of names symbolised by, for example, the enormous corporate conglomerate Hutchison Whampoa; and the insistence that little of this has been changed, little of the modern, corporate, cash-generating entity which is Hong Kong affected by the 'change of ownership' from Britain to China in 1997, the only effect of which may have been the replacement of the role of governor by that, significantly, of chief executive.

A further aspect of this modernity, then, is a certain 'transnational' aspect; where other large cities are perhaps inevitably bound to their local customs and to remote state control, there is that about Hong Kong which bespeaks a looser, more 'liquid' set of ties and affiliations. But here again, if we are to look more deeply into the psycho- and sociogeography of Hong Kong, the 'last emporium' as Ackbar Abbas has it, we see an emblematic example of the dialectic of modernity at work.

Firstly, when you look into the spaces between the skyscrapers it is to see an entirely different kind of life continuing, the evidence of a 'different' trajectory. Here you find much smaller, less 'developed' buildings, and these, of course, are where Hong Kong's basic wealth is actually generated. Hong Kong has traditionally had, and still has, one of the steepest income gradients in the world; without the thousands of small sweat-shops, the hundreds of two- or three-person printing presses, the tailors and cookshops, there would be no wealth; Golden Arcade is perhaps symbolic, a place where every kind of computer can be had, made up to order from thousands of different parts, some still bearing the name-tags of the corporations which first produced them and are, presumably, unaware of their current location as they have been swept along by the *bricolage* of modernity.

But one also needs to look further inland. Hong Kong, like a living symbol of modernity, is a façade with a hinterland. Often mistaken for the island and the small urbanised area of Kowloon, Hong Kong in fact stretches north for a further twelve miles towards what used to be the border with mainland China. Although this area is dotted with new towns, it also contains hundreds of villages which, in their folk customs and in their religion have a stronger continuity with an older China than has survived anywhere else on the Chinese mainland, because of their immunity from the excesses of the Cultural Revolution. Here again modernity shows a double face; there is an antiquity and an archaism to the so-called New Territories which underpins the onward march of central Hong Kong and both matches and parodies it in its insistence on older 'Chinese characteristics'.

There is a frequent rhetoric in Hong Kong and in China which speaks of 'modernisation with Chinese characteristics'. In part this is a language of resistance, a discourse which seeks to place a limit on the extent to which the typical brand-names of the west – Coca-Cola, Levi, even Marks and Spencer – can take control of lives which are lived athwart this mod-ernising model. The contradictions are well caught in images of school, every child neatly dressed in uniform despite the sweltering heat, learn-ing English while naturally speaking a version of street Cantonese which has virtually no written equivalent. It is well caught too in the Star Ferry, the small fleet of distinctly un-modernised boats which form one of the principal links between the island and the Hong Kong mainland.

Hong Kong is one of the world's biggest container ports, and one can look out from some of the roads outside Kowloon onto a seemingly endless landscape of stacked giant boxes containing the world's goods awaiting collection or delivery. But one can also see huge buildings being erected through the use of archaic bamboo scaffolding, in sublime disre-gard of the laws on health and safety so prized by the west yet so expen-sive in terms of competitive business practice. Modernity, then, comes at a price; but the price is always a comparative one. Hong Kong's cheap labour force, the foundation of its prosperity, exists because the social freedoms enjoyed are reckoned to be, or to have been, worth the price of comparative deprivation, in view of the worse deprivations which would have had to be endured in the villages of Guangdong province.

Modernity, then, is here specifically revealed as a psychogeography: it is a space, or a set of spaces in which there is a certain freedom to move, even when that movement can happen only in one of the most confined and overpopulated spaces on earth. It asserts, in the emblematic space of Hong Kong, that there are goals to be aspired to (here particularly in the shape of The Peak, the high place of the former governor's residence) and that capitalism provides the route map to that place of prosperity. None of this prevents the people of Hong Kong from also adhering to quite different beliefs, from throwing their luck cards into the fires of temples like Wong Tai Sin and casting the runes of chance in the hope of a better life. None of it, either, prevents Hong Kong citizens from doubling their chances of a different kind of 'better life' by buying second homes in Australia, Vancouver, the US, as insurance against the feared 'evil day' when all this modernity may be rolled back in favour of Beijing state control.

In this place, then, modernity flourishes on the margins, as an oppositional tactic; yet it cannot flourish at all without its own opposite, without the sweated labour of Tai Po, without the thousands of Chinese seamen who are virtually enslaved aboard the giant tankers which moor nightly in the aptly named Victoria Harbour. The scenario of progress and development is indivisible from the scenario of nostalgia; here modernity takes up what has been lost and translates the past into the future, 'all the electric light of new Asia' burning on the basis of lives of drudgery and obedience to the machine. Here, perhaps above all places, 'development' shows its teeth and asserts that personal betterment is available, but not exactly here, not exactly now, rather in a future scenario towards to which The Peak and all the skyscrapers point, regardless of the teeming, unclean, impure, rugged life going on down below.

11 Architecture

The phenomenon of, and controversy about, 'modern architecture' is in reality only a small and rather ephemeral part of the overall relation between modernity and architecture, which is not reducible to a matter of particular styles but rather addresses whole issues about the nature of space, time and enclosure. Essentially, the architecture of modernity privileges the public over the private, the light over the dark, the temporary over the permanent.

It is appropriate in this context to adumbrate (bring forth from the shadows) a specific modern version of the sublime. It is typified in, among other things, the airport. The airport is a space in which nobody dwells; although a 'permanent' structure in itself, it is designed as a housing for the transient and the transitory. It is not practically essential for an airport terminal building to have high ceilings; like a cathedral, the size and shape have evolved to suit symbolic norms. Everything about the modern airport signifies aspiration: this aspiration is comprised of the technological aspiration, the conquest of the vast spaces of the skies, and economic aspiration, a site from which it is possible to look down upon the users of more humble, earthbound modes of transportation and communication.

To enter a modern departure lounge is to experience a certain *frisson* of freedom; it is to enter, to put it in Virilio's terms, a world which is composed not of the static but of the intersections of various kinds of speed. The escalator, the travelator, the unmanned link train all serve to mimic the possibility of transcendence, of leaving the earth behind, of turning the body into a thing in a constant state of motion. In this brave new world the trammels of quotidian life are left behind with (all too frequently) the luggage; what is promised is a curious mythic amalgam of total freedom and total care. Here again, as we would expect, the composite dialectic of exemption and deprivation operates; just as the presence of an airport signifies, for the ground beneath, difficulties of noise and a corresponding drop in housing values, so the more menial staff of the airport become those who are condemned to live in the wastelands which the airport inevitably generates around it. In most modern western cities, these will be people from minority communities; it is, at Heathrow for example, miraculously as though the passenger has already been transported to Asia before the flight even leaves.

At a lower level (in several senses), much of this is replicated in the out-of-town shopping mall, or better, atrium: the soaring perspectives, the inclusion of a modified version of the outside world in the form of flowers, shrubs, even trees – all of this is designed to produce a certain illusion of weightlessness, a condition in which to be relieved of one's money is, paradoxically, to contribute to the overall mood of consumption. Again, of course, the mall produces its own necessary inhabitant and opposite, the 'mall rat', the denizen of a new, modernised version of the urban jungle, just as airports produce the essential corollary in the shape of at least one exile who has been trapped in Charles de Gaulle airport for many years, having the requisite papers neither to 'take off' nor to return to the 'outer world'.

Even at the level of the dwelling place, one can see a similar logic at work: to quote an old Flanders and Swann song about modern living (or 'life-style'), 'the garden's full of furniture and the house is full of plants'. Modern design seeks to render transparent and in the end erase the boundaries between the 'inside' and the 'outside'; perhaps its most apt metaphor is 'toughened glass', a kind of glass through which the inner and the outer are perfectly co-visible and yet which will not permit the intrusion of the burglar's hammer or the terrorist's bullet. At the Eden Project in Cornwall, landscapes and their vegetation from all over the world are housed in geodesic domes in which there is an apparent absolute contiguity between the outer climate and the interior microclimate; the skies of Africa merge seamlessly into the skies of the English southwest. Geography no longer presents any challenge; everything can be 'transplanted', produced on demand.

And so can every shape. From the domes of the Sydney Opera House to the London building known as the 'Erotic Gherkin', modern architects face up to the challenge of producing shapes which blur the edges of geometric rectitude. To dwell upon the 'Gherkin' for a moment, it has, interestingly, a street address, in St Mary Axe. Here again one hears the mixed tones of the absolutely new and that by which it is haunted: St Mary Axe is an ancient name, redolent of the many other medieval names which phantomise the City of London, but of course it is not that one needs to know about St Mary Axe in order to find the Gherkin, since it is visible

for miles around and entirely dwarfs the small ancient street which provides it with its earthly base; it is rather that the street name is needed to
remind us that even such a building has a human content, human
relevance; the myth might be that without such a 'tether' to history and
geography the whole building might, like an upended zeppelin, float free
from its moorings, heading off into the ambiguous 'space' the conquest
of which remains, in at least one sense, modernity's most important
mission.

The opposite end of this chain is marked by the out-of-town super-
store, which aims to construct a world of its own immune to outer light.
Huge 'do-it-yourself warehouses' have now begun to include their own
cafés; the myth is that one goes there not in order to purchase a specific
product but to become immersed in a particular world, where one can
browse among electrical tools, outdoor furniture, outré gardening equipment, whole mock-up kitchens and bathrooms in a kind of purified
parody of the messiness attendant on actually using or living in these
artefacts in everyday life. Here is the opposite of speed, a world where
everything is slowed down, where the practical need to mend a gutter or
mow a lawn is translated into an outcropping and fulfilment of 'leisure',
where there is a slow drift along the naves and aisles, accompanied here
not by the scent of incense but by the different scentlessness of a purified,
cleansed life in which every item of cookware is clean, every blade is
sharp, every electrical motor purrs delicately to life at the touch of a
switch.

What also lies behind this are the many transmutations of the concept
of the 'park' – the 'industrial park', the 'retail park', the 'science park'.
The buildings themselves may present a perfectly blank face to the world,
but their setting mimics the older style of park, as a place of quasi-
natural respite from life's tasks. Here is where we repair if we are 'weary
and heavy-laden', here is where we may be absolved of our vices, those
particular vices of procrastination and practical incompetence which
might otherwise 'throw a spanner in the works'. Here the spanner always
works, even if, when we get it home, we may still find the careful pictures
and instructions which accompany it wildly inappropriate to the ancient,
grease-caked plumbing which we have to disassemble.

12   Dirt

In 1909 Freud published 'Notes upon a Case of Obsessional Neurosis', which is more often known as the case history of the 'Rat Man'. The rat man had complicated dealings with dirt, which I want to re-read here as a proto-account of modernity's 'obsessional' dealings with dirt, with all that needs to be 'swept under the carpet'. At the end of the day, I want to contend, modernity is all about banishing dirt, banishing the rat; although since, as the urban myth often tells us, we are rarely more than a couple of yards away from a rat success in this area seems to be unavoidably limited.

A crucial paragraph in Freud's case history runs as follows:

> Once when the patient was visiting his father's grave he had seen a big beast, which he had taken to be a rat, gliding along over the grave. He assumed that it had actually come out of his father's grave, and had just been having a meal off his corpse. The notion of a rat is inseparably bound up with the fact that it has sharp teeth with which it gnaws and bites. But rats cannot be sharp-toothed, greedy and dirty with impunity: they are cruelly persecuted and mercilessly put to death by man, as the patient had often observed with horror. He had often pitied the poor creatures. But he himself had been just such a nasty, dirty little wretch, who was apt to bite people when he was in a rage, and had been fearfully punished for doing so. He could truly be said to find 'a living likeness of himself' in the rat. (Freud 1955, 215–16)

Freud with characteristic aplomb born of his familiarity with Vienna's principal cemetery, the Zentralfriedhof, decides that this 'rat', if it had been seen at all, was more probably a weasel, but this need not concern us here; what is more important is the notion of the 'living likeness of himself', which is a quotation from Goethe's *Faust*.

The critical point here is to do with abjection, with the 'throwing-off' of one's own characteristics onto the other. It can be argued – and has been, by Julia Kristeva among others – that this is a central motif of what we choose to call 'civilisation': we pride ourselves on putting behind ourselves things of the past, and thus come to inhabit a fantasy realm – which I shall here regard as the realm of modernity – in which these sad, bitter and/or embarrassing things cannot recur. We devote the efforts of civilisation to removing threat, to putting all the 'nastiness' and the 'dirt' beyond the pale; arguably that is what the west has done to Africa for generations, with results which some might consider predictable.

The link that Freud, of course, makes is between this 'cultural' imperative and the history of the individual. In order for his analysis to 'succeed', the rat man has to re-experience and re-interpret phenomena of his own personal past, and these involve him in a dilemma. In 'putting away' the rat, is it also true that he has 'put away' part of himself, that part which is here considered in two different but complementary ways, namely the part which feels sympathy for the 'persecuted' rat and the part which remembers his own 'rat-like' feelings? It is interesting, of course, that as in the parallel case of the 'wolf man' a customary titular elision has made it sound as though this unfortunate patient is some kind of hybrid, characterised *as* a rat rather than as a person whose psychological difficulties may be unravelled, at least up to a point, through the interpretation of the *symbol* of the rat.

One point of interest here is the description, no doubt Freud's own (although as always amid the multiple palimpsests of the case histories it is difficult to be sure) of the rat 'gliding along over the grave'. Here we may immediately sense the dialectic of modernity: there is that in the movement of the rat, no matter what it might have been doing immediately previously, which suggests that it exists in an exempted world which moves with a different gait from the mortal processes of life and death. In this sense, then, the rat might even be considered, against all 'common sense', to embody a fantasised purity; just as the conscious mind of the rat man wishes to 'transcend' questions of life and death

And this is not just any death: what is clearly at stake is the death of the father – and especially how this might inevitably presage the death of the son. We thus have here a by now familiar scene of haunting: the rat man would wish consciously for his father still to be with him, but at some other location inside himself he suspects that he has been feasting on his father's remains – in other words, at the cultural level, on the remains of the past. The patient is thus already caught in an impossible conundrum, which he himself approaches by wondering whether his own rat-ness, his 'self-as-rat', will be accorded the same measure of sympathy and forgiveness as he himself has afforded rats (or thinks, claims or misremembers he has) in the past.

Crucially, rats are dirty. This myth, of course, has no particular scientific basis – rats do what they have to do, and the attribution of 'dirty' is a human one, one which simultaneously anthropomorphises and abjects the rat. It may be true that rats 'carry disease', but that again is only true from the perspective of the human, not from the perspective of the rat, who indeed carries those diseases 'with impunity' – the rat, therefore, is in some sense 'immune' from its own apparent propensities, just as the child would dearly love to be 'immunised' from memories of its own humiliation and abasement, the memory of being 'greedy and dirty'.

One of the questions that therefore arises in connection with modernity is what happens to, what is done with and to, the rat (or, of course, in Kafka's case with the cockroach, or in Beckett's with old people in dustbins). The rat must be banished, confined to the underworld of the sewers, not allowed out into the bright light of modern living. The rat is not the only species to suffer this fate; a well-known (although now banned) substance for protecting crops from the depredations of badgers (also creatures who are frequently accused of 'carrying disease', in this case bovine TB) was marketed under the name of 'Badger-Off'; the abjecting reference is all too clear.

The point here would be that earlier life – whether at the personal or the cultural level – carries with it an automatic freight of dirt, contamination, infection. We would like to believe that as we 'grow up', these tendencies are surmounted, but they continue to haunt our dreams. Yet in some other way, as Freud inimitably points out, we inexorably know our own past; indeed, it is precisely because of that past – dirty, muddy, possibly, according to Carl Jung's extension of the idea, reptilian – that we make such strenuous efforts towards purification.

And this matter of purification does not merely occur within the secular culture we associate with contemporary modernity: the history of ritual purification is writ large in the history of most of the world's religions – which indeed, Freud was to suggest elsewhere, can be compared with obsessional neuroses, even of the kind from which the rat man suffered. The question would be of how to deal with this past, of how to find a mode of accommodation with its memories which would allow us to continue in the illusion that we have 'left all that behind us', that we are emerging, or forever on the brink of emerging, into a bright new age.

Rats, it becomes clear to Freud shortly afterwards, are children: free from, or yet to experience, the reality principle of social control, they are free also to throw tantrums, to get dirty, even to bite. But the task of modernity is to clean up the mess of history, to put away childish things and to proclaim a different kind of freedom. This is in general, of course, the function of taboo: to seal up the 'grave' of the past and to place a sign over it warning or prohibiting any tampering with that which has been. But as we return to the grave, we perceive further ambiguities: for we have here a feared symbiosis between the dead father and the rat. The authority which the father wielded while alive has not vanished with death; on the contrary, it has redoubled and continues to generate its living symbols, the 'rule of the rat'.

What is also at stake here is the further doubled notion of 'impunity' and 'punishment'; for what modernity also comes to bring is a certain freedom from guilt. Within the regime of modernity, we can float fancy-free and without any sense of responsibility for everything which lies without modernity's ambit; above all, we can ignore the role of capital and profit within this nexus of differentiation. The rat man and Freud could not, however:

> ... apart from this, the rat is a dirty animal, feeding upon excrement and living in sewers. It is perhaps unnecessary to point out how great an exten-sion of the rat delirium became possible owing to this new meaning. For instance, 'So many rats, so many florins' [one of the rat man's phrases] could serve as an excellent characterisation of a certain female profession which he particularly detested.   (Freud 1955, 214)

This part of Freud's interpretation depends on an identification of the rat with the penis; but it is nonetheless significant that a parallel is here made between the delightfully named 'rat delirium' and the economic motif of prostitution. We need also to see how this affects the sense of the past; for whether or not it is scientifically true that rats 'feed upon excre-ment', it does remain symbolically true that the rat man himself is char-acterising his dead father as shit. Whether the rat is doing humanity a service by ridding us of the detritus of our pasts or committing a kind of sacrilege by feasting on the 'bones of the dead' becomes an insoluble question, a 'knot' of interpretation.

The rat man cannot escape from his duality; he cannot rid himself of the suspicion that, within the 'gliding' – and thus perhaps surprisingly elegant – form of the rat, he is looking at the lineaments of his own face and body. He may now be clean, or wish to be clean, in an obsessional way such as we find in so many accounts of obsessive-compulsive disorder, but this, at some deeper level, changes nothing. Modernity may wish to proclaim its own exemption from the messiness of mortality, but its fear is that all it can do is to abject those qualities it despises onto the 'other' – and an 'other', furthermore, on which it is necessarily dependent according to an inexorable logic of economic exchange.

13 Power

It would by now seem appropriate to try to define modernity in terms of a specific regime of power, and perhaps especially the gender relations, considered in their broadest sense, enshrined in the appropriate power structures. A term which can be used to unlock modernity and power is the frequently used one, the 'glass ceiling'. This is taken to refer to the point at which career structures for women hit a maximum point, beyond which it is difficult if not impossible for them to proceed. The briefest of glances at the board-rooms and judiciaries of the western world will immediately demonstrate this to be the case, but the term touches on a whole range of issues.

Firstly, the kinds of career referred to are generally ones in which social power is at stake; it may be unusual to come across female plumbers or painters and decorators, but the term 'glass ceiling' would not be used in this context. Instead, it immediately conjures precisely the kind of atrium-based architecture of modernity we have discussed earlier; the 'glass ceiling' has to be of a certain height for it to 'count'. The rash of recent gender discrimination claims in the legal profession and in the world of finance and commerce bears this out, although of course it is double-edged; it takes a certain amount of resource and a high level of potential earnings at stake in order for cases to be brought and to attract the media attention which is, under the regime of modernity, an indispensable adjunct to – some would say the very heart of – the exercise and perception of power.

Secondly, there is in the very phrase 'glass ceiling' the dialectic of transparency and invisibility which we are coming to see as a constant trope of the modern. The (toughened) glass ceiling may be invisible to those who bump their heads against it; but it can simultaneously signify a certain degree of surveillance, implying that there are those who are in command of the placement of the ceiling, those who consider themselves best served by the exclusion of women from the corridors – or in this case walkways and elevators – of power.

We may extrapolate from this that modernity is frequently a further, 'new' expression of masculist power, within which all consists of elevation and hierarchy; the age-old dilemma of 'women succeeding in a man's world' without themselves becoming surrogate men is newly dramatised against the soaring background of the banking skyscraper, the 'board-room in the sky' which is the new emblem of corporate power. This is not a new structure in itself, especially when one regards contemporary structures as having their past equivalents in the realm of religious worship; in baroque Basque churches, for example, men used to sit in tiered galleries around the church walls, some of them as high almost as the ceiling of the nave, while women worshipped at ground level, close, as it is said, to the sepulchres of their ancestors.

What is new, however, is the spread of this structure throughout a whole regime; the phallic power expressed in the dominating skyscraper is paralleled in the structure of the space launch site, where a male-dominated hierarchy bases its most recent efforts to 'penetrate the mysteries' of the universe. What is also new is the relation between what we may thus call 'excess visibility', the desire to dominate whole landscapes, and the actual *invisibility* of corporate power, which flows down through the internet, through the conduits of international banking, through the monumental edifices of the World Bank and the World Trade Organisation, demonstrable only in its local effects, from the understanding of which people in those localities are systematically disenfranchised.

Yet even this is too simple, because along with the invisibility of the corporate there goes a need to find a simulacrum, a 'body of simulation' which will 'incarnate' unseen power, will give it a semblance of intelligibility and above all a link back to a sanctioning past, in order to prevent what might otherwise appear simply to be control by unseen forces. We might consider this example, which is from Tom Wolfe's 1987 novel, *The Bonfire of the Vanities*, and describes the place where the novel's protagonist works:

> The investment-banking firm of Pierce & Pierce occupied the fiftieth, fifty-first, fifty-second, fifty-third, and fifty-fourth floors of a glass tower that rose up sixty storeys from out of the gloomy groin of Wall Street. The bond trading room, where Sherman worked, was on the fiftieth. Every day he stepped out of an aluminium-walled elevator into what looked like the reception area of one of those new London hotels catering to the Yanks. Near the elevator door was a fake fireplace and an antique mahogany mantelpiece with great bunches of fruit carved on each corner. Out in front of

the fake fireplace was a brass fence or fender, as they called it in country homes in the west of England. In the appropriate months a fake fire glowed within, casting flickering lights upon a prodigious pair of brass andirons. The wall surrounding it was covered in more mahogany, rich and reddish, done in linen-fold panels carved so deep, you could *feel* the expense in the tips of your fingers by just looking at them.   (Wolfe 1988, 67)

Wolfe, of course, pulls no punches in his comment on the way the tower arises from the 'groin' of Wall Street. But this particular act of male display nevertheless needs to be disguised in borrowed plumage, it needs a 'coating' to make it seem credible, but more than that to relate it back to a past source and expression of power, in this case presumably the English gentlemen's club as further mediated through its adoption as a 'style' by a certain segment of the hospitality industry. Wolfe's purpose here, obviously, is to expose the 'fake-ness', the falsity at the heart of a certain dream of superiority; but it is interesting to see that he falls prey to much the same thing himself – the narrator apparently knows what 'andirons' are, but supposes that 'fender' is an archaic, regional, aristo-cratic term when in fact it is – or was, at that point in the mythical past to which we are being referred – a term in common usage.

No comments on modernity and power would be complete without a reference to the cult of 'celebrity', but it is worthwhile noticing that this too is part of a dialectic. For the people in positions of real power – the investment bankers, the venture capitalists, the advisers to central finance houses – are not themselves 'celebrities'; there are, of course, exceptions, the Richard Bransons and James Dysons of the commercial world, but for the most part the people of greatest influence could walk down a street (if they were ever to do such a thing) and not be noticed. Arguably, the cult of celebrity is therefore a massive cultural deflection: enshrined most popularly, perhaps, in Andy Warhol's famous adage that everybody can be famous for a day (a remark the irony of which has gradually drained away over the years), the notion of celebrity has become part, indeed the mainstay, of a modern circle of mutual enhance-ment involving the various cultural industries, the more attention-seeking of politicians and, of course, the media. The invisibility of power is thus evenly matched by the powerlessness of celebrity, and embedded in the constant refrain that what most celebrities want is the privilege of a 'private' life. Indeed, privacy itself is a term which has undergone a series of transmutations in modernity, from the paradoxical notion of 'private enterprise' to the cant phrase 'a very private person' which, like 'a very special person', has now become the gold standard of obituary writers within the modern regime.

At a different level, one could point to the uncanny positioning of a specific moment of modernity between an age characterised by the emergence (and demise) of the 'new woman' and an age represented by the emergence (and demise) of the 'new man'. The 'new woman' of the late nineteenth and early twentieth centuries appeared to pose a threat to masculist hegemony; the movement had, of course, its successes and failures, but structurally it represented an apparent loosening of the male grip on power. The emergence of the 'new man', dedicated to washing up and caring relationships (not always at the same time) appeared to offer a belated response in the 1980s to this formation by offering a different version of gender equality. Both were subjected to vicious and ruthless satire from those who did not want, and do not want, to see any serious challenge to the rule of 'things as they are'; both retreated into a kind of cultural melancholia, defeated by the inexorable grip on power at the heart of a money-based society. That melancholia, which has been convincingly identified by Guinn Batten as at the heart of a culture dominated by the commodity, can bring us back by a full circle to the glass ceiling and to the matching of the sense that such an invisible barrier is unbreakable and the terrible anxiety that, if it were to be broken, then the shards of glass raining down on us would be the evidence of a society which, in a thoroughly unmodern way, might be perceived to be unstable, to be crumbling at least at the edges.

14　Hatred

> It was in the material sphere that the claims of western civilisation were the most powerful. Science, technology, rational forms of economic organisation, modern methods of statecraft, these had given the European countries the strength to subjugate non-European peoples and to impose their dominance over the whole world. To overcome this domination, the colonised people must learn these superior techniques of organising material life and incorporate them within their own cultures. ... For a colonised people, the world was a distressing constraint, forced upon it by the fact of its material weakness. It was a place of oppression and daily humiliation, a place where the norms of the coloniser had perforce to be accepted. (Sangari and Vaid 1990, 237–9)

Thus Partha Chatterjee, in an essay called 'The Nationalist Resolution of the Women's Question' (1990), the very title of which indicates the complex interrelations between nationalism, colonisation, modernity and gender. Chatterjee's particular purpose is to demonstrate, in the context of the Indian subcontinent, how this modern subjugation in the material field encouraged a linkage between nationalism and various assumptions about the 'spiritual' superiority of the east; but his argument about the 'imposition' of modernity, about the west's continuing insistence on the 'modernisation' of a variety of 'traditional' cultures, has a far wider resonance. Cultures, to put it simply, are changed by modernisation; in many cases it would be appropriate to say that they are destroyed, in others that they are threatened – militarily, politically, economically – to the point where resistance to the incoming tidal wave of modernity becomes impossible.

We might also consider this passage from the Caribbean writer Jamaica Kincaid. The English colonisers, she writes in the context of her home island of Antigua,

> don't seem to know that this empire business was all wrong and they should, at least, be wearing sackcloth and ashes in token penance of the

wrongs committed, the irrevocableness of their bad deeds, for no natural disaster imaginable could equal the harm they did. Actual death might have been better. ... no place could ever really be England, and nobody who did not look exactly like them would ever be English, so you can imagine the destruction of people and land that came from that. The English hate each other and they hate England, and the reason they are so miserable now is that they have no place else to go and nobody else to feel better than. (Kincaid 1988, 41)

At first glance, this might seem a ferocious post-imperial lament at some distance from the concerns of modernity; but the book from which the passage is taken, *A Small Place*, was published in 1988 and asserts a direct contiguity between 'old' imperialism and the more 'modern' forms which, while not relying on the actual presence of the gunboat in the harbour, nevertheless assert western supremacy through a variety of more modern means, from the gross inequities of supposedly 'free trade' to the demands of the tourism industry.

At least as interesting is the direct appeal in the passage to a 'you' who can 'imagine the destruction', for it is difficult to see, within the confines of global modernity, who this 'you' could feasibly be. It is as if Kincaid is under the necessity of inventing a just, fair audience which is capable of seeing through the pretensions of colonising modernity; but we are forced to ask the question as to who this audience is since the whole force of the passage – and of the book – is directed against the very users and owners of the language in which it is written, the inheritors of imperial culture and education.

Modernity, Kincaid is suggesting, is formed around a hatred of all that threatens or resists it, all that suggests or reminds of the possibility of being dragged back into a more 'primitive' past. The further question here, though, would be of the 'other side' of modernity, of the people who are reduced to servicing a western ideal. Kincaid portrays this vividly in the Antiguan context; the black British writer Joan Riley portrays it within the 'homeland' itself, from the point of view of an immigrant who shares none of the benefits of modernity:

'They don't like neaga here'. Her father's words came unbidden and unwelcome to her ears. She would have liked to blot them out, but in her heart she knew the truth of it. She had been in England over four years and always she had seen it and now ... she was forced to live with it. 'All these white people trying so hard to hide their hate', she thought sadly. 'Yet they

> could kill you because you are different from them'. She always had to
> remind herself that they had not hurt her yet. Of course, they let her know
> she was not wanted, did not belong, but at least they were not violent like
> black people.   (Riley 1985, 69)

Modernity – like, of course, any other socio-cultural formation – involves
a dialectic of inclusion and exclusion; in order to congratulate itself on
'progress', it needs to establish that there are people who are in some
sense immune to progress, people who can be held up as examples of
how the benefits that western modernity brings sometimes fall on stony
ground.

My point in bringing forward these examples is to show the extent to
which the project of modernity, while it constantly relies upon global
aspirations, at the same time necessarily produces an 'underclass'. A
related image which comes to mind is a repetition of the eighteenth-
century formal garden: such gardens had small doors in the walls, many
of which are still visible today, through which the gardeners were supposed to disappear when ladies and gentlemen of standing came to visit.
In case this might seem an archaic image, I might add that when I lived
in an apartment in Hong Kong, a room was provided for a 'maid'; one
cardinal difference between this room and all the others in an extraordi-
narily opulent flat was that every room had a hole in the wall for an air
conditioner to somewhat ameliorate the polluted horrors of Hong Kong
weather; all, of course, except for the maid's room. At the risk of going on
about this topic for too long, it is worth mentioning that this was not a
'functional' exclusion; a hole in the wall does not cost money – if anything, in terms of building materials, slightly the reverse.

These acts of discrimination thus betray what we might by now
come to call a 'different' logic, a 'logic of purification' whereby a strict
demarcating line (perhaps a glass floor) is drawn between those who
are privileged to be part of the modern elite and those who are to be
denied these advantages. Except, of course, that this is itself too naïve a
distinction: although it may be true that the 'natives' (in many senses)
are to be denied membership of the 'modern club', they still remain
essential to the modernist project, but in specific economic roles:
as servants, sometimes as guides, always as actual or potential
consumers.

It is fair to say that much of the force of Derridean poststructuralism
has been towards finding a different way, increasingly politically and ethically engaged, of looking at these stark discriminations which charac-

terise the modern age. Here, for example, is the brilliant critic of the colonial and the postcolonial, Robert J.C. Young, on the topic:

> Between the centre and the margin Derrida finds a leeway, the lateral deviant drift and meandering movement of a dislocated economy from a resistance built into the attempted uniformity of the system, and locates its breakdown at the point at which it tries to draw its own limits, to mark the edge of its faltering reach. In any system of force there will always be sites of force that are, precisely, forced, and therefore allow for pressure and intervention. ... Derrida recognised the belatedness of the postcolonial, that the postcolonial system operates according to ... a derivative discourse, namely that the legacy of colonialism was that the postcolonial states were left inscribed with the institutions and political concepts of the west, with colonial, postcolonial modernity.   (Young 2001, 418)

There is, of course, a great deal of truth in this; for our purposes, it is probably sufficient to note that the language of 'meandering' and 'faltering' constitutes a radical alternative to modernity's central and centralising discourse of 'development' and 'progress'. But as an analysis of the complexities and duplicities of modernity, it falls some way short. To take but one example among many: many of the small Caribbean island states, despite their putative independence, still operate with judiciaries which are technically inferior to that of the ex-colonising power, symbolised, for example, in the existence of the (British) Privy Council as the final court of appeal.

This is an image worth dwelling on for a moment, perhaps as the counter-agent to Kincaid's analysis of hatred. For it signifies in two directions at once. On the one hand, it asserts that the judicial system in the Caribbean is too primitive, too unmodernised (specifically in its retention of the possibility of capital punishment) to be trusted; yet at the same time it vests responsibility in a body which is precisely the legacy of countless centuries of unreformed history, a body whose membership depends technically on the absolute prerogative of the monarch. Thus modernity reveals its archaic face; and thus power is distributed according to the dictates of its controllers and the hierarchical arrangements of pre-modern colonialism reassert themselves even under the guise of dragging, kicking and screaming, our 'native' children into a more forgiving, more just, modern world.

15　Marxism

It is impossible to assess the meanings of modernity without looking back to the traditions of Marxism and their practical and theoretical aftermath. We live in an era which, as Derrida put it in his *Spectres of Marx* (1994), remains haunted by the ruins of perhaps the most significant political and economic project of the nineteenth and twentieth centuries, and the process of trying to come to terms with this legacy remains hugely significant on the modern agenda.

What was Marxism? First and foremost, it was an analysis of modes of economic production. Marx's own writings provide a certain amount of commentary on 'older' modes of production, including feudalism and the 'Asiatic' system, but the primary focus, of course, is on capitalism, the effects of which Marx and his collaborator Engels saw all around them. The capitalism Marx saw constituted an enormous productive machine, which was engaged in transforming the world. The era of the small-scale, of 'cottage industry', was, as he saw it, coming to an end and being replaced by a form of production driven solely by the profit motive; all 'surplus value' was being drained out of the system into the pockets of the capitalists.

Marx's most famed pronouncements on the class system arise from the analysis of capitalism: power lies with those who own the means of production, or who have the resources to control it; this class Marx referred to as the then emerging bourgeoisie. Beneath this class lies the working class, the proletariat which, even if it were to come to be politically enfranchised, would nevertheless remain removed from the sources of economic power, 'alienated', as Marx had it, from the process and product of its own labour. A further critical element in Marxist theory is the notion of 'false consciousness'; the specific way in which the bourgeoisie manipulates the realm of the ideological is by producing a false consciousness according to which all members of a given society are brought to believe that what is in fact 'good' only for those in power is good for all.

This particular element of Marxist thought was further crucially elaborated by Althusser, who coined the concept of 'interpellation' to describe the way in which individuals in society are 'hailed' or addressed, and how false ideas of society are inculcated by those in charge of the means of production. What is at stake here is a lack of agency, an inability to see round the edges of the all-powerful constructions of the world which are promulgated in particular by what Althusser referred to as the 'ideological state apparatuses', which include educational and political systems and form the counterpart to the more overt 'repressive state apparatuses' which include the institutions of direct force, including the military, the police and the judiciary.

Finally, in this all too brief thumbnail sketch of Marxism, there is the crucial notion of contradiction. As Marx saw it, the ideology of capitalism was a 'superstructure' designed to conceal and misrepresent the stark facts of the economic infrastructure; if that infrastructure were ever to be fully revealed – if the workers could be brought to see the facts as they really are – then what would be shown would be a set of contradictions which would prove so gross as to promote a revolution. After this revolution, according to the more utopian strains in Marxist and post-Marxist thinking, what would ensue would be a properly 'communist' society in which the means of production would be controlled by everybody rather than by a small elite.

What it is important to say about Marx in the context of modernity is that he was not 'against' industrialisation; industrialisation was here to stay, and the question was about who should control industrial expansion. Therefore from one perspective Marx can himself be seen as a 'modernist'; he was aware that there can be no turning back from history, no retreat into a golden past. But history might, at first glance, appear to have proved Marx wrong. In the most obvious sense, there would be the question of the 'failed revolution'. The collapse of the Soviet Union and the increasing recourse to capitalism on mainland China would be the most obvious demonstrations of the ways in which revolutions have been subverted and brought back into the global capitalist fold; other contemporary examples would include Vietnam, currently embracing westernisation at an extraordinary pace. Of all the revolutions inspired by Marx, perhaps only that in Cuba retains a certain momentum – perhaps not despite but *because of* the US's unceasing attempts to destabilise the Cuban state.

Yet in another sense, modernity has proved Marx right, albeit in a shape which he was ill-equipped to perceive. Certainly he saw that the profit motive required, above all, a cheap and thus deprived labour force; in his day, however, such a labour force was available in each of the newly industrialising countries, and constraints on transport meant that it was possible to conceive of the nation state as an economically independent unit, within which specific contradictions might be exposed. This has, of course, now radically changed. One reason for this has been the exponential growth of transportation technologies, which mean that there is no longer any such thing as a 'closed' market; as we have seen, this technological expansion went hand-in-hand with the expansion dependent on the imperial and colonial systems.

Some would argue that the prosperity brought to the world's dominant countries in effect killed off the requirement for revolution; but perhaps a truer picture has emerged under the aegis of modernity. For while it is true that a huge range of factors, including trades unions and labour-saving devices, have improved the lot of what George Orwell was to term the 'respectable' working class in the west immeasurably, capitalism's basic requirement of a cheap labour force has not disappeared; it has simply been exported.

It is thus perfectly possible to mount a Marxist analysis of modern society, provided that one no longer thinks in terms of individual nation states. The Marxian 'under-class' exists in huge numbers, in countries which are subservient to the modern western regime; increasingly the whole burden of manufacturing passes to the 'far places' of the globe – for many years now this has been principally China, although the emergence of new technologies and the erosion of the peasant base suggests that this may be about to change as Chinese workers also seek basic health and safety rights which, necessarily, cost money and erode the maximisation of profit.

The old Marxian concept of revolution within the nation state therefore seems off the agenda, and this is especially so when one considers the further modifications which have occurred in recent times in terms of false consciousness. For the 'profit' which accrues to the workers in China, India, South America, is not directly economic; rather it is the phenomenon of 'Coca-Cola-isation', the enveloping of the world in a system of desire by means of which products are made in the developing world; exported to the 'metropole' where value is added sheerly by the addition of a brand-name; and then re-exported at a hugely increased price back to developing countries whose citizens have fallen prey to a 'desiring machine' which enshrines Reebok, Nike and IBM as the pinnacles of status and achievement.

This, then, is the system which is known, by Jameson among others, as 'global' or 'late' capitalism, and it is readily explicable in Marxist terms. The situation of modernity in this context would be as an articulation of desire; the hope of many from 'third-world' countries is for a new, better life in the west; or for a western education which will permit them to join the elite strata of their own nations; or, failing those, for an accumulation of western goods which will mythically transport them from poverty to plenty.

Yet behind this there also lurks another legacy of Marxism, which is difficult if not impossible to eradicate; for Marxism punctured a hole in a system which relied on things 'remaining as they are'. Many African states have in the past attempted their own version of Marxist political practice; but of course they have done so from a low base, politically, educationally, technologically and economically, and it has been easy for the global super-powers to clamp down on the aspirations which Marxism represents – although perhaps the most brutal of these many acts of repression are those committed by the US in Chile, Nicaragua and other South American countries where actual or putative revolutions have been destroyed by a combination of military might and economic pressure.

The other aspect of Marxian thought which remains of primary relevance is alienation, of which Marx talked in great detail in his early *Economic and Philosophical Manuscripts* (1844). The nub of his argument is that the kinds of work demanded by industrial capitalism are for the most part soul-less, if not soul-destroying; if pleasure is to be had at all in life it is in spheres far removed from the work-place, albeit often by the acquisition of goods and material comforts which are produced in those very surroundings. Under these conditions of production, man is alienated from his own labour; from his own product; from his 'species-being', by which Marx means his own sense of his humanity; and from his fellow-workers. It will of course be noticed that the gendered term 'man' here is not accidental; certainly in some ways Marx's thought was less developed than in others.

What has modernity to do with these kinds of alienation? Principally, it seeks to satisfy or alleviate the intellectual and emotional poverty attendant on material labour by the provision of goods – or perhaps better, by the constant *desire* for those goods produced by the advertising industry and the media. In the modern world, everything is available, but at a price; the kind of thinking pioneered by the Frankfurt School of critical theorists, and perhaps most resonantly by Marcuse in *One*

Dimensional Man, suggests that alienation is 'doctored' in the modern world by the provision of social and cultural fantasies to compensate for the drudgery of modern work.

However, we would further have to consider that it is part of the rhetoric of modernity to suggest that in fact this drudgery has come to an end, that technological advance has alleviated the plight of the worker, that, in car manufacturing for example, the advent of advanced robotics – *Vorsprung durch Technik*, as the German car-maker has it – has meant that labour is now, according to good modern principles, cleaner, safer, purer, more hygienic than ever. Again, one can only point out that insofar as this may be a gain in western countries, this is because the hard, dangerous and dirty work has passed conclusively down to labourers elsewhere who still, in sweatshops and call centres throughout the developing world, perform the most repetitive of tasks for the lowest of wages which corporate power and the local compradore class can impose.

Just as the Marxian analysis suggests that the whole endeavour of ideology is to conceal the real relations of production, so it could be suggested that modernity's love of bright, gleaming facades acts also as a kind of concealment, a remaking of the 'order of things' so that all becomes a matter of relative material progress. The provision of televisions in every village in China, and the increasing access there to computers, have had and continue to have a double effect: as well as improving the worker or peasant's material standard of living they also offer improved access to the rest of the world and reinforce a sense of deprivation which can only be incompletely addressed by material goods.

16 Children

Looking back into recent western cultural history, it has often been said that the late eighteenth-century and early nineteenth-century moment of romanticism was, in the forms of, for example, the poems of Blake and Wordsworth, the moment of the rediscovery of the child. Far from being merely an underdeveloped adult, the child in romanticism was seen as the repository of a certain special kind of wisdom born of innocence; the other side of this, especially in Blake, was renewed attention to the ways in which that innocence – his 'Chimney Sweeper' poems come to mind – could be, and was, abused in his contemporary society.

Where, then, are we to locate the child within modernity? A starting-point might be through a consideration of sexuality. Within modernity everything is apparently transparent; there are to be no dark corners, no muddy waters, and therefore everything needs to inspected, to be placed under a certain regime of surveillance. One thing that has appeared, and continues to appear, from the depths is a haunted version of childhood, a childhood endured in conditions of fear and even terror. There is a familiar conundrum at stake: does the fact that we hear about ever increasing numbers of paedophiliac encounters, ever increasing sets of abusive photographs downloaded from the internet, mean that such crimes or desires are themselves on the increase or that more of such events are now revealed by an increasingly intrusive and panoptical media?

Laurie Lee, in his classic of childhood *Cider with Rosie* (1959), in which he depicts with marvellous vividness life in a small Cotswold village in the early part of the twentieth century, remarks that, for all the soon to be eroded closeness of village life before the serious availability of non-horse-drawn transport, such matters as incest, homosexual rape and other forms of soon to be outlawed forms of sexual desire were in no way strange or unexpected; the difference was that such matters were dealt with – sometimes with extreme brutality – within the community itself.

What concerns us here, however, is the relation between these *topoi* and modernity. For within modernity there has emerged a curiously reflexive double image of the child. On the one hand there is the image of the 'innocent abroad', the child who needs to be protected at all costs from the possible attentions of the violent and the insane, prevented from playing outdoors, equipped with a mobile phone at all times so that s/he can 'call home'. On the other there is the image of, for example, the 'hoodie' – the descendant of generations of post-Second World War child miscreants from the teddy boys onwards – who brings fear and terror to the shopping mall and the suburban street, yet whose face cannot be seen, who remains in some sense 'in the shadows'.

What sews these images together is the new, modern understanding of child abuse, but this is in some ways an imponderable knowledge. Psychotherapeutically, it seems incontrovertible that people who abuse children have, for the most part, been abused themselves; and so, perhaps, it goes back through the generations. It seems appropriate here to speak again of Abraham and Torok's 'crypt', that part of the mind below even the unconscious which is the repository of family secrets too dark to be named, which can be known only in inverted form, by the shadow they cast over lives, families, communities.

In this sense, modernity in its perennial activity of window-cleaning thus opens onto a continuing darkness; it is no accident that the horror film, which is in its modern manifestation above all a record of child abuse, should have attained such heights of popularity. Here we see innocence continually threatened, damaged, raped or destroyed: despite apparent increases in knowledge and awareness, no such knowledge or awareness is sufficient to repel the dread of contact with other human beings. The problem is that we *do not understand*; the dark forces are repressed into suspicions of the supernatural, satanic abuse, as we uncover minds which, in the end, make no sense either to the general public or, in the cases of, for example, Broadmoor or the State Hospital at Carstairs, to the doctors who are entrusted with the care and, if possible, diagnosis of the most violent and irredeemable of abusers.

At stake, among other things, is the origin and the future of the family under the conditions of modernity. The very notion of the 'nuclear family' is itself an invention of modernity, the product of historically specific living and working conditions; a great deal of the political argument between conservative and modernising forces in the UK centres around the proposition that there is, or is not, some God-given, or at least natural, reputability to a certain set of living arrangements, even though it is clearly known that these living arrangements are themselves the outcrop of the labour demands of early industrialisation which effectively broke up larger, looser rural familial units in favour of a flexible and mobile urbanised work force.

The 'innocent abroad' and the 'waif and stray' are thus the two sides of a single coin, although of course it needs also to be said that those sides are inevitably striated by differences according to class and race: the face hidden under the hood may be white, but the very fact of it being in shadow suggests a certain darkness which is easily mapped onto the white western 'fear of the other'. Light and dark are thus symbolically opposed: the white assumptions of the contemporary childhood canon – the Harry Potter books, for example – serve to reinforce a certain separation, about 'growing up good' and 'growing up bad', and it is surely significant here that in urban black argot the very word 'bad' has been elevated onto a pedestal of respect.

The opposed fear and adulation of childhood is constantly reinforced by the media, who gloatingly pronounce that, with each dreadful case, either the victim or the perpetrator – or sometimes both – are the 'youngest' ever to suffer or to make suffer. Alongside this goes a curious gloss on 'innocence', which Nabokov was perhaps the first to expose in *Lolita* (1959): namely that under modern conditions such a pretension to innocence may be either a lie or, at the very least, viewed as a cover story for a frightening precocity.

17 Animal

If modernity involves a hope of putting away – perhaps putting to sleep – the past and the dark, then it also involves the crucial project of clarifying the severance of humanity from its animal roots. We can see this in all manner of ways. We can see it in the insistence of cyber-fiction on depicting organic human activities as the province of 'the meat', as opposed to the clean lines and itemisations of the pixel. We can see it, more vividly if perhaps no more damagingly, in the treatment of 'wild' species, either through their hunting to the point of extermination or through their incarceration in zoos or game parks. We can see it, as I have mentioned earlier, in the bizarre elevation of the 'pet', as beautifully depicted in the film *Best in Show* (2000), a brilliant satire on the relationship between humans and 'their' domestic animals.

Yet here perhaps we can find a further reflection of a more general modern crisis. For the environmental movement supposes, on the whole, that it is possible that we might indeed be able to 'put away' these irresponsible habits; it further supposes that the survival of species – whatever that species might be – is a good to be automatically pursued in the name of 'biodiversity'. The opposite view to this was put some years ago by James Lovelock in the shape of the Gaia hypothesis; briefly, Lovelock pointed out that the primary concern here could sensibly be regarded as the 'future of the planet'; the question of whether this would be best forwarded by human domination or by some other means, which might include human extinction, remains a moot one and in any case humanity does prove itself from time to time to be capable of self-regulation by means of war, famine and other disasters, which from an anthropocentric perspective might seem catastrophic but which might perfectly well serve the needs of planet earth.

A further extension of this argument might suggest that man's own 'species-being', to revert to Marx's term, is intimately bound up with the destruction of the other, that there is no more point in adjuring humans not to kill or lock up animals than there is in requesting lions not to eat meat or, more bewilderingly, asking bacteria to cease to exert the complexity of their benevolent and malevolent effects on the rest of nature. According to modern thinking, some kind of purification is possible; but alternatively we might suggest that the 'beast-flesh' grows back, and that attempts to repress it only sharpen the condition of desire.

The underlying question would be of a troubling of the boundaries between the human and the animal, matched at the other extreme by a similar troubling of the boundaries between the organic and the inorganic, focused in the work of Haraway and others as the emergence of the 'cyborg', the entity which is formed when technological prosthesis becomes part of the regime of living. What the cyborg also does is to trouble the further 'bourn' between life and death; a heart pacemaker may be a useful addition to the quality of an individual's life, but what it also signifies is the enduring myth of the possibility of an indefinite extension of life.

For modernity, the animal is a problem, to be endlessly teased out; but even as this is said, it becomes apparent that the terms of that problem are in a state of constant flux. The possibilities of genetic modification are such that the simple equation of species one with another remains no longer tenable. This, of course, is not entirely a new problem, but it is significant that it runs back through the history of modernity. When, one might ask, is a rose not a rose? One viable answer might be that a rose ceased to be a rose in any simple sense when Enlightenment scientists discovered the possibilities of hybridisation in order to produce plant and vegetable forms not known to 'nature'.

Monsanto and other GM firms could be said to be simply pursuing this 'enlightened' project of optimising species for their productive yield, yet here too there is an automatic process of resistance. The argument that crops with increased resistance to the vagaries of climate might better suit the appalling needs of the impoverished populations of Africa are met, not on their own terms, but with a sustained cultural plea that somehow this process is 'unnatural'. What is again at stake is the question of speed, or rate of change. The organic world mutates constantly, as we have known at least since Darwin: the question is whether we are, or should be, free to use new technologies to intervene in and speed up this rate of mutation. All dogs, after all, are mutated wolves.

Much of the modern debate on the vegetable world, if not on the animal, is around the issue of 'standardisation': about whether modernity demands that plurality and variety be abolished, whether each individual cucumber or parsnip should conform to an ideal model of a cucumber or parsnip. But such arguments, we find when we look more closely, are indeed repeated at the animal level, both in terms of productively useful animals like cows and sheep, where there is clearly an 'optimal' image at work in the complex process of agricultural cross-breeding; and, of course, at the next level in terms of the human itself, where the demands of the 'perfect body' are rampant in advertising, in the culture of the celebrity, in the rise of cosmetic surgery (with, obviously, its supposedly necessary corollary in the breeding of animals for medical experimentation).

All of these issues, therefore, fall under the same heading, which is the exclusion of the strange, the unusual, the 'faulty'; but where the situation of modernity finds itself is in precisely the curious assertion that a certain kind of hybridity is necessary in order to achieve this standard of perfection. Within hybridity, nothing therefore is exactly as it seems: the 'perfect' rose is a crossbreed of other rose-stocks, and therefore modernity on the one hand elevates and worships the crossbreed while at the same time, in human racial terms, despising and seeking to banish miscegenation. There is a lock here on development and degeneracy which we shall explore further in later sections.

18   Museums

One of the major evolving symbols of modernity can be found by examining the changing status and attributes of the museum. This could be seen as a major shift between the 'inward' and the 'outward'. The classic museum of the European nineteenth century marked an inward passage of goods, mainly from the Empire. The Pitt Rivers Museum in Oxford would be good example, with its hoards of dusty exhibits, many of them unlabelled and of uncertain provenance, and its pronounced emphasis on the weird and the macabre at the expense of the culturally typical. Indeed, even to talk of 'exhibits' in the context of such a museum – which is perhaps in any case better referred to as a 'collection' after the manner of the eighteenth-century antiquarians – raises distinct issues, for it is not clear that the artefacts here are meant to be 'exhibited' at all, or at least, if so, only to a small group of the knowledgeable, the *cognoscenti*.

The modern museum is instead focussed outward. Its supposed *raison d'être* is the education and instruction of the general public. Therefore a certain exhaustiveness which was typical of the nineteenth-century museum has been renounced; what is sought instead is 'examples', items which can make up an exemplary text which depicts a specific trajectory through time, whether this is at a local or national level or at the more ambitious level of entire civilisations. It would not be fair to say that museums are no longer places of wonderment or awe; they are – as they always have been – but there is a modern emphasis on 'interaction' with the objects on display, whether this be intellectual, oral, or indeed physical.

The 'museum of the past' used to be a dark place, full of shadows and corners and replete with the kinds of ghost story which accompany such places; stories, for example, of what might happen if one were to remain in the museum after the lights went out, and of what might then come to a peculiar kind of life. This was, of course, a reticulation of the age-old problem of museums, which is that they have never been value-free; true, some local collections were ones which had not disturbed 'foreign parts' in order to obtain their exhibits, but the vast majority of significant 'national' museums were anything but that, they represented instead the fruits of imperial labour, the bringing back and bringing together of a host of exotic artefacts, the material equivalent of 'travellers' tales'.

This is now causing a concomitant set of problems as theorists and practitioners of the museum consider the morality and legality of such collections, and are assailed by demands to return artefacts which are often perceived as either sacred, in the case of many African and native American objects, or of national importance, the most historically significant British example here being the so-called 'Elgin marbles'. Here modernity finds itself in a cleft stick: eager to shed the illusions of imperial power, it nonetheless wishes to encourage and step up its educational ambitions; at the same time, the modern west emphasises its presumed ability to provide a better care for such objects than could be provided in their frequently unstable countries of origin.

The recent upsurge of anti-western terrorism has added a further twist to this story, because it is no longer clear whether such artefacts are indeed safer in western capitals, where they may be precisely the object of bombing, or whether they would be safer returned to the 'undeveloped' lands whence they were brought. In the Louvre, there is the capstone of an Egyptian pyramid; the question of where it 'belongs' is the subject of many different narratives, as with the Elgin marbles. The question seems set to resolve itself into one not of ownership or politics but rather into the technical one of where it may best be 'displayed' – which is a question not only, if at all, of original setting, but rather of the amount and presentation of instructional material by which it can be surrounded.

All of these questions resolve themselves further into ones of context. Visiting a modern national museum, one is struck by the deliberate incongruity between most of the objects displayed and the display format itself, which is all a matter of careful lighting, brightly burnished beech finish, glass and aluminium name tags. We may see this as a marker of the way in which modernity sees itself, not as breaking with the past, but rather, as in the religious image associated with the term, as acting as a kind of *reliquary* for the past, a way of encapsulating and incarcerating the bones of the past at the same time as displaying them to an informed and suitably worshipful public.

There is, however, a further level to this description; for there are almost no museums which display the full extent of their property. As in the emblematic case of the huge Wellcome collection stored for these last many years in a Hammersmith warehouse, there is a vast substrate of ex-imperial objects in the western museum's general vault. It is now here, perhaps, where the 'haunting' is felt to its fullest effect, in the knowledge that the lust for acquisition that marked earlier moments of exploration and 'discovery' proved in many ways too much for the receiving nation or culture to hold or absorb.

As Benjamin notably outlined, the urge to collect has complex psycho-logical roots: in the thought that one might be able to possess every last example of a given type, in the need to externalise the fraying bound-aries of self into a strictly controlled and demarcated realm of carefully labelled and aetiologised articles. Modernity seeks to move beyond the set of late Victorian assumptions and to provide us instead with a care-fully edited set of narratives, clear stories we can follow through time and space. The aesthetic of collection is replaced by an aesthetic of nar-rative, static forms inserted into a moving simulation in which we as readers and participants can also have our place rather than being mere readers of an uncannily dissimilar scene.

19 Age

In its dedication to 'enlightenment' modernity, as we have seen, has historically placed a good deal of emphasis upon 'reason'. However, it would also be fair to say that there has over the last three centuries been evidence of a widening gap between reason and what at other times and in other, more traditional cultures has been regarded as 'wisdom', considered as that which can only be acquired through length and breadth of experience. In the post-war period and the 1960s there was a radical readjustment of the relations between youth and age, with the idea of 'young people' being different in kind and therefore warranting a different type of treatment, culturally and economically. This was, of course, a serious moment of anti-capitalist radicalism; but it emerged and became almost immediately embroiled in capitalism's need for ever-expanding markets.

It did, however, mark a stage in the evolution of the question of 'what to do about the old', which has since become considerably more urgent as a medical regime has developed in the west based on the prolongation of life: heart pacemakers, dialysis machines, major organ transplants have all contributed to an assault on the necessity of death at or around the biblically sanctioned age of 'three score years and ten'. The 'greying' of western populations has had and continues to have many side effects. One of these is the current UK pensions crisis: a system which evolved on the basis of actuarial assumptions about average life-span is proving rapidly incapable of dealing with changes in these basic assumptions, provoking a flurry of political gambits to try to alter or vary the standard retirement age, or in other words to juggle with the work/life balance in an ageing population while retaining the staple accents of modernity.

Alongside this, however, there has been a growing tendency in the culture of modernity, especially at the level of 'professional' institutions, to produce 'fast tracks', so that careers tend to peak ever earlier, leaving on one side the question of what to do with the accumulated wisdom – or at least experience – of those who have not been 'fast-tracked' from an early age. The difficulties are probably most dramatically seen in terms of the substantial raft of ex-presidents and ex-prime ministers who have left or been forced out of office at ever younger ages and face a choice between the unending lecture tour and superficially statesmanlike involvement in global charitable endeavour.

A further consequence is that the whole notion of education being mapped onto specific moments in the maturation and ageing process has been radically challenged, in concepts like the 'university of the third age' and in the well-meant but slightly depressing cultural focus on 'lifelong learning'. Behind this there lurks a modern anxiety about the notion of 'career' in itself, with an increasing emphasis on the 'portfolio' concept whereby individuals acquire a range of skills which can be variously deployed at different stages of life. These are undeniably modernist liberalisations of the age structure, and have a profound impact, which will surely only increase, on the 'trajectory' of individual and cultural life.

Behind all this there also stands a challenging but perpetually uneasy relationship between modernity and death. Cemetery burial, for example, is increasingly seen as old-fashioned, and indeed selfish insofar as it takes land away from the living; the crematorium, with its sanitised antechambers and neat rows of urns and memorials, is modernity's answer to the inevitably growing problem of where to house the dead. Dusty vaults and crypts are to be excised (and here we might call to mind again Abraham and Torok and recent developments in psychoanalysis), or preserved only as evidence of the outmoded beliefs and prejudices of the past, and what is perceived as the contemporary breakdown in family structures sits conveniently alongside this, since the necessity to 'visit the grave' is thereby also removed, in sequence with the earlier removal of the 'traditional' markers which set Sundays and feast days aside from the quotidian round.

Alongside this stands the whole panoply of old people's homes, hospices, carer allowances, and a full repertoire of provision for the aged and/or dying, although there is evidence of crisis in the question of quite how these admirable services are paid for, and by whom. The symbolic problem is that these services remind us of mortality; they may try to be places of light, but it is also indisputable that there is very little that can be done to reverse the ravages of time, as there is also little to be done to affect the problem that the elderly cannot conveniently be brought within the regime of speed, they affect and may even resist the universal supremacy of the dromosphere.

Modernity, we might suggest, is not in fact in thrall to the young, even though this may have seemed to be so fifty years ago; the young, to the contrary, are perceived mainly as consumers, to be catered for in the name of surplus profit. It is instead, in its present formation, the sphere of the fit, youthful middle-aged, buoyed by large salaries and discreet cosmetic surgery, encouraged and enhanced by promotions and complexly hierarchised career structures. Modernity itself peaks in the scenario of a film like *Wall Street* (1987) where, in one among many famous lines, we learn that in the corporate jungle 'lunch is for wimps', and the real business of life is conducted in the board-room, of course, but also on the squash court, notorious killer of those whose aptness for the cut and thrust of contemporary capitalism is inadequate or fake.

What lies behind this, and has done for some time, is what we may term the 'phantom science' of cryogenics, the mythical point at which death itself may be survived if the body, the meat, is caught just in time.

> And the will therein lieth, which dieth not. Who knoweth the mysteries of the will, with its vigor? For God is but a great will pervading all things by nature of its intentness. Man doth not yield himself to the angels, nor unto death utterly, save only through the weakness of his feeble will. (Poe 1998, 26)

These lines are the epigraph to Edgar Allan Poe's story 'Ligeia' (1838); he attributes them to a writer named Joseph Glanvill, but the fact that they have never been found among Glanvill's works indicates something of the uncanny structures surrounding the prolongation of life and the suspension of death. Looked at in another way, they represent an assault on the necessity of death which seems at least as comfortably at home within contemporary modernity as within the 'traditional' rhetoric within which they are here couched.

'Will', according to this analysis, would be all; we age and die only because we allow our own weakness and feebleness to overcome us. In both scenarios – the 'Glanvillian' and the modern – the opportunities for endless prolongation are there, and available for the taking; we miss these chances because we refuse to entertain the possibilities, long adumbrated by science fiction writers, for the prosthetisation of the human body, and nostalgically cling to the prospect of a 'natural' lifespan. Thus, by a curious paradox, the very old signify both the triumph of medical science over natural adversity and at the same time an irrational encumbrance on a rationally developing economy, an example of the Faustian nature of technology and of modernity's difficulties with retaining a grip on what may prove to be ineradicable facts of humanness.

20 Commodity

At the root of modernity lie a number of intertwined issues to do with the commodity and fetishism. To see this, we have only to look at some of the ways in which the 'modern citizen' is interpellated as a consumer and, indeed, as a collector. Perhaps the most bizarre but at the same time the most relevant way to approach this is via the book.

Despite constant suggestions that the book, as reading method and as artefact, is dying out in the face of multiple assaults from other media, including the resurgent realm of film and its progeny, video and DVD, it remains the case that evidence suggests that the purchase – and presumably the reading – of books is a huge business, both culturally and commercially. Major chain bookstores such as Waterstones and its more recent rivals offer vast piles of novels, often at seriously discounted prices, while publishers vie to produce a constant range of 'classic' literature in ever cheaper formats.

The question arises as to what function these ever increasing book sales represent. Books, as the old adage goes, 'do furnish a house'; more importantly, books, and especially novels, emerge in an ever increasing string of reproducible or extending formats. Rowling's series of seven Harry Potter books is perhaps the best-known, and certainly the most profitable, example of this, but the fantasy and detective genres in particular are dominated by series of books featuring the same characters. In one sense, this offers a solution to one of modernity's major paradoxes: how to persuade the public into ever greater consumption while at the same time enforcing a standardisation of format.

What is essential here is to recognise the connection between commodity and melancholia most interestingly described in the work of Guinn Batten. She situates her work within romanticism, at the very point where industrial culture was beginning to erode the bases of traditional communal life. The melancholia to which she points is caused by the removal of satisfaction in work, by the progress of alienation; for this is substituted the pleasure of reading, or perhaps of a certain kind of idealised fantasy. The unique work of art, as constructed by the individual craftsman or by a team of craftsmen, becomes obsolete in the wake of the eighteenth century; instead there comes a fetishisation of the object, a reproducibility of the kind also traced by Benjamin in 'The Work of Art in the Age of Mechanical Reproduction'. It is not that the worship of the unique disappears; it is rather that it becomes, through the mechanisms of profit and value, available only to an increasingly rarefied and wealthy stratum of society; for the rest, there have to be 'surrogate objects' onto which earlier notions of value can be projected.

This melancholia, this perceived absence of 'the real thing' (as so carefully depicted in Henry James's short story of that title) leaves a gap which can only be filled by reproduction and quantity, just as the disconnection between individual experiences can be remedied only by the continual performance of 'the same'. Perhaps Conan Doyle, in his Sherlock Holmes series, marks an early emergence of this phenomenon; certainly the repetitive fantasies of authors as otherwise remote as Raymond Chandler and Tolkien mark its apogee – at least in terms of the book; of course film series such as the James Bond movies, the Star Wars saga and the group of Matrix films represent a similar cultural development, according to which nobody significant ever dies and the protagonist simply overcomes fresh hurdles in each 'episode' of the series.

The question arises as to what the end-point might be of such a 'series'; but, perhaps more deeply, of what, within modernity, the concept of 'series' might actually mean. Essentially, it roots the audience or reader in a single place; it seeks to reduce or control audience mobility by tying him/her to one station. Thus the veneer of modernity, which has so much to do with speed, mobility, travel is in some ways revealed to be, at a deeper level, at the service of those cultural and related industries which need, above all, a fixed audience which can then be approached to yield to the greater range of goods the acquisition of which those industries are trying to provoke.

This is at its most obvious in the whole business of TV advertising; but it is now becoming far more widespread, with 'audiences' being identified by postcode and then subjected to advances which are premised on perceived lifestyle, social inclination and spending power. Modernity requires people to be part of an identifiable group, to be interpellated on the basis of class, gender, earnings, rather than as individuals. Here, perhaps, we are seeing the end and destination of the phenomenon so convincingly identified as 'possessive individualism', which from the perspective of the early twenty-first century may now look like an early capitalist formation, destined to fail and be superseded by more globally commercially viable and profitable forms.

It is interesting in this context that as the tapestry of sameness unrolls, so the need for people to claim a unique, even bizarre, individuality expands to fill the space. Perhaps the late John Peel's radio programme *Home Truths* expressed something of this; what Peel exposed, and what his successors, however faultily, continue to expose is the strangeness of what may otherwise be taken for 'ordinary family life'. The individuals and families who formed the substance of *Home Truths* were anything but ordinary; but, seen in a wider context, one might say that they were rebelling – for the most part entirely unconsciously – against the very notion that there could be anything, anywhere *called* 'ordinary family life'.

Modernity thus breeds its own inversions, but all too often these inversions – pigeon racing, stamp collecting, train spotting (in one of the usages of that term) – turn out to themselves partake of the modality of the commodity, the collection. The question would then be a Hegelian one about totality: about whether it is possible to own every last item in a particular set, and even more about whether such a possibility might occur only at the highest levels of wealth and income and everybody else might be reduced to constructing a simulacrum of total ownership – of things, but also of their own lives; whether the 'collected objects' might be a bulwark against increasingly damaging forms of alienation, a way of asserting a form of power to set against the overwhelming power of the modern corporation.

2 1   War

There are many reasons to believe that the war machine is of a different
origin, is a different assemblage, than the State apparatus. It is of nomadic
origin and is directed against the State apparatus. One of the fundamental
problems of the State is to appropriate this war machine that is foreign to it
and make it a piece in its apparatus, in the form of a stable military institution; and the State has always encountered major difficulties in this.
(Deleuze and Guattari 1987, 312)

Thus Deleuze and Guattari in *A Thousand Plateaus*. What lies behind
their argument is a fundamental opposition, as they see it, between the
force of the State, which is enshrined in boundaries, straight lines, a geo-
metricisation of the world, and the force of nomadry which is bound to
resist and oppose this notion of State order and to mount a challenge to
it from the perspective of a different kind of geography, a different kind
of travel, a different architecture of the world.

What Deleuze and Guattari are mounting, here and elsewhere, is an
assessment and critique of modernity; it can itself be further critiqued,
but first it would be better to fill out where one might agree with their
analysis. It is certainly true that the formation of a modern, State-based
war machine has been and continues to be beset with difficulties.
Emblematic of those difficulties would, until recently, have been US
operations in Vietnam and the inability of the US to find a satisfactory
military solution there on their own terms. Arguably this was due to the
guerrilla tactics of the Vietcong; at least as arguably it was due to the
level of US civilian tolerance – or intolerance – for the sight of young
men returning home in body bags.

Now, however, we can see this as only the beginning of an emerging
pattern which is being replayed in Afghanistan and Iraq. What is most
interesting for our purposes is that these battles, invasions and destruc-
tions of culture are not only political, military and economic in purpose
(although they are certainly that), but that they also represent the super-

structure of a continuing struggle for the supremacy of the modern. The ostensible problem in Vietnam was, of course, Communism; but what the war was also about was a need to demonstrate that the 'supply lines', the technological efficiency and the command structure of the US military were necessarily superior to the 'traditional', village-based, clan-backed structures of the Vietnamese polity.

It would be a moot point to declare this not the case; but insofar as the Vietnam War has now eventually been won by the west, it has happened through economic and commercial means rather than through military ones and Vietnam shows every sign of taking its 'proper' place in a western world-view of emerging eastern economies and tourist destinations. The cases of Afghanistan and Iraq are clearer; here the enemy is again ideologically based, but the principal difficulty of the US war machine is not with the ideology, it is with a kind of nomadry well expressed in the entire problematic of the 'uncivilised' caves of Tora Bora, where Osama bin Laden may or not have at some point had his headquarters.

We can therefore perfectly well see this as a war – like the unceasing low-intensity Australian war on their own aboriginal people – on nomadry, on a conception of territorialisation based not on fixed rule or capture but on more distant, non-modern memories. But it would be difficult indeed to follow Deleuze and Guattari's argument that the 'war machine' is essentially built from nomadic precepts; it would seem to follow more clearly that what is at stake here is a dialectic between two different types and wellsprings of warfare. It is true that the principle of 'nomadry' contains within it an impulse towards war, at the very least because of the contestation between tribes for elements of subsistence; but it is also true that the State itself has constantly proved itself to be at its acme *as* a State when it is 'at war' – we need only to think of the phrase 'Britain's finest hour', which has been endlessly replayed among victorious European nations.

Modern warfare, brilliantly analysed by Virilio, is based on the enactment of a certain architecture, an architecture of salients, bastions, fortresses – the very names of, for example, US military camps and aircraft carriers indicate the provenance. Yet at the same time it disempowers the significant characteristics of previous warfare; where, in a book like for example *War and Peace* (1865–9) and certainly in a whole stream of mythologised British history, the processes of war could be focussed around ideas of personal courage and sacrifice, the modern notion of war is essentially statistical. It is also, of course, economic: it was only with the great wars of the twentieth century that it became truly apparent that one of the most basic features of warfare was that it cost money, and that the money it cost would be directly dependent on the technological forces deployed – hence the necessity for that founding act of modernity, the Marshall Plan, and its putative successors in Iraq and elsewhere.

Within modernity, it is true that nomadic sites of resistance have virtually disappeared: thus part of the interest of picking a fight with Afghanistan, one of the most primordially organised of extant states. Of course it could be argued that this very vestigiality of the Afghan state was the reason in the first place for it playing host to Al Qaeda (whatever that mysterious entity might turn out to be, if the story ever has a convincing conclusion), but the fact remains that Afghanistan remained (and remains) one of the most convincingly 'nomadic' places on earth, and this could be seen to form an unsightly blot on the face of the modern world. More especially, this perceived backwardness would make such a state which is not a state a serious economic risk to other states which might have to depend on its supplies (of oil) to maintain modernity's façade.

Another, briefer, quotation from Deleuze and Guattari:

> The very conditions that make the State or World war machine possible ... continually recreate unexpected possibilities for counterattack, unforeseen initiatives determining revolutionary, popular, minority, mutant machines. (Deleuze and Guattari 1987, 313)

The argument here would be clearly recognisable if we restated it, again, as saying that modernity creates its own backlash. It is not as though there is quasi-universal war between progressive and traditional cultures: the landscape of modernity is one in which the ceaseless, restless desire for change produces its own other, its own resistance. In a very real sense, 'tradition' is *born of* modernity, rather than the other way round. If this seems counter-intuitive (and it is, and as Hegel would have said, rightly so) then one need only look to Iraq, a state which in many ways – including, not least, the emancipation of women – was one of the most progressive in the Middle East and now appears to be re-donning the mantle of the traditional as a direct consequence of the complexities of its embroilment in the western war machine.

Another term which is particularly interesting in Deleuze and Guattari's sentence is 'unforeseen', which again points up – as, in a different context, did the attacks of 9/11 – the curious paradox whereby the most advanced states of preparedness – what we might indeed call without danger of frivolity the United States of Preparedness – appear under modern conditions never to expect that which might happen. The reason for this is in one sense obvious: states which achieve superpower status do so as the equivalent of children who continue to believe in their omnipotence. When this is transgressed there is a consequent breakdown, a sudden diminution of public trust which echoes the transgressions of the playground. This in turn, as Freud said, fuels the search for a 'strong leader' who will protect against decay; when, as in New Orleans 2005, that 'strong leader' proves incapable of heading off disaster or even of adequately responding to it, the very boundaries of the State are threatened. In the absence of an external enemy to blame for a hurricane, under conditions of deprivation the animosity will be turned inwards, often to frightening effect.

Deleuze and Guattari's modern war machine, then, is a more complex beast than they imagined; the question for us would be of the extent to which it is a superstructure of the State or rather imbricated in its very foundations. Perhaps one answer to this question can be suggested by English national mythology: the notion of 'hearts of oak' would not have existed without the need to build a navy of wooden ships; more destructively, the notion that the English 'never, never would be slaves' is impossible to disassociate from the English role in encouraging and profiting from the slave trade around the world. Both of these, if you like, were acts of war, but of course seamlessly integrated into the semantic web of military patriotism, the construction and maintenance of a modern war machine which necessarily and apparently effortlessly creates its own others.

22   Repetition

I want to suggest here that, in several ways, J.G. Ballard is the emblematic writer of modernity. The first point to make would be that his entire body of work is centred around a version of Freudian *Nachträglichkeit*, a postponement or deferral of meaning. When Ballard began to write science fiction short stories in the 1960s, he rapidly evolved a certain set of symbols – of explosion, of mutilation, of media reaction – which at the time appeared new and unprecedented. It was only with the much later publication of *Empire of the Sun* (1984) that a kind of key to this symbolic landscape appeared, as Ballard wrote directly of his experience, as a Japanese prisoner-of-war, of the presence, the fantasy and the aftermath of the Hiroshima bombing.

It came to seem clear that this figured as a certain psychological and textual trauma which had been producing the effect of repetition as, according to the relevant theorists, trauma always does. This repetition operated through a number of Ballard's scenarios, and particularly through his stories and novels of disaster and survival, such as *Crash* (1973), *Concrete Island* (1973) and *High-Rise* (1975). What *Empire of the Sun* made plain was that these works were, in a sense, side-effects of the childhood self who had been in the prison camp; thus in a certain way *Empire of the Sun* worked back upon itself as it depicted the (itself traumatised) mind of the younger Ballard, arguably present at the traumatised and traumatising birth of the modern.

I refer to this as the 'birth of the modern' in the sense that, firstly, it seemed at the time as though the final horror had been unleashed on the world, a horror the continuing potential of which was to colour the entire course of the following years, the years of the Cold War and of Mutually Assured Destruction, the years of a terrifying belief in a Frankensteinian technology which had run entirely out of control; but secondly, because the story told about it was fundamentally divergent – there were, in fact, two different narratives which never have and never will come together. One was of the necessity at all costs of defeating the Japanese aggressor;

the other was of the sacrifice of hundreds of thousands of civilian lives in the service of a demonstration of irrefutable technological supremacy.

Within the framework of the modern, each story is equally true and equally impossible; they cannot exist without their other, which means that the possibility of attaining a single, homogeneous master-narrative of history recedes again from the agenda – as we are still seeing in the difficulties encountered, especially by the Chinese, with the 'revisionism' of Japanese school history textbooks. But the deeper point would be that such 'revisionism' is the essence of modernity; there is no history without its own accompanying revisions, and this is of course particularly true of the history of empire, precisely that 'empire' (not restricted to the Japanese) to which Ballard's semi-autobiography obliquely alludes.

Just as though he were undertaking his own self-analysis, then, Ballard's writings centre on the construction of symbols, in a format which might encourage one to say that the writer is 'at the mercy of those symbols', as the analytic patient is at the mercy of the mechanisms of the unconscious. This is followed (although in fact preceded) by the interpretation, or at least the demonstration, of those symbols, which then becomes firmed up into a 'case history' – a life story which, although internally validated, remains free from sanction, unclear in its justification. Ballard, we might say, was certainly in China when the bomb came down; whether he saw its effects, or indeed anything at all, remains a question which cannot be answered in textual or biographical terms – perhaps this trauma is a 'trauma of fantasy', and if so, perhaps it is indeed the 'foundational trauma' of modernity.

What is most significant, though, is that Ballard is a repetitive writer, a writer of repetition; that is not a literary-critical point but rather a statement of where writing might have to situate itself in a world where standardisation is not only the norm but also the goal of desire. Ballard speaks constantly of the way in which modernity, while appearing to permit, respect and even encourage individuality, in effect while promulgating that individuality at the same time reduces it to dust and ashes. Ballard's principal characters, if they can be said to be characters at all, are monsters of consumerism – they are interpellated as consumers, they live their lives in thrall to the object.

What Ballard might therefore reveal to us is that modernity entertains a peculiar – or perhaps it has now become a normal – relationship between those overused terms, 'subject' and 'object'. To put the terms into play: Ballard's 'subjects' conceive of themselves as 'objects'. They are 'subjected' to the ministrations of the consumer society, and their subjectivity

thus becomes impossible to enact. They may well 'object' to this reduction of their subjectivity, this subjugation, but they have no power to put
this objection – which is an objection to their 'object' (but also abject)
status – into practice; like the younger Ballard in the prison camp, they
have their world ruled for them, they are 'subjected to the empire' –
which might, from a very different perspective, look very much like
Umberto Eco's modern 'empire of signs'.

One of Ballard's more recent books, *Millennium People* (2003),
addresses the possibilities and impossibilities of this act of 'objection'. It
begins thus:

> A small revolution was taking place, so modest and well behaved that
> almost no one had noticed. Like a visitor to an abandoned film set, I stood
> by the entrance to Chelsea Marina and listened to the morning traffic in
> the King's Road, a reassuring medley of car stereos and ambulance sirens.
> Beyond the gatehouse were the streets of the deserted estate, an apocalyp-
> tic vision deprived of its soundtrack. Protest banners sagged from the bal-
> conies, and I counted a dozen overturned cars and at least two burnt-out
> houses.   (Ballard 2003, 3)

What Ballard is going to recount is a strange 'revolution of the middle
classes', rebelling against private school fees and high-level taxation; but
what is more interesting here is the 'dislocation' of the passage – a geographical 'dislocation' which has the extremely wealthy locale of Chelsea
Marina fomenting an uprising, but also a 'dislocation' (which runs
through Ballard's work, where his own home in Shepperton is continually matched with the 'unreality' of Shepperton's famous film studios)
between what might be taken for actuality and what might be taken for a
film set.

What Ballard is offering us is a modern mixed-media experience: on
the one hand there is the all too familiar soundtrack (although even this
includes its own notes of desperation and emergency); on the other there
are actual events going on, although they are too small, too 'modest', to
be noticed. Here then we have a persuasive description of the condition
of modernity: the pervasiveness of distraction, an uncertainty as to
where real events might be, a confusion born of media coverage and the
irresponsibility and lies of politicians. In the world Ballard depicts, it is
difficult to see where the 'real story' might lie. Is anybody, indeed,
capable of telling the 'real story', and what would their credentials, their
verification techniques be? The passage continues:

Yet none of the shoppers walking past me showed the slightest concern. Another Chelsea party had run out of control, though the guests were too drunk to realise it. And, in a way, this was true. Most of the rebels, and even a few of the ringleaders, never grasped what was happening in this comfortable enclave. But then these likeable and over-educated revolutionaries were rebelling against themselves.   (Ballard 2003, 3)

Another story, another partial interpretation; another sense that the real difficulty has become not merely grasping the sense of the lives of others but grasping the truth of one's own life. There is no real arbiter here, no voice of authority to whom one can appeal to make sense of these disparate shards and fragments, these inexplicable ruins. Within the very structures of modernity, within the middle-class enclave, the 'gated compound', the seeds of destruction and rebellion may be present, but they may also be unnoticed, part of a hidden story of resistance which will never see the light of day because it moves too far from the social 'horizon of expectation', too far into a terrain, a territory which modernity refuses, because it resembles too much a mirror image, to realise as its own.

23 Maps

We can summarise a great deal of modernity by thinking about the concept of the map. We might say that maps have historically moved through four phases. The first we can characterise as the 'nomadic map'. This would, of course, normally be a map held in the head, within the collective cultural memory. Its principal features would be to do with subsistence, it would hold within itself lines of animal migration, clues to the seasons, indicators of prosperity and lenity, routes and trajectories of competing tribes, locations to avoid, times to travel and times of respite. It would, in short, be a complex vernacular model of space *and time*, recognising them as indivisible if the map was to be of use for survival, for reproduction and for the strength of the social unit.

The second we can think of as the 'divine map', and here these basic facts of subsistence have become, as with the great medieval map-makers, subservient to an all-embracing picture of the world as modelled on God's creation. Thus in many of the *mappae mundi*, the centre of the world is pictured as Jerusalem. We may think of these maps as 'geo-graphically inaccurate', but this would of course be to miss the point: these maps are not guides to action or to travel – otherwise no Crusader would ever have found Jerusalem – but symbolic replicas of a presumed principle of order in the world: they celebrate God rather than assist man in his everyday actions.

The third – which embraces the bulk of post-medieval history in the west as also in the great cultures of the middle east – we might call the 'discovery map'. Here the starting-point is neither the confined reaches of tribal history, measured by the distance a man on horse or camel might be expected to cover on a day of propitious weather, nor the need to find evidence of divine planning in the geographical operations of the world, but rather the sense of the world as, at least in substantial part, as yet 'undiscovered'. These maps are constantly expanding, reinforcing, supplying yet further detail as hitherto 'unknown' parts of the world are 'filled in', from the delicate tracings of the sixteenth-century explorers trying to discover, for example, when an island is not an island, to the brutal colorations of empire which adopt a model of 'ownership' or suzerainty as the means of geographic discrimination.

Modernity's maps, however, diverge from these august predecessors and address the world in a different mode. In one interestingly paradoxical twist, one might say that they return to the nomadic map in the sense that they are governed by an economic logic, a logic no longer entirely of survival but rather of hierarchy and supremacy. These maps are not particularly erudite; I am thinking, for example, of maps which show the size of different countries not according to their land-mass but rather according to, for example, their Gross National Product; or their oil reserves; or their population densities.

Such maps can be found in every modern child's school atlas. What they recognise is that the worth of different parts of the world is not governed by their physical coordinates, but rather by their productivity, their contribution to the global economy – or sometimes according to the dictates of some highly particular trade. In the surprisingly named World Museum of Peppers in the small Basque village of Estrelette, there is probably the only map in the world which shows countries distributed according to their pepper productivity; it is one of the very few contemporary maps on which Nepal is larger than the United States, and on which Australia does not appear.

But what lies behind these perhaps trivial examples – but also behind a certain glimpsed accommodation, against all the odds, between modernity and nomadry – is a different view of the world, a world where some distances have been squashed and others have been vastly expanded. It depends (again) on how long it takes to travel over a particular terrain, and so once again these are maps in which space and time are intricately interlocked. The distance between London and Nairobi is, since regular air flights are regularly available, very small; the distance between Nairobi and any small village in Kenya is almost immeasurably large, since transport is irregularly available and subject to the vagaries of weather, road conditions and, of course, the question of the means of transport available (or unavailable) to perform the journey.

We come back again to Virilio's issue of speed: the modern map is a 'question of speed', it is about how long it might take to get from point A to point B, but within that equation it is also about how one might travel and that is ineluctably based on the question of cost. Yet, again, one might see the 'modern map', a fourth stage as I have tried to outline it in the history of the cartograph, as already on the brink of being superseded –

perhaps already so. For information technology is in an advanced stage of collapsing the process of travel altogether: most of the business-class seats on the airlines of the west are occupied by corporate clients who do not, in fact, need to travel for any practical purpose at all: the work they appear to do has already been done, or is in the process of being done, through the information superhighway, which (perhaps) has no map – because the processes of space and time have already been thoroughly conflated, instantaneous transmission renders the map useless and pointless, a relic of the past.

Yet because it is a relic, it therefore has symbolic weight. There was much need in the past for kings and princes to meet from time to time in solemn conclave, if only on the 'court' principle that a person is least dangerous when you have them within your sight. There is no such need now, yet the political business best referred to under the symbolic title of 'summit meetings' still continues, to reassure a sceptical world that leaders of different political persuasions and different religions continue to attempt to operate together for the world's good. The maps according to which they travel are largely imperceptible: they include regular airlines, but also the unrecorded routes of private jets, the meetings of corporate yachts, even the 'unscheduled' movements of the British 'Royal Train'.

'Distance' has become the prerogative of the dispossessed: it is what happens to people when they do not have the means to circumvent or overcome the everyday difficulties attendant on travel. The distances in Africa are vast, western commentators are apt to say; that is so, but it is because they are neither 'filled' by anything, nor are they 'brought together' by modern technology, which above all things is a machine for collapsing distance, in both time and space. The ancient need for travel as a means of commerce is being gradually superseded; of course, raw materials and manufactured goods still need to be transhipped, but as they are being so they fall under a different regime, that peculiar regime which 'the sea' has become, where huge tankers, their cargoes uncertain, their flags only 'of convenience', their crews (as recent disasters have revealed) incapable of talking together in a common language, ply the waves in a realm of amnesia, recognised only when they sail and when they dock – or, occasionally, when age-old forms of piracy bring them to our attention.

The *mappa mundi* is therefore now composed of a myriad points of light, points to which and from which goods and, more usefully, information can travel. The act of communication is increasingly imperceptible; perhaps the transformation of mobile phones into cameras, mentioned earlier, has a further function, in that it can remind that the momentary act is not entirely invisible, it can be at least temporarily recorded to demonstrate that it has happened, although the concomitant consequence of digitised technology is that it is no longer necessary to keep it in a state of quasi-permanence as a record of a stable past, it can be erased or discarded as the whim takes.

And modern cartography, of course, has other dimensions than this. It is no longer necessary to be restricted to mapping the earth's surface as if this is all there is: a map can now penetrate downwards, to the oceans' deeps or to and through the rocky mantle; it can penetrate upwards and outwards towards a deeper concept of 'space'. Yet we need also to ascend, or descend, from these remote reaches to recognise the importance of 'urban mapping', the mapping of social spaces which, in modern times, has become the guiding light of architects and town and country planners. For modernity's challenge remains, as it has always been, that physical bodies, 'the meat', does not go away; it offers a site of resistance to technology, to a modern cartography in which the machine would supersede the human. In this regime where the disembodied would seem to be the preferred residue of incarnation, the 'embodied' struggles back, challenging (as again in Vietnam, in Afghanistan, in Iraq) modernity to understand the importance of a different kind of mapping, which proves itself time and time again difficult of penetration to a technology equipped with radar, with satellite systems, and above all with a weaponry, typically in the form of heat-seeking missiles, which should be able to find – and destroy – a human body despite all the vicissitudes of unmapped distance.

24　Perversion

Two quotations may be useful in starting to think through the relations between modernity and perversion, and they need to be seen in the context of Jacques Lacan's more universalist claim that perversion, in some meaning of that vexed word, forms not only the limit but the also the essence of the human; it is through the exploration of perversion, through what we might term the 'dialectic of derangement', that parameters can be fixed and broken, that whole logics of invasion and resistance can be sustained and validated.

The first is from Nietzsche, and it occurs in the context of his thought in *The Genealogy of Morals* (1887) on the 'ascetic ideal', an ideal which has all too much in common with modernity's search for purity:

> We can no longer conceal from ourselves what exactly it is that this whole process of willing, inspired by the ascetic ideal, signifies – this hatred of humanity, of animality, of inert matter ... this longing to escape from illusion, change, becoming, death, and from longing itself. It signifies, let us have the courage to face it, a will to nothingness, a revulsion from life, a rebellion against the principal conditions of living.　(Nietzsche 1956, 299)

A longing to elude longing; this, we might say – to take a more modern example – is the 'plot' of Beckett's plays, a plot which is no plot, a blankness which is nonetheless still at all points – as in, for example, *Krapp's Last Tape* (1958) – haunted by the shreds of a previous remembered life, tattered curtains blowing in the wind which signify a continuing activity which is simultaneously a cessation of activity. This is the death of desire; or its subsumption into a different economy, a different logic, a logic of purification and the accurate calibration of surplus profit.

This 'surplus' is also, under the conditions of modernity, what is reclaimed off the body itself, the 'pound of flesh' which is cut off in order to fulfil modernity's promise of physical reshaping. The 'lean machine' of modernity has no apparent room for surplus; as in the case of 'excess baggage', it might slow the speed of our flight, render us incapable of matching up to 'modern needs' – for perfect fitness, for a perfect body, for the perfect lines of state-of-the-art consumer goods. The surplus, therefore, goes elsewhere: into 'fat' bank balances, into gross figures, but above all into the demeaning of shapings which might themselves figure what remains of the human, while the inevitable natural consequences of reproduction, for example, are denigrated as a paradoxical perversion of the perfect, virgin body.

And thus it may be that it is the perversions themselves, in the Freudian sense, which remain to remind us of a form of 'mercy': both of a way in which we are 'at the mercy' of desire, and also of the mercy we might show to those who cannot escape from standardisation. Modernity has, in practice, divided the perversions into two camps: the 'clean' perversions, principally homosexuality, and the 'dirty' perversions – sadism, masochism, paedophilia. Thus is the circle of the human described; but at the same time, according to this paradoxical logic, what remains 'within the camp' is itself stripped of the mess of physicality, which is relegated to that which remains outside, that which continues to howl around the camp-fire – the camp-fire, we might say, of the vanities.

The second quotation is from Keith Ansell Pearson's *Viroid Life* (1997):

> The problem with current theorising on our inhuman futures is that it ends up reifying the demonic powers it sets out to demystify. In the case of Lyotard's thinking on time today, the monstrous logic of capitalism is granted a logic of autonomy which in reality it does not enjoy. His presentation of the inhuman time of our neg-entropic destiny results in an abstract and ahistorical opposition between a pure ethicism on the one hand and the unstoppable – because cosmic – accumulative process on the other. Is this not to be seduced by capital's own desire to construct itself as the transcendental ground of all change and innovation? (Pearson 1997, 72)

The notion that the future might be – might *already* be – in some sense inhuman has permeated modern thinking from the start, an ethic of *jouissance* in supersession. To be human, to be subject to fleshly desires, is to be imperfect. To be sure, there is nothing new in this thinking: the imagery of the perfected, angelic body runs through the history of Christianity, as the undertone, the antidote, to the tortured body on the cross. But that perfected body would still – perhaps sexuality apart – retain in resurrected guise an apotheosis of human characteristics; what modernity suggests – or perhaps reminds us of – is a far more extreme possibility, which is that the human form may be a mere try-out, a guess-work stage in some further, more emancipated construction.

In the course of this construction, there is the necessity for standardis-ation: the human body will need to assume its own inherent form before it can pass through the pearly gates – or before it can perform on the heavenly catwalk. Yet of course it is immediately noticeable that moder-nity, in its most emblematic and advanced form in the US, is simultane-ously in the process of creating its own opposite. The human body, cosseted by labour-saving devices, in thrall to the passivity of media absorption, removed from the vicissitudes of its physical environment, grows not more perfected but more grotesque, more obese; the 'surplus' is returned – with interest – and the search for perfection grows ever further into the realm of the ideal.

But this, of course, is in another sense what is to be expected of modernity's capitalist formation: because the greater the distance between bodily actuality and the admired ideal, then the greater the volume of goods and desires which can be sold in order to bridge that ever growing gap. All comes to hinge on the 'cure', on the myriad of, for example, diets of which the principal outcome is one of modernity's main diseases, anorexia.

Is anorexia a perversion? It is one form, certainly, of a wider spectrum of illnesses which centre round body shape and which have relationships both, on the one hand, to the concept of celebrity and, on the other, to a complex alignment of plenty and deprivation. Although seen in an entirely opposite fashion by sufferers, it is a form of submission to an ineluctable regime, while at the same time being an apparent evasion of that regime, in the sense that it involves a complex set of mechanisms of deception, of self and others, which may be one response to an uncon-scious sense of the prevalence of modernity's panopticon.

Is addiction a perversion? Here a key witness would obviously be William Burroughs, whose commanding account of modernity involves an automatic assumption that addictions are manipulated, inculcated by the State for its purposes, that the very essence of the citizen's relation to the modern State is itself a form of addiction from which we cannot break free. In the form of his character Opium Jones, for example, he points to an inexorable logic whereby enforced addiction and its con-comitant, slavery, are built into the formation of the modern State in the same way – we may extrapolate – that corpses and totems are built into the foundations of a house or a church: to ward off evil, perhaps, but also to remind of fragility, to provide a humble memento of the temporariness of places of dwelling and of worship.

The perversions, therefore, come to serve a dialectical function. On the one hand, they serve to remind us of the residues of that which cannot be assimilated; but on the other they mimic and mock the very forms of modernity itself. Anorexia would on this reading be a parody of style and consumption; addiction and alcoholism parodies of dependence on the State; sadism would be a parody of violence; masochism a parody of subjection and submission; homosexuality a parody of a certain paradoxical purity which can thus obviously not be disconnected from the primitivism of anal fixation; paedophilia a more complex parody of the obsessive care of the child which masks a fear that a child may 'step over the traces' and thereby itself parody a certain version of adulthood.

We are thus lost in a modern hall of mirrors; as we strive towards purification the beast-flesh grows back, and modernity's 'longing' towards the future is continually thwarted, its energies absorbed into a succession of attempts to deal with the resurgent past. If only we could break free of all this and begin again – so modernity's founding myth runs – then we could proceed untrammelled towards an even braver new world; but thus modernity's clean lines become infected with a politics of impatience, a series of misunderstandings as to what people might want, especially those people – and peoples – who have yet to experience any clear benefit from modernity's many projects, or whose lives have been actively harmed, distorted, perverted by them.

And thus back to capitalism's 'monstrous logic' and to the question of whether modernity and its attendant myth of development are mere superstructures, means of coercion (to those excluded) and compliment (to those inside the web). But that is perhaps an unanswerable question; whether the core of perversion lies within or without can only be addressed by a certain recourse to the hall of mirrors, to a logic of the virus, of contamination, infection, the 'para-site', which is itself the inversion of modernity's struggle for disentanglement, its wish to deny the Freudian 'dream-knot' which marks the limit of interpretation.

Part III

Texts

25 Oscar Wilde, *The Picture of Dorian Gray*

Oscar Wilde's *The Picture of Dorian Gray* (1891) might not at first glance seem an obvious text of modernity; and yet it represents an engagement, of a startlingly complex kind, with the modern through and through. Only a few pages in, we find a lengthy rumination by one of the central figures, the artist Basil Hallward, on 'the nature of the new':

> ... there are only two eras of any importance in the world's history. The first is the appearance of a new medium for art, and the second is the appearance of a new personality for art also. What the invention of oil-painting was to the Venetians, the face of Antinoüs was to late Greek sculpture, and the face of Dorian Gray will some day be to me. ... his personality has suggested to me an entirely new manner in art, an entirely new mode of style. (Wilde 1993, 10)

It is conventional, of course, to read the developing relationship between Hallward and the youthful Dorian Gray simply as a case of homosocial infatuation, and indeed later episodes in the novel support this interpretation; but the way in which Wilde fleshes this out is very much more complicated. What the exemplary Dorian suggests to Hallward is not simply a consummation of present beauty, but rather a path of transition, the possibility of a realm beyond the 'givens' of the world, a threshold beyond which hovers the spectre of an entirely new mode of perception which will challenge our view of the everyday as we customarily know it. He continues:

> Unconsciously he defines for me the lines of a fresh school, a school that is to have in it all the passion of the romantic spirit, all the perfection of the spirit that is Greek. The harmony of soul and body – how much that is! We

in our madness have separated the two, and have invented a realism that is
vulgar, an ideality that is void.   (10)

What *Dorian Gray* stands for above all, of course – like the rest of Wilde's
work – is a rejection of 'realism', seen here as – already – an outmoded
form. It is significant here that Hallward refers to realism as something
which is 'invented': it is not at all that what is known as realism represents some verifiable proximity to 'real life'. It is not too far-fetched to
say that Wilde's aphoristic style prefaces Derrida's in its emphasis on a
certain kind of relativism, or that Nietzsche can be seen, however
improbably but as so frequently within the 'body' of modernity, as a
common forefather. What we have here is the claim that it is an illusion
to suppose that the perceiver can be removed from the equation.
'Realism' is a choice, a choice among others, and according to Hallward,
and to Wilde, it is the wrong choice: rather than opening windows onto
the 'real world', it serves to close down imaginative possibilities, and
therefore has a clear ideological and political function. In its insistence
on depicting bodies as they *are* it resists the task of depicting them *as
they may become*. In *Dorian Gray*, this need to delineate the phantasmal
form of the future begins by being nothing less than an ethical imperative, an injunction which is laid upon us to notice and represent the
forms of the future even – or indeed especially – before they have fully
arrived.

It is noticeable also that Hallward lays emphasis on material development: the movement forward into new reaches is not accomplished by
individual genius alone, it is the technology of oil-painting, for example,
that is the controlling force behind the efflorescence of the Renaissance.
Lord Henry Wotton, as we might expect, takes a rather different view of
modernity, if indeed, within the overarching regime of the aphorism, he
can be said to take a view at all:

> The thoroughly well-informed man – that is the modern ideal. And the
> mind of the thoroughly well-informed man is a dreadful thing. It is like a
> bric-à-brac shop, all monsters and dust, with everything priced above its
> proper value.   (12)

Yet even here the dialectic of modernity is at play. In order to mock the
semblance, the simulacrum of the modern which he sees around him,
Lord Henry turns it on its head, asserting that this version of the modern
is in fact a mere cover-story for the antique; rather than being able to

make daring leaps of imagination into the future, it prefers to stay encumbered with the relics of the past and to reduce itself to a mere storage chamber of the mind rather than risking an engagement with the 'abstract forms' which herald the arrival of the truly new, the forms which require us to 'body them forth'.

But the engagement with the future is not the only necessity. What *Dorian Gray* speaks of most intently is the freezing of time, the possibility of the endless prolongation of the moment of youth, the carrying forward of the perfected body into times to come. Dorian's brief but famous speech, as soon as Lord Henry's iron has entered his soul by means of its graphic reminder of the perils and indignities of ageing, reflects a regret which is simultaneously a desperate hope, a hope that the supposedly 'natural' forces of life can be overcome:

> I am jealous of everything whose beauty does not die. I am jealous of the portrait you have painted of me. Why should it keep what I must lose? Every moment that passes takes something from me, and gives something to it. Oh, if it were only the other way! If the picture would change, and I could be always what I am now! Why did you paint it? It will mock me some day – mock me horribly!   (23)

Clearly here there is a cultural bridge between romanticism and the late nineteenth century; but more importantly what is being adumbrated is a wish that the 'technological' means which permit the painting of the portrait and which will sustain it in its (relatively) changeless state could be transferred instead onto the human body itself. The desire is to pass beyond the physical constraints of mortality, to put such restrictions behind us as mere things of childhood and to move into a further sphere, a sphere also depicted in other contemporaneous and later texts such as many of those by Wells, including the aptly-named *Men Like Gods* (1923).

Within the louche presentation of Wilde's text, there begin to appear the outlines of a more steely argument. Dorian's notorious 'deal' with Lord Henry may, from the one side, appear as an updated version of the legendary 'deal with the devil'; but what is wished for is not mere immortality, it is rather an apotheosis of the 'unnatural', a sublation of the merely 'human phase' of development, a dream of progress which will take us beyond the body itself and into territories which are, in a sense, uncharted, but in another are already 'present' to us, as the seeds of the future are taken to be present in the classic texts of modernity. If Lord

Henry is no devil, neither is Dorian an angel: rather they represent a complex admixture of desire, and one which is increasingly and starkly revealed as Lord Henry shows slight but increasingly pressing signs of ageing as the story progresses, a kind of exhaustion with the effort of keeping up with 'the world' as represented by Dorian's 'flight' into the future, one of the many results of Dorian's abjection of his own frail humanity into a realm less available to inspection.

Dorian himself, of course, is in another sense the very spirit of the 'new': his mother and father died when he was a baby, and he represents the orphanic rootlessness of modernity as well as the fiction of an endless wealth which can sustain any kind of excess. Lord Henry's modernity expresses itself in other ways: 'I can sympathise with every-thing, except suffering', he says: 'I cannot sympathise with that. It is too ugly, too horrible, too distressing. There is something terribly morbid in the modern sympathy with pain' (34). What is ironically represented here by suffering and pain is that link with our animal ancestors which continually draws us back to the past, a 'weakness' which needs to be expunged from the citizenry of the future. This link is represented by pain (as it is, in a different but equally suggestive way, by Wells in *The Island of Doctor Moreau*); but it is also represented in the drab, old-fash-ioned colours of realism, as it also is by anything which smacks of conti-nuity, tradition, custom, anything which runs against the notion of the sparkling aphorism as the distinctive – and rootless – textual form of this moment of modernity. Where to a certain outlook such older regimes may resemble loyalty and fidelity, to Lord Henry they wear the opposite aspect:

> ... the people who love only once in their lives are really the shallow people. What they call their loyalty, and their fidelity, I call either the lethargy of custom or their lack of imagination. Faithfulness is to the emo-tional life what consistency is to the life of the intellect – simply a confes-sion of failures. ... The passion for property is in it.   (42)

Thus the reader is brought to see the outline of two tasks for the modern self. The first is to become a site for continual remaking; to break free from the trammels of the old and to pursue wider trajectories of possibil-ity, to become, in short, thoroughly modern. This would also involve recognising a continual movement in time; what is 'unnatural', according to Lord Henry's gospel, is the hypocritical pretence that one can remain 'the same' despite the ever-changing environment of society, culture, technology. Far from being a guarantee of continuity of spirit, such fake consistency represents a turning away from the actualities of the world, where, after all, the one rule is that nothing ever stays the same; to pretend otherwise is an act of self-reification, a removal of self from world, and ultimately a refusal of that most obvious of modern necessities, the need to 'move with the times'.

The second task is to abandon the notion of 'property'. The self as envisioned in *Dorian Gray* is a free-floating self, unbound by emotional or commercial ties. Thus the aphorism, in its extreme form of the paradox, which is the essential motif of the novel, becomes also the essential motif of the modern. What use is intellect, it is asked, if we cannot use it to play with the possibilities around us? What use is it if we use it simply to bolster ancient certainties? To engage in such activities is to engage in precisely the motion of the 'heavy' which we have discussed earlier; it involves pretending that truth is our 'property' when in fact it is we who are binding ourselves as 'property' to the ancient myth of truth. To be fully without property is also to be fully without 'properties', it is to be, in Agamben's terms, a 'bare self', a self which cannot be pinned down, which is in free fall, in continuous movement – or, of course, in continuous flight. There is no doubt that *Dorian Gray* mounts an implicit counter-critique of modernity, one in which the notion of 'escape' is seen as inextricably linked to a certain denial which is only thinly masked by the condition of 'resource exemption' which permits Dorian's life.

It follows from this, as we have seen before, that modernity must relate to a degrading, or down-grading, of wisdom and experience:

> Experience was of no ethical value. It was merely the name men gave to their mistakes. Moralists had, as a rule, regarded it as a mode of warning, had claimed for it a certain ethical efficacy in the formation of character, had praised it as something that taught us what to follow and showed us what to avoid. But there was no motive power in experience. It was as little of an active cause as conscience itself. All that it really demonstrated was that our future would be the same as our past, and that the sin we had done once, and with loathing, we would do many times, and with joy. (49)

For 'experience' here we can read the whole panoply of 'tradition' which modernity wishes to put aside or erase. In this bright new world there is no Lacanian 'law of the father': we are radically removed from context and hence free to remake ourselves and to escape from the rule of paternity (which is what, as we have seen, has already happened to Dorian). Hallward and Lord Henry are, of course, his surrogate fathers; but the relation between Dorian and Hallward is marked throughout by disrespect and eventuates in parricide, while the relation between Dorian and Lord Henry is constantly and curiously oblique, as Lord Henry continuingly marvels at Dorian's 'being-in-the-world' rather than – as he would see it – attempting to influence it. The very concept of 'formation of character' stands in opposition to all that is modern and fluid, in opposition to the real sources and advantages of power, which consist in freeing ourselves from convention and restraint and incarnating in ourselves the otherwise abstract lines of the future. What is to be avoided at all costs is the supposition that the future can be the same as the past, that old certainties can in some way guide us through the new 'moral maze'; to succumb to such a supposition would be to confine ourselves forever to the realm of the relic, the reliquary – it is no accident that Dorian toys at one point with the regime of Catholicism, but of course he sees this characteristically as one possibility of aesthetic choice among others rather than as a question of belief or faith.

But the thinking here is perhaps even more radical: in the end we are encouraged to be uncertain, sceptical as to whether there is in fact any division between self and world. There is no divine bedrock to understanding upon which we might build, or because of which we might even enter, soaring cathedrals; rather there are shifting sands on which, indeed, we might build things of beauty, but those things are ephemeral, transitory, and to mistake them for permanence is to fall into the logic of the monument, the idea that we can make something solid which will surpass ourselves – the very *topos* explored a century previously by Coleridge in 'Kubla Khan' (1798), where the task of 'new making' is again entertained only to be radically and problematically curtailed. Lord Henry, on the contrary, believes in a 'logic of experimentation': his interest in Dorian refuses to adopt a clear intellectual, emotional or sexual form, and more, he is aware that all too often 'when we thought we were experimenting on others we were really experimenting on ourselves' (49); there is a clear-sighted negativity in Lord Henry's view, in his refusal to accept the conventionalities of relationships. We notice at one point, for example, that while events have been unfolding his own marriage has broken down; but this is very much a sidelight, the real action of the world goes on elsewhere in a continuing attitude of awe and surprise at how the new might fulfil us, perhaps by taking us by storm.

So in the process of life depicted in *Dorian Gray* there is no fixity of personality but rather a continuing unmaking and remaking of character, and if the novel can be said to have an ethic, then it is one of discontinuity, an acceptance of and a revelling in the loss of certainty. When Dorian becomes engaged to be married, Hallward expects Lord Henry to disapprove, but he takes a different line:

> ... there are certain temperaments that marriage makes more complex. They retain their egotism, and add to it many other egos. They are forced to have more than one life. They become more highly organised, and to be highly organised is, I should fancy, the object of man's existence.   (62)

Within a conventional reading of Lord Henry, this admiration of the 'organised' would sit uneasily, but it works perfectly well within a context of modernity and the need to put the chaos of the past behind. We should not here read 'organised' in the sense of merely needing a more complex diary (or several diaries) with which to conduct one's life, but rather in terms of the cyborg, the evolution of the human into some further creature which can manage a more complex interaction with the world around, an interaction of which the 'self', as traditionally conceived, is not fully in control. 'More highly organised' is an important phrase: it implies a higher level of technology, and at the same time the paradoxical removal of the self from the realm of transparency and behind a veil of secrecy, such that the information which would be needed to decode human interrelationship becomes ever more difficult to obtain or disentangle. That all this proceeds in the text within the context of the iron rules of 'high society' etiquette only underlines the ironies which Lord Henry finds so delicious – indeed, perhaps, delirious: within the old, there is always the possibility of the new breaking out while those around are oblivious to the menace to order it might pose.

The modernity of *Dorian Gray* is also, of course, entangled with the complex late nineteenth-century modernities of the 'New Woman', those modernities which threaten to bring about a whole new range of mobilities, the seeds of destruction of the established order. 'I have a theory', says Lord Henry, 'that it is always the women who propose to us, and not we who propose to the women. Except, of course, in middle-class life. But then the middle classes are not modern' (64). This, of course, is again a paradox: the middle classes may well be seen, the text suggests, in some quarters as the spearhead of change, but in fact despite their vanguard economic position they are at the same time desperately wedded to the rule of property and stability. They cannot – literally – 'afford' to entertain disturbing possibilities; those must emerge on the fringes of society, and it is significant that although Dorian's life becomes progressively divided – not only between self and portrait but also between the country and the city, between Kensington and Whitechapel – what is always avoided is the stagnation which would be seen as inherent in the life of the bourgeoisie. The future emerges not at the centre of things but as a penumbra around the edges, as a half-glimpsed vision, as a phantom or spectre.

There is also here an entanglement with the whole notion of plurality, of what Deleuze and Guattari would call the rhizomatic, and with the masquerade. One of the key scenes occurs when Dorian, having proposed to Sybil Vane, takes Hallward and Lord Henry to see her act. Although Dorian has regarded her on previous nights as a consummate actress despite the squalor of the surroundings – and the text gives us no reason to doubt Dorian's word, at least on this point – on this night she is terrible, and she explains this to Dorian afterwards as being because she is 'sick of shadows', she has turned her back on the pretences involved in acting, having found the 'real thing'. To Dorian, of course, this is in turn terrible: it is precisely shadows with which he has fallen in love, the roles she plays, her seemingly endless ability to turn herself into somebody else, and shorn of the multiplicity of her roles, reduced to a state of pre-modern unity and singleness, freed from the phantasms and hauntings which have inspired his adoration, all she inspires in him as a unitary woman, a single being, is disgust and revulsion. In becoming 'the one' she has renounced the possibilities of the many, and it is immediately after this episode that the portrait shows its first signs of life (or death) as it comes to represent Dorian's hatred of that which might drag him back into the past.

When Sybil has died as a result of Dorian's violent rejection, Lord Henry again embarks upon a somewhat insouciant discourse of the modern and the transient. 'Of course', he says,

> ... now and then things linger. I once wore nothing but violets all through one season, as a form of artistic mourning for a romance that would not die. Ultimately, however, it did die. I forget what killed it. I think it was her proposing to sacrifice the whole world for me. That is always a dreadful moment. It fills one with the terror of eternity. Well – would you believe it? a week ago ... I found myself seated at dinner next the lady in question, and she insisted on going over the whole thing again, and digging up the past, and raking up the future.   (84–5)

There are clearly several different timescales being 'proposed' here. There is the Marvellian timescale of eternity, an object of horror as far as Lord Henry is concerned. However there is also, and principally, an opposition between a time which is held in the memory as though it were a solid object which can be returned to at will and a time which is forever changing, in which events occur and their meaning, if they have one at all, is held within the instant. What is at stake here is the notion that there is a final, unchanging interpretation of the past; for modernity, this is itself merely one among a tissue of fictions, and the attempt to assert some unchangeable truth is perceived as oppression, as we see in a vastly different context in the continuing opposition between modernity and fundamentalism. Referring back to that opposition, one can be sure that here too Lord Henry's refusal to acknowledge the past would have played some part in the unnamed lady's insistence on 'reminding' him of it; that which is free-floating is here seen as continually challenged by that which threatens to return it to its roots, its origin, its anchor, as though there were a single unchanging self which was the origin and motive force of action. Instead the subject is that which is 'acted through', in many senses of that phrase; it is a subject without substance, and its only discourse can be that of self-contradiction, a dialectic which is always striving to exceed but which eschews the possibility that it is proceeding in any specific direction – the constantly new for its own sake. One might therefore say that there is indeed never really any 'subject' for conversation.

'What is done is done', shouts Dorian, when Hallward is appalled by his inhumanity in the face of Sybil's death: 'What is past is past'. 'You call yesterday the past?' enquires Hallward, and this of course is exactly what Dorian, under Lord Henry's tutelage, does. 'What has the actual lapse of time got to do with it?', he asks. 'It is only shallow people who require years to get rid of an emotion. A man who is master of himself can end a sorrow as easily as he can invent a pleasure. I don't want to be at the mercy of my emotions. I want to use them, to enjoy them, and to dominate them' (91). Although Wilde's work has sometimes been treated as a last gasp of romanticism, what is evident here is that it can also be seen as in fact the reverse; many centuries of courtly and romantic love are undone in a trice in this passage, in favour of a discourse of modernity, an eclipsing and sublation of passion, a regaining of an abstract control in the name of the future but a control which is always at the mercy of change.

And this control can only be exercised when it is apparently linked to purity, although however this is a version of purity which is in direct opposition to the 'Puritanism' which Lord Henry sees as a hallmark of the age:

> Men who talked grossly became silent when Dorian Gray entered the room. There was something in the purity of his face that rebuked them. His mere presence seemed to recall to them the memory of the innocence that they had tarnished. They wondered how one so charming and graceful as he was could have escaped the stain of an age that was at once sordid and sensual.   (107–8)

In apparently 'escaping that stain', Dorian becomes himself the very principle of modernity, or at least of 'Dandyism, which, in its own way, is an attempt to assert the absolute modernity of beauty' (109). There is here the trace of the orphanic, the 'logic of the orphan', to which I have referred above, the need to avoid the 'remembrance of things past' in order to move direct into the future. In this world there is no place for the 'stained', for that which might drag one back to a 'tarnished' past; instead, there is an absolute ephemerality within which value is assigned precisely to that which is self-consciously known to be a passing fad. Dorian becomes a 'modern celebrity', much as Byron had before him and as Wilde himself became, a model to be pursued, imitated, celebrated precisely for its characterlessness, for its ability to respond to and shape each passing social whim. And in all of this what is again crucial is the future:

> ... there was to be, as Lord Henry had prophesied, a new Hedonism that was to re-create life, and to save it from that harsh, uncomely puritanism that is having, in our own day, its curious revival. It was to have its service of the intellect, certainly; yet, it was never to accept any theory or system that would involve the sacrifice of any mode of passionate experience. Its aim, indeed, was to be experience itself, and not the fruits of experience, sweet or bitter as they might be.   (110)

The necessity here, therefore, is to move not only with but indeed *beyond* the times, nothing less than the re-making of a more modern image of man. What also happens here is that the concept of 'experience' itself, which Lord Henry has previously rejected, becomes remodelled as a living in the present moment, a flight free from the bondage of time. The end-point of these meditations, one might suppose, would be a question as to whether 'representation' is possible at all or merely itself a simulacrum, a sop to the world of permanence.

Another point in Dorian's perception of the modern is that it involves, *at the same time*, the hugely detailed recapitulation of the past – which comprises, for example, Chapter 11 of the text, which is an exploration of multiple cultural reliquaries where Dorian finds himself living past lives, real and fictional, and exploring past fascinations, whether they be with jewels, scents, tapestries; but this absorption with the past has itself a curious texture:

> There were times when it appeared to Dorian Gray that the whole of history was merely the record of his own life, not as he had lived it in act and circumstance, but as his imagination had created it for him, as it has been in his brain and in his passions. He felt that he had known them all, those strange terrible figures that had passed across the stage of the world and made sin so marvellous, and evil so full of subtlety. It seemed to him that in some mysterious way their lives had been his own.   (120–1)

What we see here may be restated as a kind of apotheosis of virtuality. Dorian does not remove himself into the past; rather, he rebuilds the past as a backdrop to his own modernity. It is as if history has been merely a forerunner, a pretext, for the world of present and future, as though the past has no independent life of its own. In Dorian's imagination the past wavers and warps: it has no separable influence but is subjected to an endless remaking which is at the same time marked by an indulgence in fads and foibles. All passes under the veneer of the absolutely *now*; there is only the moment of experience, which is at the same time the shock of the new, the remaking of old materials as part of the substance of modern life. Like the architects of modernity, Dorian makes an eclectic use of materials: the point is not to revere the past but to 'bring it up to date', to subject it to a 'makeover'. If there is a death-wish here, or any-where else in the text, it is externalised; it is the remains which have to be crunched, crushed, because if granted independent life of their own they might infect the present, might remind us of the debt, that debt to history which Lord Henry (ironically) and Dorian (desperately) want, above all, to be cancelled.

So this remaking, which thus might have a great deal to do with memory, is also and intrinsically about forgetting. Later in the text, Dorian blackmails his ex-friend Alan Campbell (who is, interestingly and indispensably, a 'man of science') into disposing of Hallward's body after he has killed the painter. When taking Campbell up to the room where the body is to be found – the room which also, naturally, contains the 'hidden' painting – Dorian arrives first, takes up the 'gold and purple hanging' which usually shrouds the painting, and flings it over the picture.

> There he stopped, feeling afraid to turn round, and his eyes fixed them-
> selves on the intricacies of the pattern before him. He heard Campbell
> bringing in the heavy chest, and the irons, and the other things that he had
> required for his dreadful work. He began to wonder if he and Basil
> Hallward had ever met, and, if so, what they had thought of each other.
> (144)

In many ways these last sentences (which emblematically include the word 'heavy') represent the *mise en abŷme* of the text. Dorian has killed this man but a few hours previously, but already he is uncertain about the past – both that immediate past and the span of the past from the time when Hallward executed the fatal painting. He is instead fixated on 'intricacies', on 'pattern', on surface, on how the world presents itself in its aesthetic immediacy. Here reality trembles: the remaking of the world on which Dorian is constantly engaged is revealed as also a remaking of the self, as the birth of a rootless, origin-less self which has no past, has indeed no 'insides' at all. The purpose of Dorian hiring Campbell is to 'spirit' the body away, to make it appear as though the body (Hallward's body, but also the body in general) has never been, has never existed to provide 'evidence' for what has gone before. And as in the regime of the architectonic, for Dorian there is paradoxically no longer anything secreted, nothing hidden: the appalling secrets – his own and those of others – of which his life is composed no longer exist as a substrate, they are simply there to be manipulated, as he is manipulating Campbell and has manipulated so many others.

There can be no doubt that Dorian is moving here towards the habita-tion of a virtual reality, in which all appears transparent because the sense of an opaque, sequestered body has vanished from the horizon. All that is solid and heavy has passed into the picture (and, of course, simul-taneously passed 'out of the picture'): what is left is history as a mere tremor in the smooth, glassy façade of the new. Campbell completes his work, and Dorian says: 'You have saved me from ruin, Alan. I cannot forget that' (145). His words, of course, are double-edged, along the tra-ditional lines of the deadly effect of the shared secret – Campbell will have to die, even if at his own hand, in order to remove the further trace of the past – but more resonant here is the notion of 'ruin', that feared partial recollection of the past from which, at all costs, the truly modern must always be 'saved'. The ruin is modernity's secret, the unwelcome reminder which must be either destroyed or – to allude again to Abraham and Torok's work on the wolf-man (or, as some might see it, their re-working over of the wolf-man) – reincorporated.

What is also left, however, is the regime of addiction, Dorian's need for opium, the final, distorted residue of the demands of 'the meat'. One might see this as a peculiarly late nineteenth-century formation; but again and again the story of modernity and the alternative narrative of addiction are tangled together, as though the need to be free from the past returns in contorted form as the final subjugation of the body. Or we might say that the greater the need for modernity to free itself from the old-fashioned trammels of traditional moral law, the greater its incursion into the 'other' territory of the addict, of the subject who is finally 'not free', who has indeed entered into the pact with the devil of which Dorian is specifically accused when he meets Sybil's brother James at the opium den. Thus the very substance of the ephemeral, modernity's lust to tread lightly across the world, is intrinsically subverted by dependence; virtual reality becomes itself the drug of choice, to which the individual is 'subjected' in the very moment at which he imagines himself to have freed himself from the world's ethical demands.

But then, it remains very questionable in *Dorian Gray* where the springs of life are to be found. Towards the end of the novel, Lord Henry gives Dorian some advice:

> ... don't deceive yourself. Life is not governed by will or intention. Life is a question of nerves, and fibres, and slowly built-up cells in which thought hides itself and passion has its dreams.   (181–2)

This moment of explanation, a curious blend of the scientistic and the psychoanalytic, sits oddly with the indulgent tone of much of the text: as though the skeleton has emerged from beneath the flesh. But there is, in a sense, no doubting Lord Henry's deadly seriousness: 'You are the type of what the age is searching for, and what it is afraid it has found' (182), he continues. What 'the age' appears to be searching for, therefore, is freedom from the illusion of moral will; a life which is paradoxically free and unfree – free from the past, but unable or unwilling to place its faith in any belief or dogma – in short, in any master-narrative.

And it is at this point also that the aphoristic style of the text, and Wilde's style in general, connects with modernity. For the aphorism, the paradox, is here the distilled form of modern resistance to master-narrative. Lord Henry is never afraid to contradict himself, indeed the contradictions which occur even within the slightest of conversations or streams of thought are in many ways the very substance of the text. Small narratives erupt through the text, are pursued for a little way, and then abandoned. Boredom is a key-note: to follow an argument through to conclusions is tedious, old-fashioned, heavy rather than light. The modern intellect plays with ideas, enacts a certain *jouissance* rather than being held in thrall by them; words themselves float free, constructed purely in accordance with the momentary, transient demands of a specific social situation. Dorian, for example, recalls the resonant words of a long-lost lover: 'The curves of your lips rewrite history' (185). And, inevitably, the moment when he recalls these words is when he is looking into a mirror, given to him by Lord Henry many years before; a mirror – in some ways the antithesis of the all-consuming time machine which is the portrait – which he then destroys.

In the end the only hope left to Dorian is a further 'newness', a further remaking: 'It was better not to think of the past. ... A new life! That was what he wanted' (185). This hope, of course, is doomed; Dorian proposes to make this 'new beginning' by destroying the painting, which is the reminder of his deeds, but in doing so what he actually destroys is himself, thereby revealing at last the umbilical cord which connects him inexorably to the past and subverting his claim to modernity and to the virtualisation of reality; 'the meat' returns in the form of the blood continuing to drip from the portrait's hands, an image which recalls all the now sublated effort which has gone into the reinvention of the self.

26   T.S. Eliot, The Waste Land

In the epigraph to T.S. Eliot's *The Waste Land* (1922), perhaps the best-known work of modernist literature, the Cumaean Sybil, hanging in her cage, is asked what she wants, and she famously replies, 'I want to die' (Eliot 1963, 61). One of the major questions implicitly posed by the poem is, therefore, *why* does this ancient prophetess (long-dead, of course) 'want to die'? Is it, for example, because she has seen her prophecies come true, because she has seen the shape of the future form around her and she wants no part of it? Or is it because she has seen the futility of all prophecy, the many ways in which people ignore warnings and deny the reality and consequences of the world which they themselves are creating?

Perhaps it is both. Certainly *The Waste Land* announces itself from nearly the beginning of its first part, 'The Burial of the Dead', as a poem which is to do with prophecy and the coming to pass of prophecy, with memory and the past, with what is left in the ruins or remains of the present. *The Waste Land*, even if so often taken to be the emblematic poem of modernism, confronts us from the outset not with a celebration of the achievements of modernity but with a ruinous landscape:

> What are the roots that clutch, what branches grow
> Out of this stony rubbish? Son of man,
> You cannot say, or guess, for you know only
> A heap of broken images, where the sun beats,
> And the dead tree gives no shelter, the cricket no relief,
> And the dry stone no sound of water.   (63)

What the reader is confronted with here is a present which is radically 'unlubricated', where there is no free flow of history but instead merely the remains of a world which is now irrevocably past, which exists, if it exists at all, only in the 'dry lands' of memory. *The Waste Land* is, of course, many things, and has sustained many interpretations, some of them deliberately seeded by Eliot himself in his eccentric notes to the poem; but one of the things it certainly is is an analysis of a present plight, how civilisation has reached it, and what it would be like to try to reinsert it into a history which shows every sign of having been fractured beyond repair. It is a poem of *discontinuity*, and of the effects of that discontinuity on the cultural consciousness of Europe in the early twentieth century.

One possible response to this situation entertained in 'The Burial of the Dead' would be that of 'Madame Sosostris, famous clairvoyante', but her attempts at prediction are implicitly ridiculed, or at best reduced to one in a panoply of avoidance devices, overwhelmed by the onset of the 'virtual reality' of London conceived, as it is throughout *The Waste Land*, as a city of the dead:

> Unreal City,
> Under the brown fog of a winter dawn,
> A crowd flowed over London Bridge, so many,
> I had not thought death had undone so many.
> Sighs, short and infrequent, were exhaled,
> And each man fixed his eyes before his feet,
> Flowed up the hill and down King William Street,
> To where Saint Mary Woolnoth kept the hours
> With a dead sound on the final stroke of nine.   (65)

This is the beginning of the poem's series of portrayals of modern urban life, in terms of a city inhabited only by those who are dead or near death, inhabitants who no longer have any vitality or subjectivity, who are merely functions, vectors of the environment in which they live; their lives are summarised by the 'dead sound on the final stroke of nine', which we might take to signify history's hiatus, and at the same time as the sign of all that cannot be put right as time moves on – the echoing with time in *Orlando* is uncanny. *The Waste Land* is, we might say, a poem of radical modern dehumanisation; it offers us a world in which the 'mass' has emerged to replace the individual, and more to the point in which the individual has been invaded, infiltrated by a 'mass consciousness' which removes all possibility of spontaneous or passionate action. There are in this scenario – and they are, perhaps, the most 'solid' things about it – constant echoes of the past, a haunting set of voices from 'the tradition', as Eliot would call it; but these are subdued, only half-heard, their force has been diminished by the onset of a new set of priorities, a new – and yet at the same time curiously age-old – patterning of life wherein the subject bows him- or herself before the onslaught of an era where the springs of action are 'sullied' (to use the Shakespearean trope on 'solid'), unclear.

Perhaps this is a version of one of the sources of the Sybil's despair. Certainly *The Waste Land* consistently sets an emptiness located in the present against a nostalgic image of fullness derived from the past, as in the famous opening of the second part, 'A Game of Chess', with its allusion back to Shakespeare's *Antony and Cleopatra* (1607). Here symbols of past beauty and wealth are reduced to the scenario of a contemporary drawing-room, while the passion and terror of the story of Philomel – a story which is itself a symbol for the silencing of discordant voices – is reduced to a mere nothing:

> As though a window gave upon the sylvan scene
> The change of Philomel, by the barbarous king
> So rudely forced; yet there the nightingale
> Filled all the desert with inviolable voice
> And still she cried, and still the world pursues,
> 'Jug jug' to dirty ears.   (66)

The eloquent discourse of the past is thus seen as reduced to a meaningless chatter; the modern world is no longer capable of sustaining the history of the word – or The Word, as Eliot the religious poet would have it – and is reduced to 'withered stumps of time'. The famous line, again from Shakespeare but from *The Tempest* (1611), 'Those are pearls that were his eyes' becomes merely 'O O O O that Shakespeherian Rag' (67), as Eliot castigates a modern populism which he considers to be mere philistinism, the adoption of a loose modern phrasing which renounces any search for genuine or intricate meaning.

We might, in pursuance of this theme, also ask why so much of 'A Game of Chess' is given over to the pub closing-time conversation. One answer might be found in the repeated refrain 'Hurry up please its time' (68–9). Here it is indeed 'time', in more than one sense. It is time which is passing, largely unused in the search for soul (or for individuation, to put it in Jungian terms) which might otherwise comprise the purpose of life. It is time which has passed and remains only as the vaguest of memories as the crowds of the dead rush through a benighted London. And it is 'closing time' in the sense that the modern world appears in the poem as locked into a series of repeated actions from which meaning has been drained away. In this dried-out, exhausted world there is no possibility of real communication, but worse than that, there is no real possibility of establishing whether such communication ever *was* possible; perhaps our sense that it was so really is nostalgia, mere illusion or hallucination. If culture, in the strong sense of the term, no longer lives within the mass, then how shall we persuade ourselves that it was ever of any importance, that there was a 'time' before modernity when a certain discursive richness, a certain passional wealth, had its place in culture and society? How might we defend modernity against the accusation that it comes in order to pronounce a surcease on time, to promise us a certain atemporality which is at best an act of denial, a search for shallow pleasure, a succumbing to a desiring machine which has lost or sacrificed any definition of how such desire might be fulfilled?

Thus a further aspect of the riddle of the Sybil: she is obviously 'left over' from a previous age, a previous life, but perhaps even she has forgotten what that life might have been like or whether indeed she has ever lived in any other age than the present.

> The river's tent is broken; the last fingers of leaf
> Clutch and sink into the wet bank. The wind
> Crosses the brown land, unheard. The nymphs are departed.   (70)

So begins the third part of the poem, 'The Fire Sermon', with its half-hidden, half-revealed homage to another of the decayed 'old masters', Edmund Spenser. Whatever this world is, it is one which is spectral, haunted by half-heard echoes. And obviously whatever *The Waste Land* is, it is a poem which both makes a break with the past in terms of style and form and simultaneously critiques that break – and therefore implicitly itself – for the alternative, modern discourse it is (or appears to be) forced to use. There is an unhappy consciousness, in Hegelian terms, here, a consciousness which experiences the modern world in terms of a radical thinning down of opportunity, a dried-out discourse; the question would be whether this discourse – which is appropriate to the modern world – is simultaneously 'immersed' in that world to the point where it is unable to exert leverage, to enjoy critical perspective. Somewhere within this world – as also emblematically in Eliot's 'The Hollow Men' (1925) – there has been an emptying out, a *kenosis* which means that now it is impossible to enter into a shared perspective; what is perhaps most important is that this spectralisation of the possibility of sharing, of communication, is radically opposed to the notion of the 'mass', which, again like Deleuze and Guattari's rhizomes, spreads formlessly, spreads indeed with the hidden function of eroding form. Thus the paradox at the heart of *The Waste Land*, which is simultaneously the paradox at the heart of the modern: those very technological developments which promise to allow us to spring free from the physical at the same time, and in the same breath, enable, or force, us to forget what the physical is like, force us to abandon hopes for individual salvation.

In this world the mind is constantly hijacked, taken off on byways, as for instance in the reinvention of another of the phantomatic pantheon, Marvell:

> But at my back from time to time I hear
> The sound of horns and motors, which shall bring
> Sweeney to Mrs Porter in the spring.   (70)

The insertion here of 'from time to time' signifies again a certain, or perhaps better 'uncertain', discontinuity, an inability to see history as a connected series of events and visions: modernity comes to signify an absence, a hollowing out, above all a tiredness, an exhaustion and melancholy which can be readily connected with the phenomena of consumer fetishism we have discussed earlier. Modernity is here linked with *plurality* and *iterability*; the great discoveries of the modern, from Darwin to Freud and Marx, may well have enabled us to see more deeply into what Marx in particular would have referred to as our 'species-being', but these insights simultaneously include an effect of loss, a sense of wandering without form, ironically represented here in a poem whose formal effects are themselves so clear, so vibrant, so articulate.

All here, as is well-known to critics of Eliot, are fragments, exemplified in 'The Fire Sermon' by Mr Eugenides, the 'Smyrna merchant', whose very name signifies the dream of a purified, eugenic future but who is also 'unshaven', 'with a pocket full of currants' (71), a random, shambling figure who represents the rootlessness which is one of the poem's main themes. Here modernity is not represented in the lucid, swift forms of its major proponents; instead it exists in the remaking of ancient forms of, for example, trade in debased shape, a pre-critique, as it were, of the pretensions of corporate culture, a corruption of the past, conveyed also by the loucheness of the invitation to a 'weekend at the Metropole' (71) – that last name, of course, also signifying the hovering but always removed possibility of a presence at the 'centre' of a society which has become radically 'decentred', where master-narratives have

gone down or at least been followed, as Marx put it, by the 'farce' of a
further historical re-enactment. There is, of course, no doubting here the
implicit racism which comes to the surface so often elsewhere in Eliot's
poetry; but the critical task might be not so much to expose this racism
as to see its connection – as always with racism – with disappointment,
loss, impoverishment, the absence of a secure centre.

As opposed to figures like Mr Eugenides (whose name is also so tanta-
lisingly similar to that of the Eumenides) the next 'prophet' of the poem,
Tiresias, comes to signify, as with the Cumaean Sybil, the contrast
between the past certainty of the 'violet hour' and the contemporary
equivalents signified in

> the evening hour that strives
> Homeward, and brings the sailor home from sea,
> The typist home at teatime, clears her breakfast, lights
> Her stove, and lays out food in tins.   (71)

Yet it is of course true that the poetic persona shares in the disgust with
the body evidenced in the divan 'piled [with] stockings, slippers,
camisoles, and stays' (71). There is no exemption here: as the persona –
or Tiresias – 'strives' upwards towards an all-embracing view of the situation, he is simultaneously dragged down, forced to enter and exist in a
world of trivia – Tiresias himself 'perceived the scene, and foretold the
rest' (72), which one may interpret as suggesting that the scenario of a
world of ceaseless change may in fact mask not discontinuity but a menacing *continuity*, in which what has been played out before will be played
out again in a series of 'acts of exhaustion'. Thus what *The Waste Land*
brilliantly exemplifies is precisely a modern dialectic of continuity and
discontinuity, the struggle both to free oneself from the past and at the
same time to recall it as a place of safety and refuge, as a realm which
existed *before* – before the Fall, perhaps; or before the Great War; or
simply 'before', at some site of origin which has now disappeared from
view.

Exhaustion, then, is critical to the dealings of *The Waste Land* with
modernity:

> (And I Tiresias have foresuffered all
> Enacted on this same divan or bed;
> I who have sat by Thebes below the wall
> And walked among the lowest of the dead).   (72)

The fear here is that there is nothing new under the sun; as the sexual act
– and perhaps also the more romantic *topos* of courtship – fall under the
twinned signs of absence and repetition, so the attempt to invent or
witness the new falls back exhausted. The modern world as depicted here
is indeed a waste land. It is of course marked throughout the poem, as
Eliot constantly hints, by the mythical absence of the Fisher King,
wounded as he symbolically was in both thighs, signifying the impossibility of rejuvenation; a world which claims to be at the beginning of the
future, to be emerging from old nightmares into the light of day, is
revealed as a tired repetition of the past. The stripping away of illusions
does not reveal a new, clearer, cleaner self; rather we discover that at the
heart of what Umberto Eco refers to as the 'critical strip-tease' there is
nothing to be seen, only an echo of what might have been there some
time before, the echo signified for Eliot later, in 'Marina' (1930), by the
'woodthrush calling through the fog' (116), which announces – yet
simultaneously postpones – the possibility of the traveller's return.
Travel is indeed radically banished in *The Waste Land*; here the poetic
device of superimposition, whereby London, Thebes, Smyrna and a host
of other localities are matched, blended, dissolved together, is linked to
the problem which modernity has with recognising difference, the situation in which all locations, all trajectories and more particularly all destinations are finally the same as each other; modernity of style is thus
perceived as indissociable from the draining of affect.

Yet even so the spectral possibility of being 'at home' in this new age
cannot be entirely expunged:

> 'This music crept by me upon the waters'
> And along the Strand, up Queen Victoria Street,
> O City city, I can sometimes hear
> Beside a public bar in Lower Thames Street,
> The pleasant whining of a mandoline
> And a clatter and a chatter from within
> Where fishmen lounge at noon: where the walls
> Of Magnus Martyr hold
> Inexplicable splendour of Ionian white and gold.   (72–3)

Thus a haunting, a sense of the phantasmatic, the fleeting discernment of
'something else' beneath the practical lineaments of the present age,
perhaps even, as Blake on occasion put it, the 'lineaments of gratified
desire'. It is also perhaps worth dwelling on the church of St Magnus the

Martyr, one of Christopher Wren's most impressive creations, for a moment, for it is a church which, to quote its own guidebook, used to be one of the 'great landmarks of London ... until 20th century buildings rose up to obscure it'; it thus comes to signify a certain 'cutting down to size' of the past, and inaugurates – or perhaps, more aptly, returns to – a question as to whether and how the remains, the relics, the monuments of the past, can be accommodated within the present. There is a curious symmetry here with the fate of St Magnus himself, as recorded in his saga; his bones were frequently removed after his death in (probably) 1117, and he thus comes to signify a certain historical (and theological) restlessness, an uncertainty about origin, a difficulty about what is 'consecrated' and what is not. 'Magnus', of course, is the Latin for 'great'; and it is perhaps that sense of the possibility of 'greatness' which has been sacrificed, 'martyred', at the root of the mass culture of the modern world.

'Trams and dusty trees', the poem continues as it pursues its roundabout route through and around London,

> 'Highbury bore me. Richmond and Kew
> Undid me. By Richmond I raised my knees
> Supine on the floor of a narrow canoe'.
>
> 'My feet are at Moorgate, and my heart
> Under my feet. After the event
> He wept. He promised "a new start".
> I made no comment. What should I resent?' (74)

This would indeed be one of the crucial questions posed by *The Waste Land* – what might a 'new start' mean? It is precisely the theoretical and psychological impossibility of this 'new start' that dogs the poem, even while a new poetic style is commandingly announced. Whenever an attempt is made to begin, so the claim would be, it is thwarted, undermined by the relics of the past. They continue to sprout into their own life, like 'that corpse you planted last year in your garden' which is the subject of an earlier – and again hallucinatory – conversation in the poem. This 'sprouting' or germination, obviously, could be seen as a kind of 'new beginning', or 're-beginning'; but it is not what is required of the truly modern, it does not mark the kind of conclusive break which would banish the spectres, would indeed banish all that is signified in *The Waste Land* and elsewhere in Eliot's poetry by the enduring memory of the Great War. The 'waste land' is envisaged among other things as a ravaged Europe, ravaged in the physical sense certainly, but also the object of raids on its own culture and history, raids which, we come to fear, we might have made ourselves. In the perennial aftermath of terrible events, marooned

> 'On Margate Sands,
> I can connect
> Nothing with nothing.
> The broken fingernails of dirty hands.
> My people humble people who expect
> Nothing.'   (74)

The connections are broken, but it is questionable whether this can lead to the new purity so longed for by modernity; instead it leaves only the 'dirty' residues of the past, a lack of desire and ambition, a perpetual state of being mired in memory, an apotheosis of *anomie*. As is suggested in the next section, 'Death by Water', there is always the possibility of being drowned by these memories, of finding oneself in a position where it is impossible to rise to the surface let alone to take flight towards the future. The modern is perennially staging itself 'behind itself', trying with a certain desperation to 'keep up' even at those moments when it seems most confident of springing forward into a new future.

These thoughts, it might be said, come together in a magnificent passage in the fifth section, 'What the Thunder Said', which brings into sharp focus – if such a thing is possible – the intimations of spectrality which have coloured the poem so far:

> Who is the third who walks always beside you?
> When I count, there are only you and I together
> But when I look ahead up the white road
> There is always another one walking beside you
> Gliding wrapt in a brown mantle, hooded
> I do not know whether a man or a woman
> – But who is that on the other side of you?   (77)

In this world sight itself has become unreliable; it is not possible fully to discern figure, shape, gender or number. To put the matter more broadly: clarity of communication is always 'shadowed', there is always 'something else' to be reckoned with in the penumbra of the simplest of equations. Even a clear white road is not transparent; vision is always cloudy, incomplete, haunted. Thus it is that the clarity of modernity, however admirable as a goal and a 'guiding light', can never be fully realised: there is a 'third' which comes to menace, or at least to puzzle, and which can never be quite counted into the reckoning; yet at the same time, we must reckon with the possibility that this recognition of insufficiency is in fact modernity's greatest triumph. We are no longer at the mercy of ancient totalisations; on the contrary – and this is perhaps where it would be possible, paradoxically, to 'read the celebratory' into *The Waste Land* – we have freed ourselves into a realm of radical scepticism. We do indeed then, in one sense, 'see clearly'; but what we see is itself shadowed, haunted, not to be arranged according to the apparently clear-eyed fantasies and hallucinations of past master-narratives, be they religious, nationalistic or philosophical.

Or, to put it another way, there is here something else which 'beckons', something which threatens to turn our eyes away from the supposedly desired goal; we are pulled back into the haunting, although this may alternatively, and paradoxically, be a move into a dream of the fleshly:

A woman drew her long black hair out tight
And fiddled whisper music on those strings
And bats with baby faces in the violet light
Whistled, and beat their wings
And crawled head downward down a blackened wall
And upside down in air were towers
Tolling reminiscent bells, that kept the hours
And voices singing out of empty cisterns and exhausted wells.   (77–8)

Here again is the rhetoric of emptiness, of exhaustion, invading even those moments which might otherwise be ones of aesthetic or carnal delight; the bats come to remind us of the Gothic nightmare of the past, of the long darkness which the modern world has supposedly banished, the bells are 'reminiscent', they will not avoid repeating and thus they keep us in touch with an ancient order, whether we wish them to or not. We may suppose that the springs of the past – literally the cisterns and wells – are now behind us, but they are in fact visited by sirens, they continue to sing, although we can no more respond to their song than we can evade it; in this condition, despite the illusions of the new, we are uniquely strung between past and present. The moment of modernity is thus in one sense one of exhaustion and despondency; but we are allowed also to experience the belief that the very scepticism which is now all-pervasive constitutes a unique outlook on a 'revitalised' sense of time, a moment which is available to be seized, despite the attendant difficulties.

The poem then leads up to its climax in the voice of the thunder, with the insistent, bell-like clarity of the three resonant words 'Datta', 'Dayadhvam', 'Damyata', or as Eliot himself translates them, 'Give, sympathise, control', commanding our attention – as, we might say, only words, and words in a foreign language at that, can do. We need to consider each of these words, in the modern context, in turn:

> *Datta*: what have we given?
> My friend, blood shaking my heart
> The awful daring of a moment's surrender
> Which an age of prudence can never retract
> By this, and this only, we have existed
> Which is not to be found in our obituaries
> Or in memories draped by the beneficent spider
> Or under seals broken by the lean solicitor
> In our empty rooms   (78–9)

What indeed, the question runs, *have* we given? In other words, how have we provided an account to history; or, in more Derridean terms, how can we assess the trace of our impact on the past? There are, of course, many ways of reading this passage; but to consider it in the light of modernity would suggest an anxiety about that past, an emphasis on the obituary and on the will (in the sense of the 'last will and testament'). The moment of the 'waste land' thus represents a 'reckoning', an attempt to sum up the position of present in relation to past, and to find a path through a ruined history. Like a child who cannot leave the wreckage of his or her own anger, we are condemned to live amidst the rubble, and we cannot pretend that this destruction is not of our own doing; modernity may represent in some sense an escape from this frightening weight or burden, but the escape can never be complete and the task of modernity is to provide us with a map with which to negotiate this destroyed environment with its hesitant promises of a future ecstasy.

The speed, the trajectory of modernity is therefore always held back; there is a force of resistance to modernisation which is difficult to overcome. Obviously the earthing of these 'final terms' of *The Waste Land* in the references to the Upanishads suggests a 'different' movement of

history, one in which there remains the possibility of a divine balance, a
voice of authority which will allow us to reminisce about the past without
being bound by it, and in articulating this possibility Eliot is paradoxically uttering a hope for the new through a recapitulation of the very old.
Modernity in Eliot's hands – or rather, in his words – is revealed as
inseparable from a search for origins. The extraordinary phrase 'blood
shaking my heart' may indeed represent a moment of passion, in all the
senses of that wide-ranging term, but this simple – and terrifying –
moment of spontaneity, of rebirth, needs to be considered and res-
ponded to alongside the continuing reminders of other lives which have
not been lived, other opportunities which have not been taken, other
'gifts' which we have been reluctant to give.

The second term of the trinity is 'Dayadhvam', 'sympathise':

> *Dayadhvam*: I have heard the key
> Turn in the door once and turn once only
> We think of the key, each in his prison
> Thinking of the key, each confirms a prison
> Only at nightfall, aethereal rumours
> Revive for a moment a broken Coriolanus   (79)

What is at stake here, under the guise of 'sympathy', is also a matter of
the communitarian, of fellow-feeling. Eliot is speaking of the isolation of
modern man which is the paradoxical correlative of the incursion of the
'mass'. The underlying condition of modernity, then, would here be the
issue of how to 'accommodate' to the premises of alienation; under traditional circumstances the relation between the individual and society, the
one and the many, would have been one of a relatively unthinking acceptance; what modernity demands is that we each need to make ourselves
anew constantly. Every morning is different; in this there is an elation, a
jouissance, but also a terror in case we do not, as individual subjects,
match up to the demands which history – as remade by ourselves –
might make upon us. The 'prison' of the self – which we might fairly
compare to the 'prison-house of language', as Jameson has it – cuts us off
from 'sympathy'; but, perhaps better, and certainly more hopefully, it
confronts us with 'sympathy' – feeling together – not as a 'given' but as a
task to be continually approached, continually approximated. We do not
give up, modernity would say; rather, we appreciate the difficulties with
trepidation – now more than ever – because what has seemed natural in
preceding ages now confronts us as a question of desperation, as the

perennial need for a 'jail-break', a need to respond to a 'beckoning' from beyond, a phantasm of the future.

And the third imperative is 'Damyata', 'control'. Control of the self, certainly, in the earliest of these theological formulations; but how are we to control ourselves in the face of our excessive knowledge of the controls exerted upon us – a knowledge with which we can never rest, although of course it may be reckoned to be ethically and technologically superior to be acting, if we act at all, in the light of that knowledge rather than within the darkness of the 'unenlightened' past – and indeed the goal of all these injunctions is 'enlightenment', of a kind:

> *Damyata*: The boat responded
> Gaily, to the hand expert with sail and oar
> The sea was calm, your heart would have responded
> Gaily, when invited, beating obedient
> To controlling hands.   (79)

Perhaps the 'controlling' phrasing here is 'would have'. Within this rhetoric of a new adventure (couched, of course, within the further rhetoric of the oldest adventure of all, the venturing forth onto Homer's 'wine-dark seas') there is an implicit wondering as to whether such adventures can ever be repeated. Modernity, we might say, is *at the mercy* of knowledge; as with any condition of maturity or adulthood, there is the question as to whether we would not have been, in some sense, better off without the knowledge of the difference between good and evil, without the understanding of an ethical imperative which spoils our pleasures in the very moment when we are 'gifted' with the means to understand them. The coming of knowledge is bitter fruit; but that does not mean that we can relapse into the past, or into an internal rhetoric of circular histories; rather it means that we need to proceed even against the backdrop of a continual threat to our sense of what might be new, and indeed a continual question about why we need to feel the sense of the new at all.

It is in the light of this perception that the poem moves towards its conclusion:

> I sat upon the shore
> Fishing, with the arid plain behind me
> Shall I at least set my lands in order?
> London Bridge is falling down falling down falling down

Poi s'ascose nel foco che gli affina
Quando fiam uti chelidon – O swallow swallow
Le Prince d'Aquitaine à la tour abolie
These fragments I have shored against my ruins
Why then Ile fit you. Hieronymo's mad againe.
Datta. Dayadhvam. Damyata.
                    Shantih shantih shantih   (79)

These fragments of course have been well explored by Eliot's critics; what is also interesting, however, is the fact that the Notes translate none of them apart from 'shantih', glossed as 'The Peace which passeth understanding'. What we therefore see here is a certain ironic conception or encapsulation of a modern audience; it is obviously not that the poet expects the reader to be able to draw upon historical or linguistic resources in order to gather meaning from the text, but rather the reverse; there is some mockery here, a tone which some critics have found distasteful, but which is nevertheless designed to point up the limitations of historical transmission in the modern age.

Seen in this light, then, the final repetition of 'shantih' becomes ambiguous. Does some real hope of peace bring the poem to a close, or is it rather that the kind of 'peace' being mentioned here is a 'peace' of unknowing, a cloud of ignorance? If the latter, then there is a sense in which the poem self-destructs, becomes a piece of 'archetypal' modern ephemera, like the fragments it finally enshrines in its own reliquary. Although there may well be differences of tone and scale, we could connect this with precisely the kind of church guidebook which encourages a generalised sense of reverence which it can never fully explain, precisely the sense of a half-understood (or half-misunderstood) past which will also haunt, for example, Larkin's 'Church Going' (1954), albeit in a more minor key. It is not that a sense of reverence or the sacred has failed to survive within modernity; the question is more about what form this sense can now feasibly take, how a re-enactment of myth can continue to relate in an era where a 'different' regime of knowledge now operates.

And in the end, *The Waste Land* comes down to this question of knowledge. What kinds of knowledge are possible, or permissible, within modernity? One of the strangest of the Notes refers to the line in 'What the Thunder Said' in which the 'hermit-thrush' is mentioned:

This is *Turdus aonalaschkae pallasii*, the hermit-thrush which I have heard in Quebec Province. Chapman says (*Handbook of Birds of Eastern*

North America) 'it is most at home in secluded woodland and thickety retreats. ... Its notes are not remarkable for variety or volume, but in purity and sweetness of tone and exquisite modulation they are unequalled'. Its 'water-dripping song' is justly celebrated. (85)

This may, of course, be a reasonable description (although Audubon gives the hermit thrush a quite different Latin name and dryly records that its song 'is sometimes [*sic*] agreeable') but the question is not about Eliot's ornithological knowledge but about why the note is necessary at all. One answer to this would be that it takes its place in what we might term a 'catalogue of the forgotten' – or, presumably more accurately, of that which is in danger of being forgotten. Just as we now have, for example, a national list of 'buildings at risk', we might say that at least parts of *The Waste Land*, as of others of Eliot's poems, are lists of 'facts at risk'; or perhaps we might generalise and say that part of what *The Waste Land* is about is *fact itself at risk*. We might regard the Notes as the embodiment of a facetious facticity, a kind of waste dump of information which is improperly sorted, indexed, accessed.

But in the Notes, perhaps doubts about this facticity, this resistance to modernistic relativism, is most clearly expressed in relation to a comment which 'accompanies' the passage, quoted above, about the 'third who walks always beside you'. Eliot, as is well-known, suggests that this comes from an account of an Antarctic expedition; but clearly there is a wider relevance here. What modernity comes to remind us of – and to celebrate – is that the eye cannot be reckoned out of the equation: of course it can be said that there are only two people in this or that setting, on this or that road, but this does not obliterate the perception that there might be more – after all, 'Hieronymo's mad againe'. Modernity rests upon the claim that, after all, there is no final resolution: or if there is, it does not mitigate, dilute or even touch upon previous perceptions. The true radicalism of modernity lies in this proposition, and even if it is in radical and paradoxical opposition to the capitalist substructure which supports it, it nevertheless serves as a kind of guarantee of respect for individual perception – perhaps a respect which found its most egregious apogee in the descriptions of madness offered by R.D. Laing and David Cooper in the 1960s, where 'madness' was offered as a privileged state of being.

The 'modernity of modernism' then, as enshrined in *The Waste Land* is a composite formation, constructed on an unstable site from which the past has been partially evacuated but in which, from time to time, strange bones and relics may be found. The question then would become, within this 'archaeology of knowledge' (to use Foucault's term), how to find the tools with which, or even the position from which, to arrive at an interpretation of these ancient artefacts, which now seem separated from the present age by more than mere time. How are we, to put it in more contemporary terms, to 'process this information'? And, looming behind this question, is another: who *are* the 'we' on whose shoulders this responsibility lies, as we witness, in *The Waste Land*, the death or supersession of an interpretative clerisy, the arrival of 'the mass'? Eliot, of course, provides what may be rightly considered as a conservative answer to this question; but other answers are clearly possible.

27 William Gibson, *Neuromancer*

There can be no doubt that William Gibson's *Neuromancer*, first published in 1984, was the principal inaugurator, or perhaps the first well-known representative, of a new phase of self-consciously 'modern' fiction, sometimes since referred to as 'cyber-fiction'. And perhaps we can start to see something of the meaning of this by reflecting on the relations in *Neuromancer*, as we have done before in instances of modernity, between body and mind; or, indeed, what might be coming to succeed that age-old division, that which might be beckoning us towards a world of the 'post-human'. Essentially the body, the 'meat', is seen in the novel, as it is in many theories of modernity, as a restricting force; of itself, it does not enable action but holds us back to the past, reminding us of mortality and the passing of time. It is heavy, 'too too solid' as (again) Hamlet may have put it, a burden on the potentially free flight of the imagination, a way of being held back from further extrapolations and realms of a 'virtual' reality in which the supposedly 'real' body can play no part. This is a dialectic of supersession; even as the individual is called – or thrown, as Heidegger would have it – into being, he or she enters into a realm within which the previously apparently supreme status of the human is challenged and questioned. Various prostheses can be, of course – and in *Neuromancer*, frequently are – developed and used in order to circumvent the body's limitations and provide differing – and deferring – answers to the question of the supersession of the human; but equally, these prostheses can be reversed and made to damage the body. The link between the meat and the machine, the essence of the cyborg, is radically unstable, and this forms the basic territory which *Neuromancer* explores.

Certainly all of this is 'the case' with Case, the aptly named protagonist of the novel, whose skills lie entirely in the world 'outside' the body, in cyberspace, in a world recognisably developed from the internet and the

world-wide web but here conceived as in a far more fundamental relation with the human, such that real damage can be sustained by over-
much contact with a virtual world. Case's abilities, his skills, have been
hampered at the beginning of the text, perhaps even destroyed, by the
injection of a mycotoxin – and thus the originating problem of the
novel. In many ways it is a classic 'whodunnit'. We do indeed need as
readers to know who has done this to Case, as we need to know who is
responsible for many of the other actions, including crimes, in the
book; the difference here, however, is that the parameters have shifted.
In classic genre terms, it could be argued that *Neuromancer* – and
indeed much of cyber-fiction – has more in common with supernatural
fiction than with the crime thriller. With the crime thriller, however
macabre the events, it will turn out that they are the responsibility,
however contorted, of some individual or group of individuals with
merely human powers, however apparently vast. Here such potential
interpretations are suspended; it is not clear where power belongs or
how it is distributed. The great precursor of Gibson is, of course,
Thomas Pynchon, who in *V* (1963), in *Gravity's Rainbow* (1973), and in
Vineland (1990) has charted previously uncharted territories and
laid bare the possibilities of unearthing massive conspiracies which
connect events previously thought unconnected – Neal Stephenson's
Cryptonomicon (2000) provides a further, and later, example of what we
might call the paranoia of the modern.

To call it that, of course, is in no way to deny the real presence or
efficacy of such conspiratorial motifs; in an age of globalised technology,
it is naturally impossible on many occasions to tell where the sources of
power might be, or along what trajectories its distribution might operate.
Neuromancer can, indeed, be read, if rather pedantically, as an analysis of
the modern distribution of power.

> Power, in Case's world, meant corporate power. The zaibatsus, the multina-
> tionals that shaped the course of human history, had transcended old bar-
> riers. Viewed as organisms, they had attained a kind of immortality. You
> couldn't kill a zaibatsu by assassinating a dozen key executives; there were
> others waiting to step up the ladder, assume the vacated position, access
> the vast banks of corporate memory.   (Gibson 1984, 242)

'Human history' here, it might be said, is somewhat foreshortened,
reflecting a foreshortening of memory – which is again referred back
directly to the superior memory of the machine, which renders merely

human remembrance inefficient, antiquated and unreliable. What is being spoken of is the kind of force, the kind of scale, with which Case somehow has to cope; power is no longer in the hands of the human, the 'meat' has become subservient to the technology. The gradual but exponential increase in the 'power' – in the technical sense as well as in the political, although in this world of modernity the two have become fused – of the computer and of its concomitant, its dream and its goal, artificial intelligence, has decentred the human, abjected it. Partly this abjection is into the unwanted places in the world, thus reflecting the geopolitical actualities of our time; partly it is a different kind of abjection, a reflection of the sense the human might have of being required to quail before the might of the machine, of having to carry a numbing awareness of the poverty of individual memory and action in comparison with greater powers which work according to a different timescale – the word 'technoscape' is useful here – and according to a different set of rules in which, perhaps, human concepts of morality play little or no part. When he again becomes able to access these sources of power, Case is transformed from a mere isolated organism, an agent and victim of singularity, into part of a greater 'cyborgic' entity.

Small wonder, then, that another principal theme of the book centres on the linked terrains of addiction and delirium, the trajectory of hallucination. The concept of being a single organism held together in one place, in one time, has here become a thing of the past; instead there is the continual possibility of transcendence, of moving along more than one axis, of being part of different worlds at the same time. We can again see this as a reflection of the complications of time and space typical of late twentieth-century modernity; the question of exactly where a person *is* while moving along a pavement but simultaneously talking on a mobile phone, or texting a message, or listening to an iPod, cannot be answered in the simple terms of tradition. Such a person is simultaneously occupying different spaces, different locations: the question of gathering attention into a single spot can no longer be simply answered. Partly we can express and develop this argument in the by now familiar modern terms of speed and movement:

> Night City was like a deranged experiment in social Darwinism, designed by a bored researcher who kept one thumb permanently on the fast-forward button. Stop hustling and you sank without a trace, but move a little too swiftly and you'd break the fragile surface tension of the black market; either way, you were gone, with nothing left of you but some vague

> memory ... though heart or lungs or kidneys might survive in the service
> of some stranger with New Yen for the clinic tanks.   (14)

The image here is of a specific 'black-market' economy (the 'New Yen'
has become a common international currency, although the alternative
meaning of 'yen' as a desire or urge cannot be obliterated from the text),
but it recurs in various guises throughout the book. There is no possibility here of stasis or stability, of being 'established' in one place; the necessary trick, the essential internalisation of the trickery, is to understand
the movements, the rhythms, the trajectories of the modern eco-system,
and to align yourself with it; any other route leads towards death. These
rhythms are not set by the human; they are rhythms of the hard drive,
the unseen rhythms which pulse through the machine and which have an
eradicably altering effect on human consciousness. To understand them
is, however, also to conform to them; the future world envisaged by
Gibson, although it overflows with weirdnesses, mutants, 'strangers' in
the strong sense of the term, is essentially a world which enshrines a new
conformity; it is indeed against this that Case himself stands out, rather
as though he is a repetition of the seemingly unending motif in western
culture of the lone individual 'standing out' – in more than one sense of
the term – against an encroaching necessity of conforming to a global
standard, a norm created by power and essential to power's continuance.

It would also be necessary to trace the set of images in this passage
back to much earlier scientific discoveries, for example those of the pio-
neers of nuclear physics. The notion that 'space' (inner or outer) is
mostly empty; the vision of atoms and smaller particles being in constant movement; even the far earlier realisation of the various planetary
movements of the earth and of the consequent loss of hypotheses of stability, be they divine, geographical or merely conventional – all these
among others, it could be said, have served in a historical and intellectual
narrative which has relativised any notion of stasis. What comes instead,
according to the more recent forms of modernity, is the notion that the
world is comprised of a set of 'relative speeds', perhaps of 'gearings',
rather than of specific destinations; where you are going matters less
than the velocity with which you travel, and in *Neuromancer* if you attain
the right speed, then a certain kind of immortality is available for the
taking.

And so we can return here too to the question of geography. This, for
example, is a description of The Sprawl, the city of the future which has
spread up and enveloped the eastern seaboard of the US:

Program a map to display frequency of data exchange, every thousand megabytes a single pixel on a very large screen. Manhattan and Atlanta burn solid white. Then they start to pulse, the rate of traffic threatening to overload your simulation. Your map is about to go nova. Cool it down. Up your scale. Each pixel a million megabytes. At a hundred million megabytes a second, you begin to make out certain blocks in midtown Manhattan, outlines of hundred-year-old industrial parks ringing the old core of Atlanta ...   (57)

Perspective is all. On this map there is no simple geographical certainty based on area, latitude and longitude, distance: instead there is *measurement by power*, a simple expression of the growing truth that geography is itself dictated by power, that what may seem many miles of distance to the traveller by road or rail is virtually instantaneous in terms of corporate communication, and that what shows up, what is visible, to the 'outer' world, whatever that might be, is not a simple map but rather a 'constellation' of light and speed, electricity and motion, the real sources of power which can travel unhindered across boundaries. Deprivation is here figured as being at the mercy of boundaries; freedom is the ability to relegate those boundaries to the back (of the mind, of the planet, of time). No wonder then that one of Case's major characteristics could be so suitably described as paranoia: in this new world there is no longer any real way of knowing where anybody actually is, the individual has been reduced to a node of communication – although the question of Case's paranoia remains in many ways a floating one: there is a sense in which the conspiracies he detects are 'really there', but there is another sense in which we as readers might continue to regard them as the effects, rather than the causes, of a certain derangement which he paradoxically 'embodies' while trying at the same time to shake off the 'embodiedness' which binds him to a world where such conspiracies can matter and have effects.

Although to say 'reduced' is to succumb, of course, to a certain antimodern rhetoric. Alternatively, one could say that the old inhibitors have been removed (what Case is suffering from is an 'endorphin inhibitor', although the meaning of this is that he has become peculiarly, inhumanly, exposed to pain) and that it is now at least theoretically possible to transcend the old boundaries, to move without moving, to occupy different worlds and different spaces at the same time. The downside of this, of course, is that if this is possible for the isolated individual – and Case is above all, and paradoxically, an isolated individual in, or rather outside, the realm of corporate power – then it is infinitely more possible for those who control the means of communication and, above all, the banks of knowledge.

For *Neuromancer* is also a book about knowledge; or perhaps better, about the retrieval of knowledge. The power of the computer, the perhaps diabolical promise of artificial intelligence, does not lie in the size or scope of its memory, significant though this may be; rather it lies in its power to access that memory, to move with correct and ever-improving speed and thus to control arrays of data banks which would otherwise be overwhelming, which would frustrate, disappoint and ultimately defeat us by their sheer scale – which is an inhuman scale, and here we would properly be reminded of the uncanny connection between modernity and the sublime, between *techne* and the perverse will to be overpowered, to surrender in the face of the sheer 'cliffs', as *Neuromancer* has it, of information and data which we would have to 'scale' before we got anywhere near the 'truth', whatever that might turn out to be.

The central struggle in the book, although Case does not appreciate it until near the end, is between two super-computers. They are called Neuromancer and Wintermute, which arguably represent different kinds of memory, different types of access: the former 'new', admittedly, but bound to an old notion of 'romance', from which we might infer a certain reliance on the individual (Neuromancer is perhaps a 'simulation' of the subject as such), the latter suitably silent, fatal, thanatic, representing the death of all we believe we know to be typical of the human, that endless 'winter' in which no life can flourish or survive, a world of cold in which the silent, imperceptible movements of virtual reality can no longer be tracked by anything that lives and moves in order to have its being. In this world, the world of Wintermute, there are no longer any protecting fantasies; the comfort we derive from believing that we have individual agency is no longer available, the memory of subjectivity has become a sad, nostalgic haunting, a whistling from the wings which only serves to remind us how ill equipped we are to go on stage and act the part of a coherent character.

Or we could take another tack, as the text does, and say that in these rival computers we see a glimpse of the ambiguity of the grail of modernity, artificial intelligence. Another site of dialectic in the novel suggests to us the possibility of such artificial intelligences appearing 'in the world' – whatever that would mean, and in *Neuromancer* it is not clear – and indeed hence acquiring the ability to replicate themselves, and the necessity of restricting their powers, the responsibility of the notional regulatory authorities, no doubt by now wildly out of their depth and out of date, represented in the novel by the so-called 'Turing heat', dedicated to policing the world of the AIs but already probably doomed by the inevitable succession of the post-human.

Thus there is a struggle here between different kinds of restriction, and the difficulty of applying or abiding by any of them in a world of constant motion and fluidity. One of the outstanding symbols of this in the novel is the character (if that is the apt word) most frequently known as the 'Dixie Flatline'. The Dixie Flatline is, in some sense, a human being. He even has a name, McCoy Pauley; but McCoy Pauley is actually dead (having previously been brain-dead on three occasions on account of the risks he has taken with computer hacking) and what remains of him is a simulation, a piece of software, bodiless, without needs, but still 'embodying' the apparently matchless and envied computer skills he had when he was alive. We might say that the Dixie Flatline embodies a dream of immortality, a dream of survival. We might indeed further say that the 'dream of the text' is of the Dixie Flatline, of a life which is not a life, of the possibility of emerging into a modern, a purified world freed from the stench of meat; but matters are not so simple. 'I'm not human', says Pauley at one significant point, 'but I *respond* like one'. 'Wait a sec', says Case in reply, 'Are you sentient, or not?' 'Well, it *feels* like I am, kid, but I'm really just a bunch of ROM. It's one of them, ah, philosophical questions, I guess' (158–9), replies Pauley. 'Sometimes you repeat yourself, man', Case suggests some time later, to which the Flatline responds, with bitter irony: 'It's my nature' (160).

All of these terms – 'human', 'sentient', 'nature' – thus take their places within a kind of delirium. What is suggested, what is induced – as it is in other contexts in the novel – is a kind of free fall, and here lies something of the *jouissance* of modernity. We are here in a realm where it would be very difficult to see how any traditional moral or ethical system would operate, because the very unit on which such a system would be based – the autonomous human, or perhaps animal, subject – is in the throes of a crisis of identification. There is sadness here, even despair; but there is also the joy of the mythical high-wire artist, the constant risk of falling off the trapeze, dropping away from the apparent certainties of the world, losing the necessary speed and trajectory to maintain oneself within the illusion of being (albeit in exchange for a different and more lethal, if also more transient, speed); and this is a world in which safety nets are not allowed. In the case of the Dixie Flatline, it would be fair to think of the colloquial phrase 'no one at home'; but in fact the entire novel depicts a radical homelessness, an escape from 'roots' which has ceased to be an escape and has become instead a way of life – albeit mainly for those either privileged or bold enough to pursue it.

Yet here there is a certain circularity, by now familiar to us as we trace the trajectory of modernity, to the logic of escape and transcendence. The power of most of the corporates, for example, is, as it turns out, overshadowed by the greater power of a specific powerful 'family' or 'clan' (albeit most of them are clones) known as the Tessier-Ashpools. Their 'home' terrain (which is, naturally, orbital and therefore freed from earthly restrictions), is the Villa Straylight:

> The Villa Straylight ... is a body grown in upon itself, a Gothic folly. Each space in Straylight is in some way secret, this endless series of chambers linked by passages, by stairways vaulted like intestines, where the eye is trapped in narrow curves, carried past ornate screens, empty alcoves ...   (206)

It is obviously interesting that the Gothic motif, that motif of the 'antique', the relic, occurs here; the major significance, though, is that real power continues to reside in secrecy – indeed, real power in the world of *Neuromancer* has become specifically the power to *buy* secrecy, to buy 'reserve' where there is the constant menace of an unwanted transparency, the *power to hide*. And indeed there are further resonances to this passage; it reads, for example, very like the voice-over on a cardinal earlier modern text, albeit from a different era of modernity – the film *Last Year at Marienbad* (1961) – and like that text it is saturated in an uncanny kind of nostalgia which suffuses us with the past even as it utters the present and, by implication, a thanatic future. It may therefore come as no surprise when it is revealed that it is taken from an essay on semiotics written by a twelve-year-old, which continues in a hallucinatory rhetoric of multiplicity and proliferation:

> The architects of Freeside went to great pains to conceal the fact that the interior of the spindle is arranged with the banal precision of furniture in a hotel room. In Straylight, the hull's inner surface is overgrown with a desperate proliferation of structures, forms flowing, interlocking, rising toward a solid core of microcircuitry, our clan's corporate heart, a cylinder of silicon wormholed with narrow maintenance tunnels, some no wider than a man's hand.   (206)

This 'desperate proliferation of structures' appears to be in some sense a baroque response to the streamlined shapes of the modern, a move which is at once beyond and 'back from' the modern aesthetic. There is also here again a rhetoric of concealment, but a concealment, a secrecy which is forced to move into deeper and deeper configurations as the logic of information exchange penetrates virtually all reserves, prevents all but the richest and most powerful from entertaining the illusion of privacy. We can see here too an opposition between images of the human brain: the problem of how to describe complexity of structure alongside streamlining of performance, the further question of what it is that modernity is doing to the brain as it encourages it in its continual attempts to become 'one with the machine'.

There is here, then, a 'logic of penetration'; and it is further alluded to in the form of one of the most powerful pieces of software mentioned in the text, known as the Kuang, which 'hacks' into other systems, but does it in a 'different' way, as explained by the Flatline (the 'ice' is the rival system's security array):

> This ain't bore and inject, it's more like we interface with the ice so slow, the ice doesn't feel it. The face of the Kuang logics kinda sleazes up to the target and mutates, so it gets to be exactly like the ice fabric. Then we lock on and the main programs cut in, start talking circles 'round the logics in the ice. We go Siamese twin on 'em before they even get restless.   (201–2)

Many of the dreams of modernity intersect here. In this world, there is no need for the crudity of penetration, and obviously one might consider this under the headings of sexuality and reproduction as well as in terms of a particular kind of knowledge transfer. This dream of knowledge transfer happens unknown, silently, without any need for a show of force or violence; it is possible to find out what is happening without betraying one's own presence – the dream of cryptographers from time immemorial, but brought to a specific focus in the Second World War. There are also issues here about simulation, about who knows whom or what knows what; and about whether and how one could ever distinguish between the 'invasive force' and the 'ice' which it so perfectly replicates, that perfect ice, that perfect cold, which is also in some sense a dream of the future: a 'winter' which is 'mute', and which can only be held at bay, according to one reading of the novel's central symbolism, by a revival of 'romance' in some shape or form.

And thus back to some of the central paradoxes of modernity. What the modern appears to beckon us to is a world of transparency, a world where the ancient paraphernalia of tradition and ceremony have been sent back to the cluttered Victorian parlours which provide one of their central images. But at the same time there is an anxiety that this transparency may in fact represent a further 'withdrawal'; that wealth may remain at least as able to secure its own privileges under this new dispensation as it has in the past. As power and speed become indivisible, the ability to run at the world's speed becomes the inalienable property of a silent few.

One of the constant motifs of *Neuromancer* is the 'alibi', and this is a term which has a continuous reverberation through the concepts of modernity. In *Neuromancer* it has, of course, a literal force: nobody is ever entirely in one place at any one time, or if one is then it is a mark of a lack of technological sophistication. The power granted by the machine, by the prosthesis, is the power never to be identified as tied to a specific physical location; the danger thus inherent is the ancient mythical one, that if one severs one's connection to the 'meat', leaves one's physical body behind, then it may prove impossible to re-establish contact, one may be forever marooned in virtual space.

This, of course, is also an element of *jouissance*; riding the trajectories and 'power-lines' of the world is a mode of transcendence, as it is also a mode of escape. It is also a dream of leaving behind the parental, the problem of origin. The artificial intelligences in *Neuromancer*, as elsewhere in cyber-fiction, take their bearings from a cleansed world; but they are simultaneously contaminated by a certain haunting, the phantomatic effect of an ingrained memory of what it might have been like to have been human. This, cyber-fiction suggests, is now one of the prevailing modes of our consciousness: where traditional systems of thought might have operated along a linear trajectory, through maturation into adulthood, modernity comes to subvert those established schemes and to claim that the world is ours for the taking.

We could see this as an alibi for progression: that where modernity claims to speed us through developmental phases, what it succeeds in doing is disallowing us from leaving a fixed point. The vast engine which powers modernisation runs without cogs: it does not propel the citizen into a future world, instead it keeps him or her in place – at the controls, for instance, of a simulation machine, or ever waiting for the pinball machine to pay out – while we experience the present and the future through dark glasses, the shades Molly in *Neuromancer* has had implanted as a substitute for, or an enhancement of, or a darkening of, her merely – pathetically – physical vision.

But this too is the promise of modernity: to cannibalise the past and to use its shards and fragments as a take-off point for an ever-new voyage into the future. The goal would be an intelligence which would be wholly artificial, although the only difference between this and the way in which we more usually comprehend 'intelligence' – apart from the crucial one of scale – would be that it does not incorporate an emotional dimension. Thus artificial intelligence emerges as a dream of being free from bias, being *exempted* from the complicated world of hopes and fears, loves and hatreds – free indeed, as the Tessier-Ashpools are, from any concern with life 'down below' – down below on the planet, down below the gleaming surface of things, down below in the sexual sense, through the replacement of the messy fluids of reproduction by the techno-perfection of cloning. Thus we may see here the delineation of a value shift: a shift from depth to surface, from the inside to the outside.

The analytical psychologist James Hillman has a great deal to say about 'myths of depth', from the legendry of Hades to current dealings with the dark, the gloomy, the sequestered, and his main point is that it may be necessary to continue to address these hidden places of the heart; but the question remains – and it is one of the utmost importance – as to the extent to which modernity represents an attempt to perform just such an address, such a dealing, or to represent an evasion, a denial, of such needs. What, at base, is the human? In the end, as it were,

> The music woke him, and at first it might have been the beat of his own heart. He sat up beside her, pulling his jacket over his shoulders, in the predawn chill, gray light from the doorway and the fire long dead.
>
> His vision crawled with ghost hieroglyphs, translucent lines of symbols arranging themselves against the neutral backdrop of the bunker wall. He looked at the backs of his hands, saw faint neon molecules crawling beneath the skin, ordered by the unknowable code. He raised his right hand and moved it experimentally. It left a faint, fading trail of strobed afterimages. (286)

Everything here is 'becoming'; there is no longer any easy acceptance of what it might be like to be human. Neither is there an easy separation between the discoveries of science and the ways in which we might wish to continue to inhabit our own bodies. Alongside the evasions of modernity, there is also a strenuousness, a realisation that it will only be for so long that we can continue in our fictions of practically ignoring some of science's more devastating proclamations in the name of a pragmatic dedication to historical definitions. The body is not stable; it is an *effect*, and the cause is held somewhere else, in the 'ghost hieroglyphs', above – and beyond – all in the 'unknowable code'. Current modernity has invested a great deal of its faith in the final working out of genetic code; this would then be a knowledge which supersedes – and in some other sense also precedes – all other types of knowledge, a knowledge to which all other knowledges have been mere precursors, estimations in the dark.

And what can be fully decoded can also be deconstructed and reconstructed, in forms of difference; the malleability of the body and of the mind which we have seen earlier in such texts as *The Island of Doctor Moreau* is here with us again. We do not inhabit a stable space or time; we are a set of nodes, a set of points, which represent the intersection between different physical and mental spaces. The 'difference' – and the problem – is that while that may always have been the case, now we know it, we are aware of it, we can no longer reside in old holistic fictions. We need, therefore, a new set of narratives, narratives which will relativise the human, which will see our human-ness not as a trend, however difficult and devious, towards some kind of human sublation but rather as one which brings us ever closer to the supersession of the human, to a world in which it will be revealed that our narratives have been fundamentally wrong all along, because we have persisted, like frightened children, in asserting our own centrality while meanwhile the great machines of the universe have been telling a quite different, silent, powerful story, in which we have merely been bit-part players, destined in the end to abandon our hold on that centrality and available to be sent off stage when the 'real' characters, in whatever inhuman glory they may reside, finally arrive.

28 M. John Harrison, *Light*

M. John Harrison may be best known for his short series of fantasies based in the realm called Viriconium, in which characters move in the shadows of a Gothicised city where every place name – Margarethestrasse, the Luitpold Café, Montrouge – and the name of every character – Ashlyme, the Grand Cairo, Paulinus Rack – appears to come from a different geographical and/or literary background. Divided between the High City and the Low City, Viriconium is a place of doubts and uncertainties, crumbling mansions and pointless journeys, where nothing can ever be seen clearly and all is exhaustion and etiolation. A cross between Gormenghast and Edinburgh on a rainy evening, Viriconium is a place with no boundaries, no straight lines; everything flickers and warps in an uncertain vision.

Or he may be well known, if to a rather more select few, as the author of a remarkable book which takes him back to an older heritage, *Climbers* (1989). *Climbers* is, as far as I am aware, the only example of a sub-genre which can only be called the 'Gothic of rock-climbing'. It is billed as a novel, and perhaps it is; but it reads more as a collection of numinous experiences amid the high crags, held together only by the power of the rocks and fells themselves, a book which effects a remarkable *rapprochement* between the hard detail of the sheer difficulty of scrambling up cliffs and the haunted feelings which accompany this savage way of relating to the 'natural'. In the end, a kind of bridge is thrown between the resistant material and what Harrison will later, and in more modernistic terms, refer to as the 'wetware', the organic, in this case – but not always elsewhere – the human.

Or, to follow that thread for a moment, he may be best known as a modern science fiction writer, the best of science fiction writers, according to Iain M. Banks. Probably his most well-known work in this genre is *The Centauri Device*, published in 1974; but it is his 2002 novel, *Light*, which solicits our attention here as an emblematic text of modernity. It would be a difficult novel to summarise, but it is necessary to at least try to offer a reading; because it is, in part, a novel about reading under modern conditions, as it is also a novel about light, but a light which may not illuminate, may have little to do with a rhetoric of 'enlightenment', but which may instead attract by its wildness, its variety, its resistance to any traditionally known form of life.

Michael Kearney is a scientist who is searching quantum theory for answers to problems about something called 'Kielpinski space', K-space, in a time which sufficiently resembles the present. Seria Mau Genlicher, in the year 2400, is the captain of a K-ship; becoming a captain has meant that she has had to renounce, or at least atrophy, her body and become effectively a part of the spaceship, a ship which is effectively run by the 'shadow operators', ghostly beings whose reality status never becomes entirely clear, and also by a computer known only as 'the mathematics'. The third central character, whom we originally know as 'Chinese Ed' but whose name turns out to be Ed Chianese, is a twink, a man addicted to 'tanks', which are essentially virtual reality scenarios, within one of which we first, to our readerly confusion, find him.

Michael Kearney could be summed up as a man with a number of problems. One of them is with penetrative sex, which he finds impossible for a number of hinted and complicated reasons. Another is that he is pursued by, or perhaps haunted by, a being known – to him at least – as the Shrander, a macabre figure who appears before him wherever he goes, and from whom he has, for no apparent reason, stolen a set of dice. Seria Mau also has problems which require resolution; the main one is that, having renounced her body, having apparently transcended the organic, she is continually confronted by temptations to return to it. Another problem she has is that she is in touch with Uncle Zip the Tailor:

> Uncle Zip the tailor ran his operation from a parlour on Henry Street down by the Harbour Mole. He had been famous in his day, his cuts franchised in every major port. A fat, driven man with protuberant china-blue eyes, inflated white cheeks, rosebud lips, and a belly as hard as a wax pear, he claimed to have discovered the origins of life, coded in fossil proteins on a system in Radio Bay less than twenty lights from the Tract itself. Whether you believed that depended on how well you knew him. He had shipped out talented and come back focused, that was certain. Whatever codes he found, they made him only as rich as any other good tailor: Uncle Zip wanted nothing more, or so he said. He and his family lived above the

> business, in some ceremony. His wife wore bright red flamenco skirts. All
> his children were girls.   (Harrison 2002, 31)

There are a number of further problems here. The mentions of the
Harbour Mole and Radio Bay, to take but two examples, are not as cosy
as they might seem; they are instead non-terrestrial. We are talking here,
as elsewhere, about 'locations' on a galactic scale, even if they are modelled on a more familiar type and nomenclature of territory. And being a
tailor in 2400 AD has nothing to do with cloth, and nor do 'cuts'; what
Uncle Zip does is virtual genetic engineering, producing bodies and
states of mind to go with them to order – which also means that although
Uncle Zip chooses to project himself (we are not talking here about real
people meeting each other, that would be a rare event indeed in the
modern world of *Light*) as a cross between a fairground accordion player
and W.C. Fields, this has nothing to do with any 'reality' we might
associate with Uncle Zip, because there is none to be had. The fact that
he similarly chooses to project himself as a man with a family is his,
unverifiable, choice, another way of constructing a virtual image in
cyberspace.

A further problem Seria Mau has, which constitutes the cornerstone of
the text, is that Uncle Zip has sold her a 'package', which does not appear
to 'work', whatever that might mean – a package of 'code', because code,
in 2400, is virtual currency, the most valuable commodity, a commodity
for which people dare and die. This package, however – whose physical
identity we never see, because Uncle Zip has tailored it in accordance
with the aesthetics of his own chosen world – seems to be on a continual
loop; all it does when opened is to ask for one 'Dr Haends', who appears
to choose to present himself in virtual space as a top-hatted conjuror.

The person who runs the tank farm frequented by Chinese Ed is one
Tig Vesicle, and he is, in terms by now familiar all through modernity, a
'New Man', but a 'new man' in the world of *Light* is not what you might
think:

> Drawn by the radio and TV ads of the twentieth century, which had
> reached them as faltering wisps and cobwebs of communication (yet still
> full of a mysterious, alien vitality), the New Men had invaded Earth in the
> middle 2100s. They were bipedal, humanoid – if you stretched a point –
> and uniformly tall and white-skinned, each with a shock of flaming red
> hair. They were indistinguishable from some kinds of Irish junkies. ... To
> start with, they had great optimism and energy. Everything about Earth

amazed them. They took over and, in an amiable, paternalistic way, mis-
understood and mismanaged everything. It appeared to be an attempt to
understand the human race in terms of a 1982 Coke ad. They produced
food no one could eat, outlawed politics in favour of the kind of bureaucracy you find in the subsidised arts, and buried enormous machinery in
the subcrust which eventually killed millions. After that, they seemed to
fade away in embarrassment, taking to drugs, pop music and the twink-
tank which was then an exciting if less than reliable new entertainment
technology. (36)

So: in the world of *Light*, everything is tangential to what it seems, the
conventionalities of origins are turned on their heads. Ed Chianese's
world is recognisable in relation to our own, but the question of how
things got to be that way receives a different answer, an answer which
appears to display the fluidity of modernity while at the same time
rejecting its hold on location and space.

Back in the present day, Kearney's paranoia is developing apace. He
continually uses the dice he stole from the Shrander to plan out his
actions, but since the symbols on them are incomprehensible it is hard
for him, or for us as readers, to know what meaning this has. And he has
another problem: a surprising number of the actions he consequently
undertakes consists of killing people, especially women. But what is most
puzzling to Kearney, who appears to have become inured to his status as
a serial killer, is that whatever he does he never gets caught, even when
he drowns in the Thames the boss of a corporation which is trying to
take over the IT company which he runs with his friend Brian Tate.
Exactly what Kearney and Tate are trying to work out in the endless
hours they spend on their machines is never made entirely clear, but certainly it becomes an obsession with developing a new mode of perception and understanding, and one which costs Tate his life.

We are not very far into the book yet, but perhaps it is time to pause for
a little thought. What *Light* appears to be offering us is a world of modernity which consists of disconnected bits and pieces, disconnected through
space and time; most of these shreds (and perhaps the Shrander is a thing
of 'shreds') of evidence belong in a structure which is, in the obvious
poststructuralist sense, 'postal' – one which is 'after' this or that discovery,
most of which are 'relativising' discoveries about humanity, decentring
acts which relegate the most common features of the human, whether it
be physicality or causation, to a more primitive world which has already
been, in some sense, surpassed. And so, perhaps inevitably and not for

the first time in the history of modernity, the question becomes one of whether these bits and pieces, these 'fragments' shored against an imminent dissolution of all order, can be made to yield a pattern.

Kearney, certainly, is seeking for a pattern, searching through wave after wave of data, some of which he summons up, some of which appear to be simply integral to the techno-world he largely inhabits. This might be a mathematical pattern of the universe; but in his case it is perhaps also a simpler one. He is looking, he says, for some way of breaking down the barrier 'between me and me'. If there is a barrier to be broken down, we might say, then there must be a difference between these two 'me's', these two selves, and hence a way of sealing a gap between present and future, and perhaps there is, but if this is so then the trajectory to be undertaken is not an obvious one. Rather it is a question of perspective. One could put it like this. Kearney has been, from his childhood, 'entranced' with the possibilities of science, and particularly with the power of pure number, with the way in which the apparently solid arrangement of subjects and events can be alternatively seen as a side-effect of a different kind of patterning. We might consider, for example, this moment of interaction between a computer programme and a 'real' cat (if anything in *Light* is 'real'):

> A new programme launched. There was a flash of arctic-blue light; the female oriental stiffened on Kearney's shoulder; then the earlier test result bloomed in front of them as the Beowulf system began faking space. This time the illusion was much slower and clearer. Something gathered itself up behind the code somewhere and shot out across the screen. A million coloured lights, boiling and sweeping about like a shoal of startled fish. The white cat was off Kearney's shoulder in a second, hurling herself at the display so hard it rocked. For fully half a minute the fractals poured and jerked across the screen. Then everything stopped. The cat, her coat reflecting ice-blue in the wash of the display, danced about for half a minute more, then lost interest and began to wash herself affectedly. (119)

Clearly here the boundary between two worlds is going down; but what might interest us most about this passage (although such an interest might always be eccentric to the main 'plot', if indeed there can be a plot, the simplicity of an accepted narrative in this alternative world where nothing is exactly what it seems) is the relation between the two uses of the word 'wash' towards the end, the 'wash' of the display and the cat 'washing itself'. *Light*, as a novel, is lost in this world of duplication, where each attempt to discover a metaphor is instantly drowned in immediacy, where every attempt at intimacy is immediately frustrated by a recession into metaphor. This, then, would also be a description of a certain moment of modernity, where all is 'becoming', but where also the very process of metaphorisation is consequently under temporary erasure, where the future implodes back into the present with potentially devastating results.

And this, perhaps, is one of the roots of Kearney's difficulties, if one can refer to a panoply of problems which include an addiction to random killing as a 'difficulty': that he has, as he claims, seen a glimpse of the boiling arithmetical heart of the universe, and beside this the relatively antique 'reality' of meat and bone appear merely as a 'wash of colour' across an otherwise colourless universe. History, then – personal, cultural or cosmic history – becomes merely an effect of the desire for pattern; what would it take, indeed, if we revert to an earlier conception of the modern, to 'disturb the universe'? What would it take, to take up the obvious sexualisation of the metaphor, to 'penetrate the secret', and what terrors might hold us back from the attempt?

But the paradox here is that as Kearney continues on his murderous quest, he becomes precisely the victim of the Shrander, who might appear, at least at first, to be a principle of disorder; or might, obviously, be a psychotic projection from Kearney himself. The Shrander is described as resembling a 'horse's skull' – not, Kearney is careful to say, a horse's head, but a skull, perhaps with 'shreds' of flesh hanging from it, but at any rate a violent image of dry jaws snapping (which may, at another level, be a rather obvious image of the unstated castration anxiety which prevents him from penetration or, at a more cultural level, of the fear of what might happen if we were to penetrate, perhaps prematurely, too far into the future). As Kearney moves around London and the US, in flight from the Shrander, he also knows that it is to the Shrander that he will and must return, because the Shrander is the missing link, the image for all that is lacking in the arrays on the screen but perhaps also the point at which the cat's reaction to a virtual shoal of fish will be demonstrated to have some connection, the point at which his physical obsessions and ritualisms will prove to correlate with the on-screen patterns, the mathematical models which simultaneously represent and distort a presumably underlying reality.

It could, of course, be at this point that one might think again about effecting the elusive connection with the Gothic, for there is an underlying hypothesis here of distortion, along with a desire for the, perhaps psychotic, perception of an underlying order. Another such connection might be through the 'shadow operators'. Nobody knows where these beings have come from; nobody has any idea of the 'origin' of those who actually take care of the menial tasks which, among other things, allow spaceships, however sophisticated, to fly. But what is certain is that the shadow operators are, in some sense, more 'human' than the other inhabitants of the spacecraft of Seria Mau's future world; when she acts, for instance, to kill a suspect human cargo she has taken on, it is not she but the operators who enact the possibility of guilt, whispering about her cruelty in corners, expressing inarticulate grief, mourning for all that has been lost in a way that Seria Mau herself, who is merely following her childhood dream of being a K-ship captain, is unable to. The 'shadow operators' are a kind of Greek chorus, mopping and mowing over man's inhumanity to man; bodiless, unrestricted by physical constraints, they nevertheless remain as a repository of those qualities of the 'human' which humanity, especially in the shape of the cyborg which is Seria Mau and the K-ship, is gradually shedding. They 'represent' the 'escape' of modernity, but they do so by a recourse to a world of the ancient, by a 'reincorporation' of superseded emotions, even passions, into a 'ship' – a vehicle in the broader sense – from which all such passions have been supposedly excluded – as well as being in partial control of the ship, they are also in some sense stowaways, which suggests all manner of thoughts as to what it might be like to be a stowaway on a ship which is taking up a trajectory towards the future.

Within all this there lurks the mystery of a deep-space terrain known as the Kefahuchi Tract, and further mysteries linked to it – for example, the mystery of non-contradiction:

> ... the boys from Earth were awed despite themselves by the things they found there: but worse, their science was in a mess. Every race they met on their way through the Core had a star drive based on a different theory. All those theories worked, even when they ruled out one another's basic assumptions. You could travel between the stars, it began to seem, by assuming anything. If your theory gave you a foamy space to work with – if you had to catch a wave – that didn't preclude some other engine, running on a perfectly smooth Einsteinian surface, from surfing the same tranche of empty space.   (139–40)

The Kefahuchi Tract figures as another space which cannot be penetrated, a riddle which cannot be solved, a place both modern and beyond the modern where the mathematics run out. This, of course, provides a kind of ironic solution to the old science fiction problem of the 'novum', the inexplicable 'new thing' that has to be added to current scientific assumptions in order to provide a ground for fiction and a trajectory into the future. At the literary level, we could say that the universe of *Light* is constructed in such a way that *every* 'novum' works, and thus the problem is removed to a further level: *why* do they work, and what might this tell us about the relations between mind and matter and about what it might mean to inhabit a truly modern space in which the old oppositions are cancelled out, in which the grit has been removed from the machine by an ultimate lubricant, the dream of modern engineers, and indeed architects, the world over? But there is, naturally, also the direct opposite of this ultimately pliable universe in the shape of the Tract, which 'contains' what is referred to as an 'uncontained singularity' which resists interpretation and exploration.

And meanwhile, in following the lure of these two stories, what of the third story, the story of Chinese Ed? Ed is living with a physically mutated rickshaw-girl the size of a small horse and has taken on a job as a prophet in the Circus of Pathet Lao, a circus run by an algorithm which most often presents in the form of an oriental-looking woman called Sandra Shen (another partial anagram of the Shrander). The difficulty here is that although he apparently prophesies, he never remembers doing so. Having previously been an explorer of outer space, a cowboy 'entradista' – before succumbing to the twink addiction, that is – he is now gradually turned into an explorer of some kind of inner space. Among the exhibits in the circus is a moving hologram of Michael Kearney and Brian Tate, at their computer console all those hundreds of years ago, and so some bits and pieces of the puzzle begin to fall into place.

But the underlying problem here remains: what is physical and what is not? Consider, for example, a specific 'planet' – if that is what it is:

> Though a little large, it was strictly a moon. Tidal heating in its core had raised the surface to temperatures resembling Earth's, generating also a loose and wispy atmosphere which featured the gases that support life. Against a curious greenish arc of sky ballooned the salmon-pink bulk of the nearest gas giant. A single fractal structure occupied the entire planet. Though from a distance this resembled vegetation, it was neither alive nor dead. It was just some mad old algorithm which, vented from a passing navigational system, had run wild then run out of raw materials. The effect was of endless peacock feathers a million different sizes: a clever drawing

ramped into three dimensions. Mathematics trying to save itself from death. (226-7)

Here again the issue is one of perspective. What might look like organic life seen from one position is merely an effect of 'the mathematics': below the apparent surfaces there beats another, entirely different kind of 'life', if even 'life' is the right word. Hence, in another sense, the specifically modern version of the age-old need to find pattern: but in *Light* most of the characters are at least as frightened by the possibility of pattern as they are attracted to it. When Chinese Ed performs his fortune-telling tricks in front of a paying audience, it seems to them as though he is predicting the future; but what he himself sees, or at least what he remembers when he returns from the blankness which attends his prophecies, is a series of trips back into what might have been his own past – not that he is ever quite certain about that either.

Cause and effect again:

> The Kefahuchi Tract almost filled the sky, always growing as you watched, like the genie raging up out of the bottle, yet somehow never larger. It was a singularity without an event horizon, they said, the wrong physics loose in the universe. Anything could come out of there, but nothing ever did. Unless of course, Ed thought, what we have out here is already a result of what happens in there ... (237)

This, perhaps, is one of the crucial conundrums of *Light*. Somewhere in the universe, as we continually expand our modern understanding of it, it is possible that there might be a 'key to all mysteries'; but if you are the experiment in which the possibilities of an answer are being tested, then it becomes impossible to find the way to an answer. Here we at least see, writ large, a modern, or perhaps postmodern, trope: one might see the Kefahuchi Tract precisely as the end, or beginning, of all master-narratives; in which case the entradistas, the mad space cowboys who dive time and time again into the Tract, never to return, are not looking for an answer. True to their dislocation, their post-teenage sense of 'throwing it all away', they are looking instead for the final way of avoiding having to find an answer. Advance and denial are completely inter-locked; the very process of searching for knowledge is entwined at its root with a sense that that knowledge is irretrievable. 'Why', as Heidegger put it, 'is there something instead of nothing?' But here the twist goes a little further, because it is not clear in what sense there *is* anything at all: all is simulacrum, a world where anything apparently scientific or technological in which you believe for long enough may become operational, but only because the matter with which it is dealing is ephemeral, transitional, evanescent, the by-product of an inexplicable mathematics which is both the source and the carapace of all secrets.

Yet there is still, perhaps unsurprisingly, choice somewhere within these processes. Seria Mau chose to become a K-ship pilot (which is, in effect, to become a K-ship itself). The process is described in nauseating detail, of which this is a small part:

> By then they have broken most of your bones, and taken some of your organs out: you are blind and deaf, and all you are aware of is a kind of nauseous surf rolling through you forever. They have cut into your neocortex so that it will accept the software bridge known ironically as 'the Einstein Cross' from the shape you see the first time you use it. You are no longer alone. You will soon be able to consciously process billions of billions of bits per second; but you will never walk again. You will never laugh or touch someone or be touched, fuck or be fucked. You will never do anything for yourself again. You will never even shit for yourself again. You have signed up. It comes to you for an instant that you were able to choose this but that you will never, ever, ever be able to unchoose it.   (259)

Perhaps the closest thing to a key to this process would be in the phrase 'You are no longer alone'. This has, at one level, to do with the past personal disasters which Seria Mau, like Chinese Ed, has suffered (and whether they are, or have been in some other space and time, brother and sister is a suggestion which is never clearly followed through); but it has more to do with a question about the price which needs to be paid in order to be 'hooked up' to a thoroughly modern perception of the 'real' processes of the universe. In order, one might say, truly to understand 'the story', whatever the story might be, it is necessary to be dehumanised (or at least partly so, and it is because this dehumanisation is only partial that Seria Mau, lying or thrashing in her tank of fluids, encounters such difficulties); and here one might think of a whole theory of reading, and wonder what it is within the modern subject that truly engages with the text. For *Light* is certainly about trying to engage with the 'text' of the universe, and about the sacrifices which might have to be made in order to achieve this goal; one question about Seria Mau in particular, who has had to experience, if briefly, the symptoms of MS, lupus and schizophrenia as part of the process of her remaking, is whether the remnant of her that continues in physical existence is in any verifiable sense sane at all.

One of the features that does remain here, however, is the 'remains' of the human voice. Time and time again, amid the ruinous collisions of the human and the not-human, there is phraseology reminiscent of the cheapest of thrillers; but of course in the world of *Light* there are multiple explanations of this. There are, for example, the 'cultivars': beings, possibly human in the remotest of senses, who have exchanged their bodies – or rather, had their bodies 'tailored', often by Uncle Zip, the best of them all – for bodies drawn from late twentieth-century B-movies; what they enjoy is risk and death, while knowing all the time that the kind of death which their virtually engineered bodies continually encounter will not be permanent, that it will simply mark off a point in the progression of lives which have gone beyond the human, perhaps even beyond time – not that this stops them from talking in gangster clichés, or from enjoying themselves with archaic flick-knives, guns drawn from ancient US survival manuals, drugs which are primitive compared with the *other* 'one-shot' drugs which are continually remaking them into modern shapes of narcissistic desire.

Another way of looking at the key to all this is in terms of excess. The Shrander's final vision to Kearney is of a universe where there is always more, but it is ambiguous, for the 'more' at stake is, in a sense, more of the same: lights within lights, tears within tears, all perfectly shaped to match the level above them. The elements of the 'code' manifest themselves as silver motes, continually extruding from the eyes, continually calling into question the reality of the higher forms which are comprised of them. There is a show of beauty, the peacock's feathers again, but a remaining question about variety. Similarly, the vision vouchsafed to Seria Mau when she finally decides to take back something approximating her human form, is of a magic-shop window:

> All around ... were stacked the things she had seen in her dreams – retro things, conjuror's things, children's things. Ruby-coloured plastic lips. Feathers dyed bright orange and green. Bundles of silk scarves that would go into the top hat and hop out as live white pigeons. There were hanks of fake liquorice. There was a valentine's heart which lit itself up by means of loving diodes within. There were 'X-Ray Specs' and elevator shoes, trick eternity rings and handcuffs you couldn't take off. There were all the things you wanted when you were a child, when it seemed there would always be more in the world and always more after that.   (303)

Seria Mau is introduced to this apocalypse by the character who has haunted her dreams, the top-hatted conjuror who turns out to be, at one level at least, the very Dr Haends who has been summoned by the mysterious box which Uncle Zip has sold her; one of the main tropes here is about 'what comes in and what comes out', and again we are on the terrain of the possibility – or impossibility – of some kind of hidden generator at the heart of the universe which is responsible for producing the world of modern effects and simulacra amid which we ordinarily live our lives, a structure of structures whose purposes and designs cannot be questioned. Perhaps penetrating the Kefahuchi Tract will provide these answers; perhaps, on the other hand, it is there precisely to provide a continual reminder of the impossibility, despite all technological development, of seeking answers.

We can return to the term 'wetware'; to peacock feathers and tears. At the end of the day (which in the case of the ending of the text of *Light* will also be termed 'The Beginning') there is still a faint possibility that all this has been a trip into sentimentality – or, perhaps even more disarmingly, an exercise in psychotherapy disguised as a trip through unknown galaxies. And so back again to the question of the humanity, or otherwise, of the modern reader. What do we become as we read? What *are* we as we read? Which part of our unassimilable selves, the 'perpetual star, multifoliate rose', is deployed as we perform mind-numbing travels to distant worlds which are, in any case, not *there* at all?

The guides here, it turns out, have all been the same: the Shrander, Dr Haends, Sandra Shen. Almost-anagrams: near misses in the attempt to find order in the world. And as the conclusion nears, so does the increasingly obvious denouement, finally imparted to Ed as he stands alone on a distant asteroid – or perhaps only the semblance of one – with the Shrander:

> ... we built you, Ed. We built you from the amino acids up. We made a guess at what we didn't have, and we built your ancestors to evolve into what we couldn't be. It was a long-term project, as long-term as anything here on the Beach. OK, maybe not as visible as some of this solar engineering stuff. But, you know, did any of that actually *work*? Look around you; I'd say it didn't. We thought our investment had a chance, Ed. It was low-end and elegant both at the same time; even more interesting, we gave the universe a hand in it and left some things to chance. All this time I was watching over it. (315–16)

The Shrander is the last of her race, she is the failure of the organic to keep pace with the evolution of modernity; the final throw of a species that tried to penetrate the mystery of the Kefahuchi Tract and failed, deciding instead to entrust the unlocking of the secret to its own creation, the human race, a further projection of the techno-modern which might have a chance where others have, bitterly, failed. But in the end although Ed, the entradista, the daredevil, the gambler, takes Seria Mau's K-ship into the Tract, still nothing comes back. Reading ends; the act of interpretation ends; nothing is certain – not even the Shrander's dice, which were, she says, old even when her ancient race found them, and whose meaning they too never discovered.

And what, in all this, of Uncle Zip the Tailor? Uncle Zip is an emblem of modernity; he can remake anything, even if he cannot explain its antecedents. Long years ago, it turns out, he too was an entradista, searching for fragments of the code in distant corners of the universe – including, of course, the strange box which absorbs Seria Mau's attention. But, in a kind of parody of the Shrander, he has turned to producing clones to do his work for him. It does turn out, however, that it is he who has been trying to find 'the solution', perhaps the Shrander's most advanced product; but this does not save him from being blown apart in an inevitable cataclysm. This may be because Uncle Zip is also a figure for corporate greed: his motivations are not really to do with knowledge, with penetrating the arcane, but rather with the accumulation of wealth, security, exemption, the final removal of his physical self from the world.

How, then, might we summarise modernity from the viewpoint of *Light*? First, of course, there is the matter of the title. The irony contained within it is multiple. The 'enlightenment' we seek in the text is never delivered: although to an extent there is plot resolution, as the Shrander reveals that she has been constantly intervening in human history in order to maximise our chances of discovering the secret, there is no light shed on the endless 'lights' of the Kefahuchi Tract. It remains as goal, as destination, as the problem which dwarfs all others, even as the shape of the notion of 'problem' itself, in both mathematical and philosophical senses, continues to elude our framing of the concept of 'solution'. It is not clear what would happen were 'the problem' to be solved; the Tract is ringed with the rusting hulks of spaceships, deep-space scientific stations, manufactured planets and suns, all parts of attempts to 'solve the problem'. Humanity understands none of them, cannot work out what inconceivably ancient races built or ran them; they are now used only for 'mining', for salvaging some of the rare metals and complex techno-structures which can be found in them. There is no light to be found here, no hope of a modernistic transcendence.

Second, there is the whole question of science itself. Where it might be conventional to regard science as an accretive process, *Light* suggests a world in which a certain barrier has been broken down. It is no longer a matter of explaining the universe; it is a matter of explaining the notion of explanation. The universe is not simply an entity which lies inertly around; instead it is an effect, a product, a cover-story. If you listen very closely to the planets or the asteroids, what you hear is not the organic, or even the inorganic, processes of matter; what you hear is the song of the code, the unending voice of the most basic units of all, and that underlying and perhaps meaningless song signifies the end of all possibility of 'enlightening' meaning.

Third, we might point to the radical possibilities of dehumanisation with which Harrison deals. Seria Mau has been connected up to a 'bridge'; in that process she has lost most of her physical body, entered into a 'new' relation as part of – and simultaneously the whole of – a cyborg. But, interestingly, this process has not destroyed or removed her emotions: she still feels anger, impatience, incredulity, but her only way of acting upon these emotions is through prosthesis. The principal prosthesis here is the 'mathematics': calm, dispassionate, an almost Jeeves-like figure (although, of course, without a physical manifestation since it/he consists of billions of bytes of memory), he offers all that is alternative and at the same time complementary to Seria Mau.

And this naturally brings up again the question within modernity of memory itself. Michael Kearney, Ed Chianese, Seria Mau all have memories: but they can only access them in dream-states or their equivalent. Just as they continually adjust to the demands of 'modern living', they are continually haunted by the past, but they can make little sense of these memories. It is not as though such memories are their own; rather, that one of the forces which operates on them (in some cases all too literally) is a 'plane of memory' which can no longer be in any sense regarded as individual. Just as Seria Mau lives her life flooded in her tank of hormones and drugs, so memory is an all-encompassing medium; it is larger, deeper, than our selves, and the small portions of ourselves with which we think and act, as in classic Freudian theory, are adrift on this vast sea which is, of course, also imaged in deep space itself.

Above all, perhaps, there is a dealing with risk. Seria Mau finally proves herself incapable of risk; she needs in the end to return to at least a semblance of human shape, to revert to a time before modernity's conjuror-like dealings with human form. Similarly Kearney, many centuries before, in the end proved himself incapable of completing the work he started, as the Shrander sadly remarks as she shows Ed his remains. It is left for Ed, the ultimate figure of risk, to take over where the others failed and to attempt the final journey through the wormhole and into the heart of the Tract, because for him life has always been risk – either that, or the relapse from risk represented in the addiction to fantasy represented in the figure of the twink, doubled images of the relation between modernity and the human endeavour, between adventure and addiction.

One could therefore see a very traditional plot structure gleaming through the hi-tech surface of *Light*: the old science fiction assumption that what the human race has to contribute to the universe is the taking of risk, an inexplicable compulsion to find out, as it were, what is round the next corner. But, in a further twist, in order to get there Ed has to undergo the K-ship process himself, to reduce his humanity down to what Agamben might call 'bare life', strip himself of inessentials and enter into a final compact with the machine. And if Ed were ever to discover the secret, a possibility which seems highly unlikely at the 'ending' of the text, a further question would remain: who, or what, now is it that *has* made the discovery?

A modern reliance on prosthesis, then, is everywhere; in the case of Uncle Zip, there is nothing left at all but prosthesis, no reliable human shape, no verifiable account of causes and effects, only the trading in an infinitely malleable universe within which desires are granted and die nightly; a world which curiously mingles the modern and the Gothic and in which acceptable subjectivity counts for nothing, and the only beings that hold the secret to themselves are, as we might now expect from the complications and pleasures of modernity, the 'shadow operators'. What *Light* comes to remind us of us is, indeed, the dialectic of light and shadow, the question of what happens, as we emerge into the light, to the shadows we leave behind, and of whether what we perceive under the regime of light has any greater – or indeed lesser – validity than the realm of shadow with which we prefer not to engage – perhaps to our disadvantage, perhaps, indeed, to our terror as the shadow masses behind the realm of light.

Conclusion

By way of a polemical conclusion, I should like to engage directly with an argument which I have only approached obliquely in earlier pages, namely the relation between the culture(s) of modernity and the findings of psychoanalysis. This is critical, among other reasons, because both modernity and psychoanalysis have dealings with what we might loosely term the 'pleasure principle', albeit in very different ways.

For example, many arguments about modernity, and many of the habits of representation typical of modernity, rely upon a rhetoric of the 'surface': on the 'skin show', on fashion, on the emptying or hollowing out of the depths. In this sense modernity can be seen to be radically opposed to psychoanalysis which, despite the potency and revolutionary status of its approach, serves precisely to foreclose any possibility of the disconnection of clean surface from messy innards, or of contemporary presentation from archaic residue. The question would yet again be one about 'trajectory', about whether and in what sense one can be 'propelled' free from the present and the past, be placed in a new kind of orbit around the linear dimensions of history – and these, of course, are considerations which have come to have a fuller force in more recent versions of modernity as the very constraints of gravity, the compulsions of the 'earth-bound', have come to seem more relative, less subject to an absolute or divine embargo.

Alternatively, one might say that the opposition between modernity and psychoanalysis is less one of substance than one of time. Modernity, that is to say, would be deliberately, even perhaps grotesquely, synchronic. In its attempts to deny or circumvent death, in its assertion of temporary transcendence, in its embarrassed rejection of ageing, it offers instead a series of snapshots of 'favourite moments', where everybody is young and beautiful. And, of course, in many cases dead – perhaps at the moment the ultimate emblem is the anorexic, addicted super-model, whose allure is directly connected to the imminence of her collapse, an image of the 'body on the edge', the 'body of edges' which beckons us to a future kingdom where all shall be free from sin – not because of any specific morality but because of a politics of exhaustion wherein desire itself is laid to rest as the body takes on the 'hard edges' which stand against all that might be reproductively, messily possible under other, now defunct regimes.

Modernity comes, above all, to free us from tradition and prejudice; it comes to promote a world of free fall, free flight. Here lies its greatest strength; it assures us that it is indeed possible to be born again, for something to rise from the rubble – and hence its frequent embroilment with the aftermaths of war. War clears a site for modernisation: this could be said to be the sub-narrative of recent conflicts in Afghanistan and Iraq, but it could be equally relevantly said of the Roman invasion of Britain or of the expansionist aims of France in the aftermath of the 1789 revolution.

I want to suggest that psychoanalysis figures as modernity's other, as its 'reminder', in that its own desire is ceaselessly to want to know the story behind the family album; it wants to know not only what the photographs (these may be war photographs, photographs of happy families, or indeed photographs which remind us curiously of intervening traumas through which there may be no obvious passage) appear to portray, but also what is written on the back of them, it wants to relativise the world of 'disembodied' images and to supply an aetiology, an account of how we have got to where we are, of how we have travelled and what we have thought we have left behind. Although, of course, what is perfectly possible (as so often in the real world of which this is but a series of images, or dreams) is that there is nothing written on the back of the photos, that all is under continuing erasure, that the narrative of the world is being continuously rewritten and that any attempt at excavation is doomed to failure. The opposition between modernity and psychoanalysis might be equally written as an opposition between modernity and archaeology, both in its immediate sense and in the further reticulations suggested by Foucault's 'archaeology of knowledge'.

Or: perhaps, if indeed nothing is written on the back of the photos, then we might alternatively say that what is written on the back of the photos is, precisely, 'Nothing': 'nothing' is what is scrawled on the smoked glass, spray-painted on the subway walls – 'nothing', of course, in the case of graffiti with a singularly incomprehensible signature effect attached or inscribed. Perhaps the thought of photography, with its early imbrication with spiritualism, might remind us that the thought has to be entertained, and modernity over the centuries has entertained it, that the re-conjuring of the past is all smoke and mirrors: that there is nothing 'behind' the present moment which might hamper the fluidity of the relationship between present and future, that all is a question of perspective and desire – one alternatively might think, for example, of the ways in which a Cubist painting absorbs and replicates the past without, for the most part (although Picasso himself is an obvious exception here) commenting on it or allowing it standing-room on the expressway – or the mode of expression – into the future.

And what would be insufficient would be to confront modernity with its own structure of disavowal; rather, a certain type of disavowal would be the necessary gesture for clearing the ground, clearing away the undergrowth, which will allow for forward movement. 'Disavowal', perhaps, is the heart of the gesture of modernity: there may be all manner of ancestors beckoning back towards the past, but it is only by ignoring or transcending their sireniac blandishments that the genuinely 'new thing' can be discovered and valued. The essential response to a world grown simultaneously too tumultuous and too bland is the repetitive call to 'get a life', to resist the call of convention and to strike out to distant shores, thereby naturally replicating and developing the desire of the adventurer through the ages. If psychoanalysis – and here I am only taking psychoanalysis as an example of those 'resorts' which might connect us to the (social, cultural, familial, personal) past – might rely upon the formula 'By what they ignore shall ye know them', then modernity has its own riposte, and a powerful one it is: by what is recognised, in its full weight, its full 'heaviness', shall ye be dragged down. The 'oceanic' may represent nurture, but it also represents, as we have seen, the possibility of death by drowning, of succumbing to the lure and the snare of the 'lonesome ocean'.

One side of this argument, then, would say – and from Iran to the Congo, from Russia to Chile, it is one of the most compelling and urgent arguments being conducted today – that the issue is indeed one of 'reminder', and there is where psychoanalysis takes its stand, on the necessity of being 're-minded' of what is past, because otherwise there will be no sure footing into the future. The other side would say, however – and here the constant rhetoric of 'closure' is relevant – that what is critical is the possibility of forgetting; because unless we consign what is past to the past – here again the culture of apology is symptomatic – then there will be no possibility of 'moving on', which may, cliché though it has become, be a codex for the ultimate modernistic gesture.

Or one might look upon the analytic and the modernistic projects as alternate versions – which despite their most potent present incarnations have no doubt proceeded in different forms through history as the 'ancients' and the 'moderns' have fought their necessary battles – of the crucial category of fascination. The image that might be most relevant here is that of Janus, the figure which looks both ways at once and thus guards the borderland, the threshold, while simultaneously holding within itself the limitless possibilities of the liminal, the ever-present threat of betrayal. It is also an image of infatuation, of being held in thrall between two competing desires, the desire to return and the desire to progress: between these two desires we are, as Edward Young said so long ago in his *Night Thoughts* (1742), an enduring commentary on the aims and goals of enlightenment, an ever-present reminder of the pull towards the dark which shadows the possibility of our emergence into the light, forever strung; or, as in more recent post-Darwinian formulations, we are divided between a desire to return to the bestial, to the quiet yet violent sleep of the pre-human, and the desire to perfect the species even if – or perhaps especially if – that requires a redrafting of the terms of what it is to be human in any case, a submission to the demands – which we have ourselves created – of a posthuman world in which we will, no doubt, continue to struggle to find our place and our being.

Fascination, as Kierkegaard remarked, requires immediately a concept of sin. And it would follow, then, that modernity is deeply enmeshed with sin, with taboo and transgression, with the pleasure of excess, even if the mark of its enmeshment is also of the status of a disavowal. Modernity knows what it does not want to know; it knows that the vision of a clearer, cleaner, purer world may be receding day by day, but it also knows, with desperation, that unless the illusion of possibility is main-tained then the opposite of its vision will grow daily more crystalline, it will be constantly confronted by its potentially overwhelming alterna-tives. Within this regime, there is a complex terrain – most ably delin-eated, as I have suggested, by Deleuze and Guattari – on which it is not clear whether the mythical, 'arborescent' features of growth and develop-ment will eventually succeed or suppress the slow, quiet growth of that which will continue to prove irrepressible, the 'rhizomatic' growth which proceeds under our feet, all the time. The most apt image is perhaps a commonplace, suburban one: the image of fractured pavements, lifted slabs, which 'proceed' from the underground growth of tree roots which have always been too large, too powerful to submit to the demands of mere stone, concrete, tarmac.

Then again, perhaps none of this matters. As modernity confronts its own others it simultaneously, it would appear, gains the power to drag them through the looking glass – at the moment the image of a modernising China, of a 'modernism with Chinese characteristics', is the outstanding example of this. The question would now be one of what the roots of modernity itself are, of whether there is such an irresistible link between the modern and the west that no other possible paths are available.

Perhaps we can conclude with an image from Derek Walcott, a poet who is above all concerned with modernity, its promises and its encroachments, in which he confronts and opposes two attitudes to the past. Which of these characters, the painter Gregorias or the poet-narrator, we might ask, is the closer to the modern trajectory, which the one who continues to seek a different, as yet inexpressible, connection between past, present and future?

> Gregorias laughs, a white roar ringed with lamplight,
> gigantic moths, the shadows of his hands
> fluttering the wall, it is his usual
> gesture now, the crucifix.
> 'Man I ent care if they misunderstand me,
> I drink my rum, I praise my God, I mind my business!
> The thing is you love death and I love life'.
> Then, wiping the oracular moustache:
> 'Your poetry too full of spiders,
> bones, worms, ants, things eating up each other,
> I can't read it. Look!'
> He frames a seascape in a chair,
> then, striding back, beyond a table littered
> with broken loaves, fishbones, a gut-rusting wine,
> he smites his forehead.   (Walcott 1992, 206)

Annotated Bibliography

Anderson, Benedict, *Imagined Communities: Reflections on the Origin and Spread of Nationalism* (London: Verso, 1991)

> Although at first glance issues of nationalism may not appear to be at the root of modernity, in this remarkable text Anderson demonstrates that they are, and that the world we consider to be 'modern' has been fundamentally shaped by national symbols, national rivalries and nationalist aspirations. First published in 1983, Anderson's work underpins a great deal of later work in postcolonial theory; but more importantly, it sets out critical ways in which modernisation is, or is forced to be, the primary mode through which nations develop, whether that is from an already 'developed' base or elsewhere in the world. Stimulatingly, tersely written, and with an extraordinary global range.

Barthes, Roland, *A Lover's Discourse: Fragments*, trans. Richard Howard (London: Jonathan Cape, 1979)

> This is a work not only 'on' modernity but also 'within' modernity. It is 'on' modernity in the sense that it points, in a wide range of examples, to some of the crucial features of desire under specifically modern conditions; it is 'within' modernity in the sense that it eschews the possibility of a master-narrative and works instead within the form of the fragment, the miniature, indeed the individual word itself, divorced and estranged from its surroundings and thus allowed a peculiar life of its own. A highly valuable stripping away of illusion is accompanied by, indeed represented by, a 'different' fascination, a fascination with the unrepresentable and consequently the ambiguous, fluctuating role of language.

Bauman, Zygmunt, *Liquid Modernity* (Cambridge: Polity Press, 2000)

> This book forms the concluding part of a series which also includes *Globalisation: The Human Consequences* and *In Search of Politics*, but

it is in a sense the most interesting and alarming of them all. Essentially, it describes the movement between two concepts of the modern: the first 'heavy', based on hard technology, industry, manufacture and the consequent revolution in social and labour relations; the second 'light', as these imperatives are replaced by the prioritisation of information and the 'soft' technologies necessary to spread the 'knowledge economy'. Further at stake here are issues of political freedom, and how they might be affected by cultural and technological transition in an economically unevenly distributed world.

Benjamin, Andrew, ed., *The Problems of Modernity: Adorno and Benjamin* (London and New York: Routledge, 1989)

This book contains essays by a fine range of writers on modernity: Peter Dews, Peter Osborne, Jay Bernstein, Andrew Bowie, Joanna Hodge, John Rignall, Janet Wolff and Irving Wohlfarth as well as Andrew Benjamin himself. Essentially, they remind the reader that the philosophical roots of a self-conscious consideration of modernity lie very much within the work of Theodor Adorno and Walter Benjamin, in their fragmentary writings and in their representation of the fragmentary state of the modern world itself. This is an excellent composite introduction to the two thinkers, but it also reminds us of the tremendous spread of their work, and thus, elliptically, of how modernity is always connected with barriers being broken down as the fragments of previous beliefs and ideologies are set in renewed motion.

Benjamin, Walter, 'The Work of Art in the Age of Mechanical Reproduction', in *Illuminations*, ed. Hannah Arendt (London: Jonathan Cape, 1970)

In this much-quoted essay, Walter Benjamin sets out to demonstrate the changes in cultural context and interpretation consequent on the increasing 'reproducibility' of the work of art. Under modern conditions, concepts like 'uniqueness' and 'genius' come under siege; this not only affects the reception of works of art, but feeds back into the tasks artists set themselves and how they conceive of their work. There was a time, Benjamin suggests, when art possessed an 'aura', a sense of the sacred. But modernity comes to dispel that aura; alongside the beneficial effects of 'making art available to the masses', there also lies a more problematic question about the present and future relation between art and authenticity.

Berman, Marshall, *All that is Solid Melts into Air: The Experience of Modernity* (London: Verso, 1982)

> A hugely wide-ranging and, to an extent, a personal book about modernity. Berman charts the social revolutions of the nineteenth century and relates these to significant texts by political thinkers (principally Marx) and creative writers (Goethe, Dostoevsky and others); he then proceeds to ponder on what these changes might portend. In particular, he is concerned with the potential liberation to be derived within societies freed from traditional certainties, but also with the difficulty of managing this liberation while materialistic, economistic credos hold sway. Through a series of analyses which also look at modern urban settings, Berman poses a crucial question about how it is possible for the individual, the citizen, the subject to cope with the problems of living in a situation of fluidity.

Connor, Steven, *Postmodernist Culture: An Introduction to Theories of the Contemporary* (Oxford: Basil Blackwell, 1989)

> In its focus on the postmodern, this challenging book naturally seeks to differentiate its topic from merely another moment in the long history of modernity. Nevertheless, the argument and documentation Connor provides are of great help in thinking through the specificity of the modern, and also what we mean when using that notoriously slippery word 'contemporary'. Chapters on theory, the visual arts, literature, performance, TV, video, film and popular culture lead the reader towards some powerful closing speculations on 'critical modernity' and on the deeply contested realm of modern cultural politics.

Docherty, Thomas, *Criticism and Modernity: Aesthetics, Literature and Nations in Europe and its Academies* (Oxford: Oxford University Press, 1999)

> This is an unusual and demanding book. Seen from one perspective, it seeks to trace a series of connections between modernity and the nation-state; but it also relates these issues to the development of modern institutions, and specifically universities. A question

insistently posed is the relation between these factors and the issue of 'democracy', which is seen as a problematic area rather than as a 'given'. Also centrally at stake is the question of what the very notion of criticism itself means under the specific historical conditions of modernity and the role that might be played by literary disciplines in the development and retention of critical purchase on an increasingly technologised and bureaucratised world.

Eagleton, Terry, *The Illusions of Postmodernism* (Oxford: Blackwell, 1996)

This is not a book about modernity; instead, it is a book which seeks to debunk some of the fallacies of postmodernism from a neo-Marxist perspective. But as it does so, it raises important questions – about modernity, certainly; but also about what modernity might conceal or revise, in the classic manner of an ideology which denies the contradictions with which it claims to deal. There is a particularly valuable treatment of the all-important concept of the subject in modernity: what is it we are becoming, how are we dealing with that which is withheld from us in a globally divided society? A certain degree of relativism in approaching the world's problems may indeed by necessary, even healthy; but is this part of yet another cover-story on the part of dominant interests?

Frisby, David, *Cityscapes of Modernity: Critical Explorations* (Cambridge: Polity Press, 2001)

This excellent book takes the reader through seven approaches to the modern city – the city 'observed', 'detected', 'interpreted', 'compared', 'designed', 'dissolved' and 'rationalised'. Under each of these headings, Frisby deploys both detailed and complex information about urban and architectural planning and a continuing narrative of how modern cities have been represented in literature, art and theory. As in many other works (and this is, clearly, open to argument) the city is taken as the typical site of modernity, and consequently as the terrain on which modern modifications of subjectivity need to be reinterpreted; what is distinctive here is the enormous wealth of detail which brings alive the entire process of urbanisation which is so frequently taken for granted.

Giddens, Anthony, *Modernity and Self-Identity: Self and Society in the Late Modern Age* (Cambridge: Polity Press, 1991)

> Anthony Giddens is probably most famous for being the acknowledged intellectual progenitor of the New Labour project, the 'third way'. But in this book, he turns his attention less to political programme than to the nature of the self under modern conditions. The self, obviously, is not a given; the question becomes one of what kind of self it is necessary to construct in order for modernity to plant its imprint and in order for there to be a viable harmony between individual and state. Particularly interesting is the recurrent focus on chance and risk as essential factors in modern experience, which sharply differentiates it from the nature of selfhood within traditional societies while at the same time enabling a certain reflexivity within the modern (Western) concept of citizenship.

Goody, Jack, *Capitalism and Modernity: The Great Debate* (Cambridge: Polity Press, 2004)

> This book builds on Goody's long experience as an anthropologist concerned primarily with non-European societies and thus delivers an extremely interesting perspective on the rise and continuation of European and American dominance of the modern world. It may be true that it leaves the reader with more questions than answers, but the questions are valuable ones, if only as they help to dislodge the unthought belief that there has been something historically 'necessary' in European domination and thus to open our minds to other possibilities and to the transience of political, economic and cultural empire. Within this constellation, capitalism is clearly an important term; but Goody adds considerably to our understanding of its specific intersection with modernity.

Habermas, Jürgen, *The Philosophical Discourse of Modernity: Twelve Lectures*, trans. Frederick Lawrence (Cambridge: Polity Press and Basil Blackwell, 1987)

> This is a complex and difficult book, but nevertheless an indispensable one for the study of modernity. Habermas takes issue with a number of well-known contemporary thinkers, Derrida and Foucault among them, in order to advance a delicately balanced critique of the

relationship between modernity and reason. In the process, he exhumes many arguments from thinkers such as Hegel and Nietzsche and gives them a distinctive twist in order to add to the debate on the modern and to situate it within a wider historical and philosophical trajectory. Above all, Habermas reminds us of the ever-problematic relationship between the discourses of philosophy and the pragmatic force of everyday communication.

Haraway, Donna, *Simians, Cyborgs and Women: The Reinvention of Nature* (New York: Routledge, 1991)

At the heart of this book is an argument about how 'nature' is not a neutral category inlaid into scientific investigation, but is rather a constantly changing and developing construct. Thus, in modern times, the concept of nature has changed continuously under the pressure of different biological theories, and apparent evidence gathered from the animal kingdom needs to be subject to radical revision. Similarly, the contemporary debate about the cyborg – the juncture of cybernetic and organic components – needs to be seen in ideological terms, and as part of the (male-centred) revision of concepts of human nature in a time of vast technological change.

Horkheimer, Max, and Theodor W. Adorno, *Dialectic of Enlightenment*, trans. John Cumming (New York: Herder and Herder, 1972)

The central question posed by this book is: what is it that emerges to thwart the hopes and postures of 'enlightenment'? Although there may be no doubt as to the value of progress, nevertheless unless such progress is seen dialectically and its problems carefully measured, then the apparent liberation which results may prove to drag terrible consequences in its wake. In its diagnosis of the ills of contemporary western societies, this has been seen as a deeply pessimistic book; it would be better to see it as a reminder that many contemporary problems occur not despite enlightenment but as necessary corollaries to the gaps and hiatuses which persist within enlightenment thought.

Jameson, Fredric, *Postmodernism; or, The Cultural Logic of Late Capitalism* (London: Verso, 1991)

This crucial book is again, perhaps, not directly about modernity; but it is about the postmodern, arguably modernity's latest avatar, and it has been much hailed for its complex demonstration of the ways in which the postmodern, while it affects the playful and the free-floating, a world of *jouissance*, is in fact inevitably striated by its affiliation to the economic formation to which Jameson refers as 'late capitalism'. Arguably, a question is begged as to in what terms the current phase of capitalism is 'late', which would also be a question about what will succeed it; what, in other words, will be the next form of – undoubtedly global – modernity.

Lash, Scott, and Jonathan Friedman, eds, *Modernity and Identity* (Oxford: Blackwell, 1992)

Among the contributors to this collection of essays are Marshall Berman, Richard Rorty, Peter Bürger, Paul Rabinow and Peter Burke. Its central argument is that we do a disservice to both high modernism and postmodernism when we attempt to capture them in a series of fixities; the 'essence' – to use the term paradoxically – of the modern is to reside in fluidity, change, reflexivity. Similarly the attempt to find master-narratives which will explain such movements will inevitably fail, because what we are confronted with on the modern stage is the claim of the local, the need to disentangle specificities of supply and demand (at the economic and cultural level) from global dictates.

Lyotard, Jean-François, *The Postmodern Condition: A Report on Knowledge*, trans. Geoff Bennington and Brian Massumi (Minneapolis: University of Minnesota Press, 1984)

The question that lies behind this highly regarded book is about how we know, in the modern world, what is true. That is to put the point rather baldly: Lyotard is more concerned with what he refers to as the issue of legitimation, and where we might find sources of authority that might convince us that our experience can be fairly regarded as generally shared. What, then, *is* knowledge under contemporary conditions? Do we, in fact, mind or care, or are we participants in a consumer culture in which promotion and branding constitute their own hierarchy of values? If we are, as subjects, simply constituted by the flows of 'knowledge' in which we are constantly immersed, then by what means might we find a place from which to view this flood of information objectively?

Pile, Steve, *Real Cities: Modernity, Space and the Phantasmagorias of City Life* (London: SAGE Publications, 2005)

> It is best to summarise this remarkable book about how the modern city figures in our imaginative life – and in turn structures that life – by quoting the headings of its four principal sections: 'The Dreaming City, in which cities turn into dreams and dreams turn into cities'; 'The Magic City, in which we are careful about what we wish for'; 'The Vampiric City, in which blood runs free'; and 'The Ghostly City, in which the city is haunted and haunting'. Perhaps nothing more needs to be added: this is a book which asserts that, under the conditions of modernity, we live within and manifest phantasmagorias; cities are places where the artificial barriers between dream and 'reality' break down; and this is as true for 'urban planners' as it is for urban *flâneurs*.

Swingewood, Alan, *Cultural Theory and the Problem of Modernity* (Houndmills: Macmillan, 1998)

> Centrally, this is a survey of theories of culture from Marx onwards, with a particular emphasis on what might be called 'mass culture'; but it does contain an underlying argument – as well as a specific chapter – on modernity and culture, which provides a highly readable account of some of the major theorists of modernity. It also addresses some of the crucial concepts of modernity – hegemony, cultural materialism – in a helpful and understandable way which nevertheless does not undermine the complexity of thought we need to develop in order to address the modern from, as it were, within its own confines.

Turner, Bryan S., ed., *Theories of Modernity and Postmodernity* (London: SAGE Publications, 1990)

> There are essays here on the film *Wall Street*; on urban space; on Habermas, Lyotard and Weber; on women 'between fundamentalism and modernity' and 'between modernity and postmodernity'. All of them are of interest and, indeed, concern; but what makes this book particularly interesting is the recurring emphasis on nostalgia as a specific ingredient of the modern condition. Nostalgia, it could be argued, is impossible in 'traditional' societies; it can only emerge after a specific, reflexively identified break. Thus the origins of the

modern are inseparable from its own sense of loss; the project towards the future is always accompanied and coloured by the haunting recognition that the past remains behind us, even as it is continually recapitulated in the present.

Wilson, Elizabeth, *Adorned in Dreams: Fashion and Modernity* (London: Virago, 1985)

This book was, and remains, an inspiration to those who seek to probe the meanings of modernity in areas which have been traditionally ignored by scholarship. In an extremely erudite way, it explores the impact of fashion on history, and the shaping of fashion by history. In turn, it suggests that the 'real history' which we might think we are seeking often passes us by, because it is a function of a world which we choose to ignore; there are many important lessons to be learnt about past and present societies – and even the possible directions of the future – by looking closely at how adornment, and even the idealised shape of the human (and, in this case, usually female) body changes over time, and what this reveals about larger social structures.

Bibliography

Abraham, Nicolas, and Maria Torok, *The Shell and the Kernel*, trans. Nicholas Rand (Chicago: University of Chicago Press, 1994)

Achebe, Chinua, *Anthills of the Savannah* (London: Heinemann, 1988)

Adorno, Theodor W., *The Culture Industry: Selected Essays on Mass Culture*, ed. J.M. Bernstein (London: Routledge, 1991)

Adorno, Theodor W., *Prisms*, trans. Samuel and Shierry Weber (London: Neville Spearman, 1967)

Agamben, Giorgio, *Infancy and History: On the Destruction of Experience*, trans. Liz Heron (London: Verso, 1993)

Albrow, Martin, *The Global Age: State and Society beyond Modernity* (Cambridge: Polity Press, 1996)

Allen, John, Peter Braham and Paul Lewis, eds, *Political and Economic Forms of Modernity* (Cambridge: Polity Press and the Open University, 1992)

Anderson, Benedict, *Imagined Communities* (London: Verso, 1991)

Appadurai, Arjun, *Modernity at Large: Cultural Dimensions of Globalisation* (Minneapolis and London: University of Minnesota Press, 1996)

Badcock, C.R., *Madness and Modernity: A Study in Social Psychoanalysis* (Oxford: Blackwell, 1983)

Ballard, J.G., *Concrete Island* (London: Jonathan Cape, 1973)

Ballard, J.G., *Crash* (London: Jonathan Cape, 1973)

Ballard, J.G., *Empire of the Sun* (London: Victor Gollancz, 1984)

Ballard, J.G., *High-Rise* (London: Jonathan Cape, 1975)

Ballard, J.G., *Millennium People* (London: Flamingo, 2003)

Barker, Francis, Peter Hulme and Margaret Iversen, eds, *Postmodernism and the Re-reading of Modernity* (Manchester and New York: Manchester University Press, 1992)

Barlow, Tani E., ed., *Formations of Colonial Modernity in East Asia* (Durham: Duke University Press, 1997)

Barnett, S.J., *The Enlightenment and Religion: The Myths of Modernity* (Manchester: Manchester University Press, 2003)

Barthes, Roland, *A Lover's Discourse: Fragments*, trans. Richard Howard (London: Jonathan Cape, 1979)

Batten, Guinn, *The Orphaned Imagination: Melancholy and Commodity Culture in English Romanticism* (Durham, N.C.: Duke University Press, 1998)

Baudrillard, Jean, *The Evil Demon of Images*, trans. P. Patton and P. Foss (Annandale: Power Institute, 1987)

Baudrillard, Jean, 'Mass-Media Culture', in *The Consumer Society: Myths and Structures*, trans. Chris Turner (London: SAGE Publications, 1998)

Baudrillard, Jean, 'Water, Empire, Gold, Primitive Stage', trans. Serhan Ada, *Atlas*, 1999

Bauman, Zygmunt, *Globalisation: The Human Consequences* (Cambridge: Polity Press, 1998)

Bauman, Zygmunt, *Liquid Modernity* (Cambridge: Polity Press, 2000)

Bauman, Zygmunt, *Modernity and Ambivalence* (Ithaca, NY: Cornell University Press, 1991)

Bauman, Zygmunt, *Work, Consumerism and the New Poor* (Milton Keynes: Open University Press, 1998)

Bech, Henning, *When Men Meet: Homosexuality and Modernity*, trans. Teresa Mesquit and Tim Davies (Cambridge: Polity Press, 1997)

Beck, Ulrich, *The Reinvention of Politics: Rethinking Modernity in the Global Social Order*, trans. Mark Ritter (Cambridge: Polity Press, 1997)

Beckett, Samuel, *The Complete Dramatic Works* (London: Faber and Faber, 1986)

Begam, Richard, *Samuel Beckett and the End of Modernity* (Stanford, Calif.: Stanford University Press, 1996)

Behrend, Heike, and Ute Luig, eds, *Spirit Possession, Modernity and Power in Africa* (Oxford: James Currey, 1999)

Bell, Michael, *Literature, Modernity and Myth: Belief and Responsibility in the Twentieth Century* (Cambridge: Cambridge University Press, 1997)

Benjamin, Andrew, ed., *The Problems of Modernity: Adorno and Benjamin* (London and New York: Routledge, 1989)

Benjamin, Walter, 'The Work of Art in the Age of Mechanical Reproduction', in *Illuminations*, ed. Hannah Arendt (London: Jonathan Cape, 1970)

Benjamin, Walter, 'This Space for Rent', in *One-Way Street and Other Writings* (London: Verso, 1996)

Bennett, Clinton, *Muslims and Modernity: An Introduction to the Issues and Debates* (New York: Continuum, 2005)

Berger, Peter L., *Facing up to Modernity: Excursions in Society, Politics and Religion* (New York: Basic Books, 1977)

Berman, Marshall, *All that is Solid Melts into Air: The Experience of Modernity* (London: Verso, 1982)

Bewes, Timothy, *Cynicism and Postmodernity* (London: Verso, 1997)

Bhabha, Homi, *The Location of Culture* (London and New York: Routledge, 1994)

Bhabha, Homi, ed., *Nation and Narration* (London: Routledge, 1990)

Bocock, Robert, and Kenneth Thompson, eds, *Social and Cultural Forms of Modernity* (Cambridge: Polity Press and the Open University, 1992)

Boyle, Frank, *Swift as Nemesis: Modernity and its Satirist* (Stanford, Calif.: Stanford University Press, 2000)

Bradbury, Ray, *Fahrenheit 451* (London: Rupert Hart-Davis, 1954)

Breward, Christopher, and Caroline Evans, eds, *Fashion and Modernity* (Oxford: Berg, 2005)

Bristol, Michael, and Kathleen McLuskie, eds, *Shakespeare and Modern Theatre: The Performance of Modernity* (London: Routledge, 2001)

Buck-Morss, Susan, *The Dialectics of Seeing: Walter Benjamin and the Arcades Project* (Cambridge, Mass.: The MIT Press, 1993)

Bunnell, Tim, *Malaysia, Modernity and the Multimedia Super-corridor: A Critical Geography of Intelligent Landscapes* (New York: RoutledgeCurzon, 2004)

Bürger, Peter, *Theory of the Avant-garde*, trans. Michael Shaw (Minneapolis: University of Minnesota Press, 1984)

Cacciari, Massimo, *Architecture and Nihilism: On the Philosophy of Modern Architecture*, trans. Stephen Sartarelli (New Haven: Yale University Press, 1993)

Calinescu, Matei, *Five Faces of Modernity: Modernism, Avant-Garde, Decadence, Kitsch, Postmodernism* (Durham, NC: Duke University Press, 1987)

Cascardi, Anthony J., *The Subject of Modernity* (Cambridge: Cambridge University Press, 1992)

Chatterjee, Partha, 'The Nationalist Resolution of the Women's Question', in *Postcolonial Discourses: An Anthology*, ed. Gregory Castle (London: Blackwell, 2001)

Chattopadhyay, Swati, *Representing Calcutta: Modernity, Nationalism and the Colonial Uncanny* (London: Routledge, 2006)

Coleridge, Samuel Taylor, *Poetical Works*, ed. E.H. Coleridge (London: Oxford University Press, 1967)

Comaroff, Jean, and John Comaroff, eds, *Modernity and its Malcontents: Ritual and Power in Postcolonial Africa* (Chicago: University of Chicago Press, 1993)

Conan Doyle, Arthur, *The Memoirs of Sherlock Holmes*, introd. Kingsley Amis (London: John Murray and Jonathan Cape, 1974)

Connolly, William E., *Political Theory and Modernity* (Oxford: Basil Blackwell, 1988)

Connor, Steven, *Postmodernist Culture: An Introduction to Theories of the Contemporary* (Oxford: Basil Blackwell, 1989)

Conrad, Joseph, *Heart of Darkness*, ed. Paul O'Prey (London: Penguin, 1983)

Cooter, Roger, Mark Harrison and Steve Sturdy, eds, *War, Medicine and Modernity* (Stroud: Sutton, 1998)

Craib, Ian, *Modernity* (London: Routledge, 2003)

Crary, Jonathan, *Techniques of the Observer: On Vision and Modernity in the Nineteenth Century* (Cambridge, Mass., and London: The MIT Press, 1990)

Dandeker, Christopher, *Surveillance, Power and Modernity: Bureaucracy and Discipline from 1700 to the Present Day* (Cambridge: Polity Press, 1990)

Davey, Kevin, *English Imaginaries: Six Studies in Anglo-British Modernity* (London: Lawrence and Wishart, 1999)

Debord, Guy, *The Society of the Spectacle*, trans. Donald Nicholson-Smith (New York: Zone Books, 1994)

Deleuze, Gilles, and Félix Guattari, *Anti-Oedipus*, trans. Robert Hurley, Mark Seem and Helen R. Lane (Minneapolis: University of Minnesota Press, 1983)

Deleuze, Gilles, and Félix Guattari, *A Thousand Plateaus*, trans. Brian Massumi (London: The Athlone Press, 1987)

Derrida, Jacques, *The Post Card: From Socrates to Freud and Beyond*, trans. Alan Bass (Chicago: Chicago University Press, 1987)

Derrida, Jacques, *Spectres of Marx: The State of the Debt, the Work of Mourning, and the New International*, trans. Peggy Kamuf (London and New York: Routledge, 1994)

Devji, Faisal, *Landscapes of the Jihad: Militancy, Morality, Modernity* (Ithaca, NY: Cornell University Press, 2005)

Diderot, Denis, 'Conversation between D'Alembert and Diderot', in *'Rameau's Nephew' and 'D'Alembert's Dream'*, trans. Leonard Tancock (London: Penguin, 1966)

Dimendberg, Edward, *Film Noir and the Spaces of Modernity* (Cambridge, Mass.: Harvard University Press, 2004)

Doane, Mary Ann, *The Emergence of Cinematic Time: Modernity, Contingency, the Archive* (Cambridge, Mass.: Harvard University Press, 2002)

Docherty, Thomas, *Criticism and Modernity: Aesthetics, Literature and Nations in Europe and its Academies* (Oxford: Oxford University Press, 1999)

Domingues, José Mauricio, *Social Creativity, Collective Subjectivity and Contemporary Modernity* (Basingstoke: Macmillan, 2000)

Duggan, Lisa, *Sapphic Slashers: Sex, Violence and American Modernity* (Durham, NC: Duke University Press, 2000)

Eagleton, Terry, *The Illusions of Postmodernism* (Oxford: Blackwell, 1996)

Egan, Greg, *Diaspora* (London: Millennium, 1997)

Eisenstadt, S.N., *Tradition, Change and Modernity* (New York and London: Wiley-Interscience, 1973)

Eliot, T.S., *Collected Poems 1909–1962* (London: Faber and Faber, 1963)

Eliot, T.S., *Selected Essays* (London: Faber and Faber, 1951)

Ellmann, Richard, and Charles Feidelson, eds, *The Modern Tradition* (Oxford: Oxford University Press, 1965)

Entrikin, J. Nicholas, *The Betweenness of Place: Towards a Geography of Modernity* (Basingstoke: Macmillan, 1991)

Ewing, Katherine Pratt, *Arguing Sainthood: Modernity, Psychoanalysis and Islam* (Durham, NC: Duke University Press, 1997)

Felski, Rita, *The Gender of Modernity* (Cambridge, Mass.: Harvard University Press, 1995)

Ferguson, Harry, *Protecting Children in Time: Child Abuse, Child Protection, and the Consequences of Modernity* (Basingstoke: Palgrave Macmillan, 2004)

Flanagan, Kieran, and Peter C. Jupp, eds, *Virtue, Ethics and Sociology: Issues of Modernity and Religion* (Basingstoke: Palgrave, 2001)

Foucault, Michel, *Discipline and Punish*, trans. Alan Sheridan (London: Allen Lane, 1977)

Franklin, Adrian, *Animals and Modern Cultures: A Sociology of Human-Animal Relations in Modernity* (London: SAGE Publications, 1999)

Freud, Sigmund, *Civilisation and its Discontents*, in *The Standard Edition of the Complete Psychological Works*, eds James Strachey *et al.*, Vol. XXI (London: The Hogarth Press, 1964)

Freud, Sigmund, *Notes upon a Case of Obsessional Neurosis*, in *The Standard Edition of the Complete Psychological Works*, eds James Strachey *et al.*, Vol. X (London: The Hogarth Press, 1955)

Frisby, David, *Cityscapes of Modernity: Critical Explorations* (Cambridge: Polity Press, 2001)

Frosh, Stephen, *Identity Crisis: Modernity, Psychoanalysis and the Self* (Basingstoke: Macmillan, 1991)

Frow, John, *Cultural Studies and Cultural Value* (Oxford: Clarendon Press, 1995)

Fuller, J.F.C., *The Influence of Arms on History* (Paris: Payot, 1948)

Galgan, Gerald J., *The Logic of Modernity* (New York and London: New York University Press, 1982)

Gallo, Rubén, *Mexican Modernity: The Avant-garde and the Technological Revolution* (Cambridge, Mass.: The MIT Press, 2005)

Gandelsonas, Mario, ed., *Shanghai Reflections: Architecture, Urbanism and the Search for an Alternative Modernity* (New York: Princeton Architectural Press, 2002)

García Canclini, Néstor, 'Hybrid Cultures and Communicative Strategies', in Renato Rosaldo, Néstor García Canclini, Christopher L. Chiappari and Silvia Lopez, *Hybrid Cultures: Strategies for Entering and Leaving Modernity* (Minneapolis: University of Minnesota Press, 1997)

Geffré, Claude, and Jean-Pierre Jossua, eds, *The Debate on Modernity* (London: SCM, 1992)

Gentile, Emilio, *The Struggle for Modernity: Nationalism, Futurism and Fascism* (Westport, CT: Praeger, 2003)

Gibson, William, *Neuromancer* (London: Victor Gollancz, 1984)

Giddens, Anthony, *The Consequences of Modernity* (Cambridge: Polity Press, 1990)

Giddens, Anthony, *Modernity and Self-Identity: Self and Society in the Late Modern Age* (Cambridge: Polity Press, 1991)

Giddens, Anthony, and Christopher Pierson, *Conversations with Anthony Giddens: Making Sense of Modernity* (Cambridge: Polity Press, 1998)

Gilbert, David, David Matless and Brian Short, eds, *Geographies of British Modernity: Space and Society in the Twentieth Century* (Malden, Mass.: Blackwell, 2003)

Gilroy, Paul, *The Black Atlantic: Modernity and Double Consciousness* (London: Verso, 1993)

Glancey, Jonathan, 'Who would live in a world like this?', *The Guardian*, 17th November, 1997

Goody, Jack, *Capitalism and Modernity: The Great Debate* (Cambridge: Polity Press, 2004)

Graham, W.S., *New Collected Poems* (London: Faber and Faber, 2004)

Gray, John, 'Three Mistakes about Modernity', lecture delivered at London School of Economics, 2nd March, 2000

Green, Garrett, *Theology, Hermeneutics and Imagination: The Crisis of Interpretation at the end of Modernity* (Cambridge: Cambridge University Press, 2000)

Greenfeld, Liah, *Nationalism: Five Roads to Modernity* (Cambridge, Mass.: Harvard University Press, 1992)

Gronberg, Tag, *Designs on Modernity: Exhibiting the City in 1920s Paris* (Manchester: Manchester University Press, 1998)

Habermas, Jürgen, *The Philosophical Discourse of Modernity: Twelve Lectures*, trans. Frederick Lawrence (Cambridge: Polity Press and Basil Blackwell, 1987)

Hall, Stuart, and Bram Gieben, eds, *Formations of Modernity* (Cambridge: Polity Press and the Open University, 1992)

Hall, Stuart *et al.*, eds, *Modernity: An Introduction to Modern Societies* (Cambridge: Polity Press, 1995)

Hall, Stuart, David Held and Tony McGrew, eds, *Modernity and its Futures* (Cambridge: Polity Press and the Open University, 1992)

Haraway, Donna, *Simians, Cyborgs and Women: The Reinvention of Nature* (New York: Routledge, 1991)

Harrison, M. John, *The Centauri Device* (London: Orion Millennium, 1974)

Harrison, M. John, *Climbers: A Novel* (London: Gollancz, 1989)

Harrison, M. John, *Light* (London: Gollancz, 2002)

Hartt, Julian N., Ray L. Hart and Robert P. Scharlemann, *The Critique of Modernity: Theological Reflections on Contemporary Culture* (Charlottesville: University of Virginia Press, 1986)

Harvey, David, *Paris, Capital of Modernity* (New York: Routledge, 2003)

Heelas, Paul, with David Martin and Paul Morris, ed., *Religion, Modernity and Postmodernity* (Oxford: Blackwell, 1998)

Hegel, G.W.F., *The Phenomenology of Mind*, trans. James Baillie (London: Allen and Unwin, 1966)

Hegel, G.W.F., *Philosophy of* Right, trans. T.M. Knox (Oxford: Oxford University Press, 1967)

Heynen, Hilde, *Architecture and Modernity: A Critique* (Cambridge, Mass.: The MIT Press, 1999)

Horkheimer, Max, and Theodor W. Adorno, *Dialectic of Enlightenment*, trans. John Cumming (New York: Herder and Herder, 1972)

Hughes, Robert, *Shock of the New* (New York: Random House, 1988)

Huxley, Aldous, *Brave New World* (New York: Vintage, 2004)

Hvattum, Mari, and Christian Hermansen, eds, *Tracing Modernity: Manifestations of the Modern in Architecture and the City* (London: Routledge, 2004)

Israel, Jonathan I., *Radical Enlightenment: Philosophy and the Making of Modernity, 1650–1750* (Oxford: Oxford University Press, 2001)

Jameson, Fredric, *Postmodernism; or, The Cultural Logic of Late Capitalism* (London: Verso, 1991)

Jameson, Fredric, *A Singular Modernity: Essay on the Ontology of the Present* (London: Verso, 2002)

Jardine, Alice A., *Gynesis: Configurations of Woman and Modernity* (Ithaca, NY: Cornell University Press, 1985)

Johnson, Paul, and Pat Thane, eds, *Old Age from Antiquity to Post-Modernity* (London and New York: Routledge, 1998)

Keats, John, *Works*, ed. Elizabeth Cook (Oxford and New York: Oxford University Press, 1990)

Kellner, Douglas, *Critical Theory, Marxism and Modernity* (Cambridge: Polity Press, 1989)

Kincaid, Jamaica, *A Small Place* (New York: Penguin, 1988)

King, Anthony D., ed., *Culture, Globalisation and the World System* (Binghamton: University of New York at Binghamton, 1991)

Kurasawa, Fuyuki, *The Ethnological Imagination: A Cross-cultural Critique of Modernity* (Minneapolis: University of Minnesota Press, 2004)

Laclau, Ernesto, 'Politics and the Limits of Modernity', in *Universal Abandon? The Politics of Postmodernism* (Minneapolis: University of Minnesota Press, 1988)

Laing, R.D., *The Divided Self: An Existential Study in Sanity and Madness* (London: Tavistock, 1960)

Laing, R.D., and David Cooper, *Reason and Violence* (London: Tavistock, 1964)

Larkin, Philip, *Collected Poems*, ed. Anthony Thwaite (London: The Marvell Press and Faber and Faber, 1988)

Larmore, Charles E., *The Morals of Modernity* (Cambridge: Cambridge University Press, 1996)

Lash, Scott, and Jonathan Friedman, eds, *Modernity and Identity* (Oxford: Blackwell, 1992)

Lash, Scott, Bronislaw Szerszynski and Broan Wynne, eds, *Risk, Environment and Modernity: Towards a New Ecology* (London: SAGE Publications, 1996)

Law, John, *Organising Modernity* (Oxford: Blackwell, 1994)

Lawrence, D.H., *Lady Chatterley's Lover*, introd. Richard Hoggart (Harmondsworth: Penguin, 1961)

Lee, Laurie, *Cider with Rosie* (London: The Hogarth Press, 1959)

Leighton, Daniel, 'Searching for Politics in an Uncertain World: Interview with Zygmunt Bauman', *Archive*, 10.1, 2001

Love, Nancy S., *Marx, Nietzsche and Modernity* (New York: Columbia University Press, 1986)

Lovelock, James, *Gaia: A New Look at Life on Earth* (Oxford: Oxford University Press, 1979)

Löwy, Michael, and Robert Sayre, *Romanticism against the Tide of Modernity*, trans. Catherine Porter (Durham, NC: Duke University Press, 2001)

Luhmann, Niklas, *Observations on Modernity*, trans. William Whobrey (Stanford, Calif.: Stanford University Press, 1998)

Luke, Timothy W., *Social Theory and Modernity: Critique, Dissent and Revolution* (Newbury Park, Calif., and London: SAGE Publications, 1990)

Lyotard, Jean-François, *The Postmodern Condition: A Report on Knowledge*, trans. Geoff Bennington and Brian Massumi (Minneapolis: University of Minnesota Press, 1984)

Lyotard, Jean-François, *The Differend: Phrases in Dispute*, trans. Georges van den Abeele (Manchester: Manchester University Press, 1991)

Malik, Iftikhar, *Islam and Modernity: Muslims in Europe and the United States* (London: Pluto Press, 2004)

Marcus, Steven, *Freud and the Culture of Psychoanalysis: Studies in the Transition from Victorian Humanism to Modernity* (London: Allen and Unwin, 1984)

Marcuse, Herbert, *One Dimensional Man: Studies in the Ideology of Advanced Industrial Society* (Boston: Beacon, 1964)

Marinetti, F.T., 'The Founding and Manifesto of Futurism', in *Let's Murder the Moonshine: Selected Writings*, ed. R.W. Flint (Los Angeles: Sun and Moon Classics, 1991)

Marshall, Barbara L., *Engendering Modernity: Feminism, Social Theory and Social Change* (Cambridge: Polity Press, 1994)

Marvell, Andrew, *The Complete Poems*, ed. Elizabeth Story Donno (Harmondsworth: Penguin, 1972)

Marx, Karl, 'Speech at the Anniversary of the People's Paper (1856)', in *The Marx-Engels Reader*, ed. R.C. Tucker (New York: Norton, 1978)

Marx, Karl, *Economic and Philosophical Manuscripts of 1844*, trans. Martin Milligan (Moscow: Foreign Languages Publishing House, 1961)

McCormick, Peter J., *Modernity, Aesthetics and the Bounds of Art* (Ithaca, NY: Cornell University Press, 1990)

McGuigan, Jim, *Culture and the Public Sphere* (London: Routledge, 1996)

McMahon, Darrin M., *Enemies of the Enlightenment: The French Counter-Enlightenment and the Making of Modernity* (Oxford: Oxford University Press, 2001)

McQuire, Scott, *Visions of Modernity: Representation, Memory, Time and Space in the Age of the Camera* (London: SAGE Publications, 1998)

Mellor, Philip A., and Chris Shilling, *Re-forming the Body: Religion, Community and Modernity* (London: SAGE Publications, 1997)

Milic, Louis T, ed., *The Modernity of the Eighteenth Century* (Cleveland, Ohio: The Press of Case Western Reserve University, 1971)

Misa, Thomas J., Philip Brey and Andrew Feenberg, eds, *Modernity and Technology* (Cambridge, Mass.: The MIT Press, 2003)

Nabokov, Vladimir, *Lolita* (London: Weidenfeld and Nicolson, 1959)

Nava, Mica, and Alan O'Shea, eds, *Reflections on a Century of English Modernity* (London: Routledge, 1996)

Nietzsche, Friedrich, *The Genealogy of Morals*, in *'The Birth of Tragedy' and 'The Genealogy of Morals'*, trans. Francis Golffing (New York: Doubleday, 1956)

Ogborn, Miles, *Spaces of Modernity: London's Geographies 1680–1780* (New York and London: The Guilford Press, 1998)

Orwell, George, *1984* (Harmondsworth: Penguin, 1954)

Osborne, Peter, *The Politics of Time: Modernity and Avant-garde* (London: Verso, 1995)

Owen, David, *Maturity and Modernity: Nietzsche, Weber, Foucault and the Ambivalence of Reason* (London: Routledge, 1994)

Owen, David, *Nietzsche, Politics and Modernity: A Critique of Liberal Reason* (London: SAGE Publications, 1995)

Palmié, Stephan, *Wizards and Scientists: Explorations in Afro-Cuban Modernity and Tradition* (Durham, NC: Duke University Press, 2002)

Parsons, Deborah L., *Streetwalking the Metropolis: Women, the City and Modernity* (Oxford: Oxford University Press, 2000)

Pearson, Keith Ansell, *Viroid Life: Perspectives on Nietzsche and the Transhuman Condition* (London and New York: Routledge, 1997)

Pile, Steve, *Real Cities: Modernity, Space and the Phantasmagorias of City Life* (London: SAGE Publications, 2005)

Poe, Edgar Allan, 'Ligeia', in *Selected Tales*, ed. David van Leer (Oxford and New York: Oxford University Press, 1998)

Pomerance, Murray, ed., *Cinema and Modernity* (New Brunswick: Rutgers University Press, 2006)

Poole, Ross, *Morality and Modernity* (London: Routledge, 1991)

Pope, 'Essay on Man', in *Poetical Works*, ed. Herbert Davis (London: Oxford University Press, 1966)

Porush, David, 'Cybernetic Fiction and Postmodern Science', *New Literary History*, 20:2, 1989

Pound, Ezra, *Selected Poems*, introd. T.S. Eliot (London: Faber and Faber, 1948)

Pred, Allan, and Michael John Watts, *Reworking Modernity: Capitalisms and Symbolic Discontent* (New Brunswick: Rutgers University Press, 1992)

Prendergast, Christopher, 'Codeword Modernity', *New Left Review*, 24, November–December 2003

Preziosi, Donald, *Brain of the Earth's Body: Art, Museums and the Phantasms of Modernity* (Minneapolis: University of Minnesota Press, 2003)

Prior, Nick, *Museums and Modernity: Art Galleries and the Making of Modern Culture* (Oxford: Berg, 2002)

Pynchon, Thomas, *Gravity's Rainbow* (London: Jonathan Cape, 1973)

Pynchon, Thomas, *V* (London: Jonathan Cape, 1963)

Pynchon, Thomas, *Vineland* (New York: Vintage, 1990)

Rahnema, Majid, 'Development', in *The Future of Knowledge and Culture: A Dictionary for the 21st Century*, eds Vinay Lal and Ashis Nandy (New Delhi: Penguin, 2005)

Rattansi, Ali, and Sallie Westwood, eds, *Racism, Modernity and Identity on the Western Front* (Cambridge: Polity Press, 1994)

Rengger, N.J., *Political Theory, Modernity and Postmodernity: Beyond Enlightenment and Critique* (Oxford: Blackwell, 1995)

Repstad, Pål, ed., *Religion and Modernity: Modes of Co-existence* (Oslo: Scandinavian University Press, 1996)

Riley, Joan, *The Unbelonging* (London: The Women's Press, 1985)

Rocco, Christopher, *Tragedy and Enlightenment: Athenian Political Thought and the Dilemmas of Modernity* (Berkeley, Calif.: University of California Press, 1997)

Rosenberg, Harold, *The Tradition of the New* (London: Thames and Hudson, 1962)

Rundell, John F., *Origins of Modernity: The Origins of Modern Social Theory from Kant to Hegel to Marx* (Cambridge: Polity Press, 1987)

Salvatore, Armando, *Islam and the Political Discourse of Modernity* (Reading: Ithaca, 1997)

Sangari, Kumkum, and Sudesh Vaid, eds, *Recasting Women: Essays in Colonial History* (New Delhi: Kali for Women, 1990)

Sanyal, Debarati, *The Violence of Modernity: Baudelaire, Irony and the Politics of Form* (Baltimore, MD: The Johns Hopkins University Press, 2006)

Saunders, Kriemild, ed., *Feminist Post-Development Thought: Rethinking Modernity, Post-colonialism and Representation* (London: Zed, 2002)

Savage, Mike, and Alan Warde, *Urban Sociology, Capitalism and Modernity* (Basingstoke: Macmillan, 1993)

Schaebler, Birgit, and Leif Stenberg, eds, *Globalisation and the Muslim World: Culture, Religion and Modernity* (Syracuse, NY: Syracuse University Press, 2004)

Schelling, Vivian, ed., *Through the Kaleidoscope: The Experience of Modernity in Latin America* (London: Verso, 2000)

Schluchter, Wolfgang, *Paradoxes of Modernity: Culture and Conflict in the Theory of Max Weber*, trans. Neil Solomon (Stanford, Calif.: Stanford University Press, 1996)

Scott, David, *Conscripts of Modernity: The Tragedy of Colonial Enlightenment* (Durham, NC: Duke University Press, 2004)

Shakespeare, William, *Antony and Cleopatra*, ed. Barbara Everett (London: Penguin, 1964)

Shakespeare, William, *The Tempest*, ed. Robert Langbaum (London: Penguin, 1964)

Shelley, Mary, *Frankenstein*, eds D.L. Macdonald and Kathleen Scherf (Ontario: Broadview Press, 1994)

Shields, Rob, *Places on the Margin: Alternative Geographies of Modernity* (London: Routledge, 1991)

Smart, Barry, *Facing Modernity: Ambivalence, Reflexivity and Morality* (London: SAGE Publications, 1999)

Stephenson, Neal, *Cryptonomicon* (London: Arrow, 2000)

Stoker, Bram, *Dracula*, ed. Glennis Byron (Ontario: Broadview Press, 1998)

Swingewood, Alan, *Cultural Theory and the Problem of Modernity* (Houndmills: Macmillan, 1998)

Taxidou, Olga, *Tragedy, Modernity and Mourning* (Edinburgh: Edinburgh University Press, 2004)

Terdiman, Richard, *Present Past: Modernity and the Memory Crisis* (Ithaca, N.Y.: Cornell University Press, 1993)

Therborn, Göran, *European Modernity and Beyond: The Trajectory of European Societies, 1945–2000* (London: SAGE Publications, 1995)

Thompson, John B., *The Media and Modernity: A Social Theory of the Media* (Stanford, Calif.: Stanford University Press, 1995)

Tolstoy, *War and Peace* (London: Penguin, 2006)

Toulmin, Stephen, *Cosmopolis: The Hidden Agenda of Modernity* (Chicago: University of Chicago Press, 1992)

Touraine, Alain, *Critique of Modernity*, trans. David Macey (Oxford: Blackwell, 1995)

Turner, Bryan S., ed., *Theories of Modernity and Postmodernity* (London: SAGE Publications, 1990)

Turner, Charles, *Modernity and Politics in the Work of Max Weber* (London and New York: Routledge, 1992)

Van der Veer, Peter, *Imperial Encounters: Religion and Modernity in India and Britain* (Princeton, NJ: Princeton University Press, 2001)

Vattimo, Gianni, *The Transparent Society*, trans. David Webb (Cambridge: Polity Press, 1992)

Vattimo, Gianni, *The End of Modernity: Nihilism and Hermeneutics in Postmodern Culture*, trans. Jon R. Snyder (Cambridge: Polity Press, 1998)

Venn, Couze, *Occidentalism: Modernity and Subjectivity* (London: SAGE Publications, 2000)

Virilio, Paul, *The Critical Space* (New York: Semiotext(e), 1984)

Virilio, Paul, *Bunker Archaeology* (New York: Princeton Architectural Press, 1994)

Wagner, Peter, *A Sociology of Modernity: Liberty and Discipline* (London: Routledge, 1994)

Walcott, Derek, *Collected Poems 1948–1984* (London: Faber and Faber, 1992)

Wang, Gungwu, *China and the World since 1949: The Impact of Independence, Modernity and Revolution* (London: Macmillan, 1977)

Wang, Orrin N.C., *Fantastic Modernity: Dialectical Readings in Romanticism and Theory* (Baltimore, MD: The Johns Hopkins University Press, 1996)

Ward, Patricia A., with James S. Patty, *Baudelaire and the Poetics of Modernity* (Nashville: Vanderbilt University Press, 2001)

Watenpaugh, Keith, *Being Modern in the Middle East: Revolution, Nationalism, Colonialism and the Arab Middle Class* (Princeton, NJ: Princeton University Press, 2006)

Watt, W. Montgomery, *Islamic Fundamentalism and Modernity* (London: Routledge, 1988)

Weber, Max, *Max Weber on Law in Economy and Society*, ed. Max Rheinstein (Cambridge, Mass.: Harvard University Press, 1954)

Weinstein, Michael A., *Culture/Flesh: Explorations of Post-civilised Modernity* (Lanham, MD: Rowman and Littlefield, 1995)

Wellmer, Albrecht, *The Persistence of Modernity: Essays on Aesthetics, Ethics and Postmodernism*, trans. David Midgley (Oxford: Polity Press, 1991)

Wells, H.G., *The Island of Doctor Moreau*, ed. Brian Aldiss (London: J.M. Dent, 1993a)

Wells, H.G., *The Time Machine*, ed. Michael Moorcock (London: J.M. Dent, 1993b)

Wilde, Oscar, *The Picture of Dorian Gray*, ed. Peter Faulkner (London: J.M. Dent, 1993)

Williams, Alastair, *New Music and the Claims of Modernity* (Aldershot: Ashgate, 1997)

Wilson, Elizabeth, *Adorned in Dreams: Fashion and Modernity* (London: Virago, 1985)

Wolfe, Tom, *The Bonfire of the Vanities* (London: Jonathan Cape, 1988)

Wood, Ellen Meiksins, and John Bellamy, eds, *In Defence of History: Marxism and the Postmodern Agenda* (New York: Monthly Review Press, 1997)

Woolf, Virginia, *Mrs Dalloway*, introd. Elaine Showalter, ed. Stella McNichol (London: Penguin, 1992)

Woolf, Virginia, *Orlando*, introd. Sandra M. Gilbert, ed. Brenda Lyons (London: Penguin, 1993)

Woolf, Virginia, *To the Lighthouse*, introd. Hermione Lee, ed. Stella McNichol (London: Penguin, 1992)

Xenos, Nicholas, *Scarcity and Modernity* (London: Routledge, 1989)

Yeats, W.B., *Collected Poems* (London: Macmillan, 1965)

Young, Edward, *Night Thoughts*, ed. Stephen Cornford (Cambridge: Cambridge University Press, 1989)

Young, Robert J.C., *Postcolonialism: An Historical Introduction* (Oxford: Blackwell, 2001)

Yue Dong, Madeleine, and Joshua L. Goldstein, eds, *Everyday Modernity in China* (Seattle: University of Washington Press, 2006)

Index